AL

PARROTLOPAEDIA

A Complete Guide
To Parrot Care

Annette De Saulles and
Neil Forbes BVetMed MIBiol CBiol DipECAMS FRCVS

D1341014

RINGPRESS

Published by Ringpress Books,
A Division of Interpet Publishing
Vincent Lane, Dorking, Surrey RH4 3YX

ISBN 1 86054 285 9

Manufactured in Singapore

10 9 8 7 6 5 4 3 2 1

CONTENTS

seeds, grains, and pulses (Growing sprouts; Types to try); Home-grown wheat grass; Special diets; Seasonal diets; Cutting down on fat; Converting the fussy eater; Supplements; Eating with the family.

7. CARE AND MANAGEMENT 63

General care principles; First aid (First-aid kit); The cage as a sanctuary (Size and construction; Cage accessories); A busy parrot is a happy parrot (Human company; Toys; Playstands; Food for thought; The need to chew); Exercise; Grooming (Bathing; Nail and beak clipping); Rest and sleep; Is my parrot lonely? (Bird rooms); Wing clipping (Pros of clipping; Cons of clipping; Baby birds; Ask the experts); Recovering a lost parrot (What can I do?); Parrot thieves; Securing the future.

8. BEHAVIOUR AND TRAINING 81

Introduction; Mutual trust; Body language (Whistling and chattering; Growling; Wing spreading; Food regurgitation; Head lowering; Displaying; Lying on his back; Flashing eyes; Yawning); Socialisation; Training (Baby parrots; Basic training; Do's and don'ts of training; Stepping on to your hand; Stepping down; "Come here!"; "No!"; Cuddling up; House-training); Problem behaviour (Biting; Screaming; Feather plucking; Vandalism; Over-bonding); Speech training (Speech training lessons); Teaching tricks (Learning to play; Simple tricks); Flying free.

9. BREEDING PARROTS 99

Introduction; Points to ponder (Which species?; Time; A lifetime commitment; Costs; Neighbours; Profits; Unsold stock; Starting out; Breeding from pet parrots; Sexing the breeding pair; Introductions; Hand-rearing; Special diets); Aviaries (Building an outdoor aviary; Indoor aviaries; Nest boxes; Home, sweet home); Routine care (Special diets; Worming); Breeding (Timing; When nothing happens; Egg laying); Checking the nest (Closed-circuit TV; Eggs; Chicks; Incubation and fostering; Closed banding); Hand-rearing (Nests; Feeding; Weaning); Selling young stock; Breeding Cockatiels (Housing with other species; How many breeding pairs?; Aviary; Eggs and chicks); Breeding African Greys (Housing; Young in the nest; Hand-rearing Greys; Weaning); Notes on other aviary parrots (Cockatoos; Macaws; Amazons; Alexandrine Parakeets; Pionus; Lories and Lorikeets).

SECTION TWO: PARROT HEALTH
By Neil Forbes

INTRODUCTION

Of the many bird species that share our world, parrots have always been especially prized for their outstanding beauty, intelligence, and personality. Pet parrots show a remarkable capacity for affection, usually bonding for life with their human keeper and enjoying nothing better than a cuddle on the sofa or sharing a snack at the dining table. It is because these birds are so intelligent and inquisitive that many can be taught sophisticated tricks – Macaws and Cockatoos, for example, can master such unnatural activities as tightrope-cycling and skateboarding. Most notably, the parrot's uncanny ability to mimic speech, whistles, and all kinds of other sounds, has endeared them to us over many centuries.

PARROT VARIETIES

The parrot family (also known as *psittacines*, parrot-like birds, or hookbills) includes the smaller parakeet species, such as Budgerigars, Lovebirds and Parrotlets. The larger parrots include Macaws, such as the Hyacinth and Scarlet, and the impressive Black Palm Cockatoo, while there are also medium-sized parrots, such as Amazons, Greys, Eclectus, Alexandrines, and various species of Cockatoo and Conure.

The parrot's most distinguishing feature is his large, powerful, hooked upper mandible, which fits over the shorter, lower beak. This strong beak is used to crack open seeds and nuts, as well as for gripping and climbing. The appearance of the psittacine beak varies according to the species, having evolved as a result of diet – whether seeds, tough-shelled nuts, or insects. For example, the grass-seed-eating Australian parakeets have comparatively modest-sized beaks; the Macaws's large beak is large and strong enough to crack open the toughest Brazil nut; while the Slender-billed Conure and the Kea have an unusually thin upper mandible, which can more easily probe for roots or insects.

Parrots are further recognisable for their stunning plumage, large heads, and stocky body shape. They perch with two toes pointing forwards and two back, unlike other birds, which have three toes pointing forwards and one back. The parrot's unique feet make him adept at grasping branches as well as pieces of food.

Every colour combination is to be found among more than 300 parrot species living in the southerly continents of Africa, South America, Australia, the Far East and India. Some are forest, mountain, or scrub-dwelling birds; others thrive in arid, desert conditions. They eat whatever fruits, nuts, seeds, buds, or flowers are in season, and take grubs and insects for extra protein.

PARROTS TODAY

In many parts of the world, parrots are seriously declining in numbers, but in other areas they breed in large numbers. For example, the South American Monk Parakeet, and some of the Australian Cockatoos, have bred so successfully that they are now considered a serious pest by arable farmers, who are culling these birds to protect their crops. Some aviary escapees – notably Alexandrines and Ring-necked Parakeets – are flourishing in feral colonies in the UK and other non-indigenous countries.

PARROTS AS PETS

Since the days of the early seafaring explorers, parrots have been tamed and taken to far-flung corners of the world, to be kept as house pets in what, to them, is a totally alien environment. It is this astonishing ability to live and bond with humans in a domestic setting that has led to the parrot's popularity as a pet.

Undoubtedly, parrots can make exceptionally affectionate and playful pets. If you are thinking of acquiring one of these birds, or have recently acquired a parrot and want to know more, this book aims to show that there is much more involved in parrot keeping than just providing a cage and a bowl of seed. Please do not choose a pet parrot just because you want a pet that can talk – you may be disappointed. Not every parrot – even the normally garrulous African Grey – chooses to mimic. In any event, pet parrots have much more to offer than mere mimicry; even if a bird does not talk, he will communicate clearly with his body language, calls, and facial expression.

By knowing something of the wild habitat of the species you are keeping, you will be able to provide a suitable environment and diet. Proper socialising and training of your bird will be of enormous benefit to you both. Taking the time and trouble to understand your parrot is always worthwhile – what you get out of your relationship will depend on what you put in. Your bird has great potential for adapting and learning, and will repay many times over the attention and affection you give him. With no input from the keeper, a parrot will become bored and may develop antisocial habits. For example, if a parrot bites, his keeper may become afraid and keep the bird confined to his cage. This is a common situation and one that may continue for many years, the parrot having become a neglected prisoner. At the other end of the scale, with patient training, an exceptionally well-bonded pet parrot can be trained to fly freely out of doors and return to his keeper. Although the latter is not recommended to anyone without expert knowledge of parrot behaviour and training, these two extreme cases show just how important a role the keeper plays in the wellbeing of the bird and a mutually happy relationship.

The best advice, if you are thinking of keeping and perhaps breeding parrots, is to read as much as possible on the subject, talk to experienced bird keepers and – most importantly – consider your future lifestyle plans before taking on one of these long-lived birds. Only then will you be ready for a new, exciting and rewarding way of life with your feathered family member.

Annette De Saulles

CHAPTER I

LIFE IN THE WILD

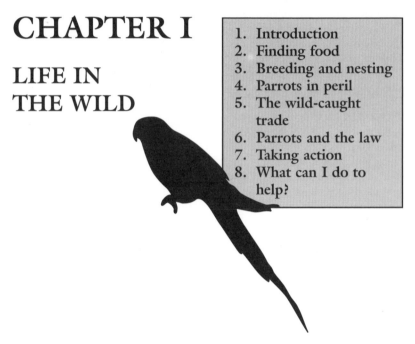

"If we save the parrots, we might yet save ourselves. We need the rainforests as much as the parrots do" – Mike Reynolds, Director of the World Parrot Trust.

1. INTRODUCTION

Parrots originate from the southerly continents and outlying islands of South America, Africa, the Far East, and Australia.

Approximately 330 species of *psittacine* have evolved, flourishing in widely differing habitats, adapting to varying climates, food, and nesting sites. The rainforests of South America are home to Amazon parrots and Macaws. Africa's wild parrots include the Congo and Timneh Grey, Senegals and Lovebirds, while the dry scrub of Australia supports many species of Parakeet and Cockatoo.

2. FINDING FOOD

Parrots are mainly vegetarian. Their diet varies according to species and the availability of food, but largely includes fruits, seeds, grasses, nuts, palm fruit, buds, flowers, and green foods. Some parrots supplement their diet with grubs and insects.

Lories and Lorikeets (from Australia and the Far East) are the exception. These vividly coloured birds have evolved a brush-like tip to their tongue for extracting pollen and nectar from flowers, although they also eat other foods such as fruit, seeds, and insects.

Parrots and Parakeets spend much of their time flying in search of food, often raiding farm crops as their natural habitats become depleted.

DID YOU KNOW?
There are 32 different types of parrot living wild in the Peruvian rainforest reserve of Tambopata – a tenth of all the world's parrot species.

---

3. BREEDING AND NESTING

Parrots begin to breed and nest as spring approaches, when daylight hours increase and food sources are at their richest and most abundant. In this way, the young have the best chance of surviving and fledging. In almost all areas, habitat destruction means there are fewer suitable nesting sites available to the breeding pairs, and competition can be fierce. Holes in rotting tree trunks are a favourite nesting place for many species, notably the large Macaws such as the Hyacinth, and the Blue and Gold. However, the depletion of natural habitats means these are scarce.

Parrots lay clutches of white eggs. A clutch can consist of one or two eggs, to more than eight, depending on the species. The incubation periods range from three to four weeks. In most cases, the hen incubates the eggs while the cock forages for food to bring back to her.

Once the chicks have hatched, they are fed by both parents until they are ready to leave the nest. They stay close to their parents at this stage, learning flying and landing skills, how to find food for themselves, and how to recognise and avoid predators.

INTERNATIONAL TRADE IN PARROTS
Rare and endangered parrot species, included in Appendix I of the CITES listing (the Convention on the International Trade in Endangered Species) cannot be bought or sold without the required legal documentation. Appendix I includes several species of Amazon and many of the large Macaws.
Unfortunately, CITES cannot intervene with internal trade in the parrots' countries of origin. Corruption in many areas, as well as local politics, are a severe hindrance to the efforts of conservationists.

---

4. PARROTS IN PERIL

Until recently, colourful flocks of parrots were a common sight in their natural habitats, feeding together in tree tops, or calling to each other as they flew over scrubland and desert. However, over the last few decades, the situation has changed drastically. In some parts of the world, parrots have bred so successfully they are considered a threat to food crops, but this applies to a few species only. Deforestation, and trapping for the pet trade, have put nearly 100 species in danger of extinction. More than half the world's forests have already disappeared, and, in the late 1990s, widespread forest fires destroyed the wild habitats of many Asian parrots. Dam-building projects, and the laying of pipelines and new roads through virgin rainforest, are steadily wiping out food sources and nesting places. Up to 30 species of parrot have already become extinct.

Unfortunately, there is also a thriving trade in wildlife, with parrots making up a substantial proportion of the $5-billion turnover.

> **DID YOU KNOW?**
> *With few suitable trees remaining, man-made nest boxes are being installed and monitored in the Pantanal region of Brazil, to give Hyacinth Macaws somewhere to nest.*

5. THE WILD-CAUGHT TRADE

For every five parrots taken from the wild, only one will survive the trauma of capture and export. The cruel trade in wild parrots will stop only when there is no longer a market for these birds. No one who is aware of the stress wild-caught parrots undergo during capture and exportation would want to promote this activity by buying one of them. Illegally caught parrots are stuffed into small boxes or tubes, many of them dying of suffocation before they reach their destination. Sadly, exporting wild birds and animals is still legal for many species. Ensure the bird you are buying is captive-bred – more on this later.

A different perspective is given by some parrot keepers, who argue that there can be a need to take highly threatened individuals into a captive breeding programme to avoid extinction of the species.

> **DID YOU KNOW?**
> *Humans are not the only threat to wild parrots. In the rainforest, nests are regularly plundered by toucans, skunks and other creatures, so that only half the eggs survive. In Australia, conservationists wrap the trunks of nesting trees with sheets of tin to prevent the large native lizards from climbing up to steal the eggs of the Major Mitchell (Leadbeaters) Cockatoo.*

6. PARROTS AND THE LAW

Conservationists in the US were successful in helping to bring about the Wild Bird Act of 1992, which ended the illegal import of parrots. Endangered species have been given protection under the act, and many other species of pet parrots now need an import permit.

Cruelty laws and penalties vary in detail between each American state. In the UK, legal protection for parrots is outdated and inadequate. Local authorities are responsible for following up any complaints of neglect or abuse. The RSPCA has only limited powers to safeguard the welfare of parrots, as follows:

- Parrots cannot be sold to children less than 12 years of age
- Parrots must not be sold on the street
- Caged birds must be able to fully extend both wings in all directions
- A keeper is liable for prosecution if a bird has been left unattended for more than 48 hours.

If cruelty is proven, the keeper may be fined up to £5,000 and/or receive six months' imprisonment for each bird involved. However, it can be a difficult and lengthy process to bring a case to court and successfully prosecute.

Alleviating the plight of parrots at home and in their countries of origin, by means of improvements to existing legislation, depends entirely on the strength of public protest.

7. TAKING ACTION

Fortunately, awareness of the wild parrot's plight is growing and many conservation initiatives are now under way.

One success story is that of the Echo Parakeet, which has recovered from the brink of extinction in its native Mauritius. Captive-bred individuals are being carefully released into the wild, and the wild population is slowly recovering. Another successful captive breeding and re-release scheme, carried out by Jersey Zoo, has restored numbers of the St Lucia Amazon from tens to hundreds in its native Caribbean islands.

The World Parrot Trust, which has branches in many countries, has several ongoing projects aimed at protecting, captive-breeding, and rehabilitating, rare species. The Trust is now involved in a total of 37 species conservation projects.

Specialist zoos and bird parks, such as Loro Parque in Tenerife and the Jersey Wildlife Preservation Trust, are joining forces in these long-term and painstaking efforts to save the birds and their natural habitats from further decline.

Illegally exported wild parrots, if intercepted and confiscated, need to be carefully rehabilitated before being re-released into the wild. Captive-bred birds, if they are to survive once released into the wild, have first to be taught how to fend for themselves, how to recognise predators, and how to find food. This can be a lengthy process. The birds are introduced gradually to the wild environment by being released initially into large flights.

Conservation involves protecting remaining habitats as well as the birds themselves. This cannot be done without the co-operation of local people. The main problem is the widespread poverty in many of the countries where parrots live. Trapping parrots for the pet trade, or killing them for food, is one of the few sources of income for many people. In addition, cattle are grazed on cleared forestland that is unsuited for pasture. Consequently, the herds are moved on frequently, with more trees felled in the process.

Long-standing local traditions and a lack of awareness play a further part in the parrot's demise. Some indigenous peoples regularly kill Macaws for their brightly coloured tail feathers, which are made into ceremonial head-dresses and other ornaments.

Illegal markets continue to thrive in the parrots' countries of origin, where birds and other wild creatures are kept in cramped, dirty conditions before being sold for small sums of money.

7.1. ECO-TOURISM

One hoped-for solution to the problem is the involvement of local inhabitants with the growing eco-tourist market. In this way, parrots will come to be regarded as a valuable natural resource and one that should be actively protected. Wildlife sight-seeing holidays bring much-needed financial help to poor areas, and, if the right balance is struck, both parrots and humans can benefit. One example is the huge clay lick at the Tambopata Reserve in South-East Peru, which is visited every day by many different species of parrots seeking out detoxifying minerals. This spectacular site is now the focus of eco-tourist holidays in the area.

8. WHAT CAN I DO TO HELP?

For some reason, in the past, parrots have been regarded as figures of fun, although this attitude is now changing. John Cleese, the comic actor who featured in the famous Monty Python 'Ex-Parrot' sketch, is now a campaigner for the World Parrot Trust and World Wildlife Fund.

If no-one bought another wild-caught bird, whatever the species, the illegal trade would stop almost immediately. Likewise, if we insist on buying wood products from sustainable sources only, there would be no market for rainforest trees and logging would end. Governments and local authorities, if they are to remain in power, eventually have to listen and do what the populace demand. You can help the parrots by not buying a wild-caught bird for a pet (even if you feel sorry for it, please don't be tempted – the supplier will soon replace it with another).

Don't buy furniture, building materials and other items made from mahogany, rosewood, teak or ebony. These are rainforest woods. Go for purpose-grown wood, such as pine, instead. If possible, do not buy bananas! Even the organic variety is produced at great cost to the rainforests, which are cleared to plant banana trees. Eat locally produced, organic foods; I buy recycled paper products; I use energy-efficient transport, heating and lighting. This may all seem extreme and far removed from protecting parrots, but our demand for such things as hamburger meat, hardwood and oil, is the reason the rainforests are being decimated.

Join a parrot conservation charity or make a donation in your will; go on a protest march; get involved in a conservation or wildlife action day; take your (tame) parrot to the local school and give a talk to the children; let your member of parliament or congressman know your views. If enough people make a stand, things will start to change for the better.

CHAPTER 2

THE PSITTACINE SPECIES

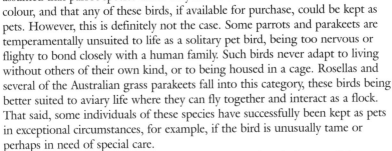

1. INTRODUCTION

If you are new to parrot keeping, you may have assumed that parrot species differ only in size and colour, and that any of these birds, if available for purchase, could be kept as pets. However, this is definitely not the case. Some parrots and parakeets are temperamentally unsuited to life as a solitary pet bird, being too nervous or flighty to bond closely with a human family. Such birds never adapt to living without others of their own kind, or to being housed in a cage. Rosellas and several of the Australian grass parakeets fall into this category, these birds being better suited to aviary life where they can fly together and interact as a flock. That said, some individuals of these species have successfully been kept as pets in exceptional circumstances, for example, if the bird is unusually tame or perhaps in need of special care.

The strikingly coloured Lories and Lorikeets are also obvious candidates for the aviary. Their fruit and nectar diet produces liquid droppings, which can make a considerable mess when fired at speed through the cage bars! However, these parakeets are such charming, lively little characters that some keepers are prepared to put up with the mess and adapt an indoor cage for them.

All parrots are noisy, but some much more so than others. This is another good reason to house your birds outside, rather than in your living room. Some of the Aratinga Conures, Cockatoos and Macaws, as well as the little

Quaker Parakeets, fall into this category. If you plan to keep these birds, it is a good idea to check with any close neighbours first, or you may fall out over the noise issue.

The most rewarding pet parrots are those species that actually enjoy the company of humans and will welcome interaction and affection from their keeper. Hand-reared Amazons, Pionus, Greys, Caiques, Cockatiels, Senegals and Budgerigars are some of these more popular species. Well-trained Macaws and Cockatoos also make lovely pets, provided you have the space and time for them.

2. PARAKEETS

Smaller and livelier than their larger relatives, parakeets are nonetheless true parrots. In the wild, they live and travel in flocks, and, for this reason, many parakeets are more suited to communal aviary life than to being kept as household pets. However, there are some notable exceptions to this rule – Budgerigars and Cockatiels, for example, make excellent companion birds, as do some Lovebirds, such as the Peach-faced.

For the newcomer to bird keeping, parakeets are a good choice. They are less expensive than larger parrots, many species are relatively easy to care for, and many will breed readily in captivity.

Noise can be a problem with larger aviary parrots, and housing needs to be really sturdy to withstand the surprising strength and ingenuity of those powerful beaks. Children will find it easier to handle and care for a parakeet, and its relatively small beak is an important safety consideration. Some pet parakeets will become very tame and even learn to say a few words. Take care if you also keep a cat or dog. A slow-moving African Grey or Macaw might well command respect from other pets, whereas a free-flying parakeet darting about the sitting room is more likely to provoke the natural hunting instinct.

One fascinating aspect of breeding parakeets is the development of new colour mutations. Jim Hayward, a UK aviculturist of many years' standing, has made a careful study of colour breeding and has written widely on the subject *(See Appendix)*.

Before buying a parakeet, think carefully about what you want from your bird. If you hope for a larger species that will also make a tame and playful pet, a hand-reared Alexandrine might be the right choice. Parakeets can be long-lived – a Cockatiel can live for 25 years, for example. It is, therefore, a good idea to read up carefully on the species that attract you before committing yourself.

Consider the natural environment and climate of the species. Some, such as the Australian grass parakeets, will require a weatherproof aviary. Peach-faced Lovebirds can be prone to frostbite, so they need an enclosed retreat in winter. Other species, such as Cockatiels, are more hardy and can acclimatise to cold weather.

Breeding parakeets is unlikely to be very profitable, so monetary gain is not a good reason for taking up the hobby. The more common species fetch very little in today's market, and indeed, it may be difficult to find suitable homes for all the young stock. With experience, however, the rarer and more demanding species may be successfully bred by the dedicated aviculturist, with a view to increasing the numbers of those parakeets now under threat. Given below are the species more commonly seen in captivity, with details about their availability, and their suitability as pets or aviary birds.

2.1. BUDGERIGARS (MELOPSITTACUS UNDULATUS)

Since the mid-19th century, when Budgerigars were first exported from their native Australia, these cheerful, colourful little parakeets have become firmly established as pets in Europe, America, and throughout the world. Australia no longer permits the export of any parrots, but the Budgerigar has proved easy to breed in captivity, so that young birds are always available.

Budgerigars are ground-feeding parakeets that range widely over Australia, travelling in large flocks and eating seeding grasses and other seeds and green foods. The wild Budgerigar was originally a green and yellow bird. Nowadays, however, with the interest in colour mutation breeding, almost every combination of green, blue, yellow, grey and white can be seen. Approximately 8 inches (20 cms) in length, these parakeets may live for 10 years or more in captivity (less in the wild).

If you want to make sure you are buying a young bird, look for barred feathering across the top of the head. This shows that the Budgerigar is less than four months old – after which time the barring disappears. As the birds mature, the sexes can be distinguished by their ceres (the nostril area above the beak). The adult male's cere is blue, the hen's brown.

Budgerigars are ideal for children, the beginner, or anyone wanting an affordable, low-maintenance, affectionate and intelligent companion bird. One of the important advantages with these birds is that their beaks don't really hurt even if they do nip you.

Budgerigars are sometimes discounted as commonplace and uninteresting, largely because they have been around for so long and are such familiar cage birds. This is far from the case, however, as these little birds have lots to offer. As with all pet birds, their level of tameness, response and interaction will depend on the amount of time and attention given by the keeper.

Although hand-feeding is not usual with Budgerigars, young parent-reared birds can be tamed easily if given plenty of attention and handling. Some individuals, particularly the males, can be taught to mimic. However an older bird, especially one used to aviary life, may take longer to tame than a youngster and will probably not want to bother to learn to talk.

Budgerigars are flock birds and they are happiest interacting with others of their own kind. A lone budgie in a small cage is a sorry, all-too-common sight. These are active birds and should be given plenty of scope for flying, whether in the aviary or out of the cage during supervised free time.

Keeping two or more pet birds does not involve much extra work or expense, and they will be good company for each other. These little parakeets are also an excellent choice for the first-time parakeet breeder who wants to keep an aviary flock. Non-aggressive, and not unduly noisy, Budgerigars are hardy little birds that will readily breed.

2.2. PARROTLETS

There are seven species of the tiny *psittacines* known as Parrotlets. These little birds, which come from Central and South America, are ideal for the first-time parrot keeper, for children, or anyone wanting a small, easily-maintained bird.

Parrotlets grow up to 6 inches (15 cms) in length, and several colour mutations have been developed by breeders. These little birds live for approximately 25 years and they can be taught to mimic a few words.

2.3. COCKATIELS *(NYMPHICUS HOLLANDICUS)*

A close relative of the much larger Cockatoo, this highly popular Australian parakeet makes an excellent and affectionate pet, and a rewarding aviary bird. Cockatiels grow to about 12 inches (30 cms) in size, and can live for up to 25 years in captivity. Cockatiels will bond closely with their keeper and can be taught a few words, as well as whistles or songs. The male birds are more likely to talk than the females. The size and friendly disposition of these birds also makes them a good choice for children. Tame, captive-bred Cockatiels are widely available at modest cost.

In their natural habitat, Cockatiels are seed-eating flock birds, travelling over the Australian scrubland in search of food and water. Their natural colouring is grey, with a yellow head and crest, orange cheek patches, and white wing flashes. The female can be distinguished by her muted head colouring and her striped tail and rump feathers. Young birds resemble the adult hen until their first moult, after which their gender becomes apparent. Captive-bred Cockatiels are available in other colours, with breeders developing many striking colour alternatives.

These birds make charming, tame and docile pets, and they enjoy nothing better than a tickle on the back of the neck. They are also ideal for newcomers to aviculture, who want a straightforward, hardy aviary bird that will readily breed. They can, however, be fairly noisy at times, when kept as a breeding flock. Cockatiels thrive on a diet of various seeds and green foods and enjoy chewing on natural branches. They need a spacious aviary flight or plenty of free time out of the cage if kept as pets, as they are active flyers *(see page 72)*.

2.4. RED-FRONTED KAKARIKIS *(CYANORAMPHUS NOVAEZELANDIAE)*

These rather unusual and comical parakeets come from New Zealand. They are best suited to aviary life as they are particularly active birds, darting about and running swiftly up the aviary wire or scratching about on the floor and in their food pots. They have a distinctive laughing call. They mature early and are productive breeders.

Red-fronts are about 10 inches (25 cms) in length. The colouring is bright green, highlighted with a red forehead. They do not live for very long, five years being the average lifespan.

The less-often-seen Yellow-fronted Kakariki *(C. auriceps)* is an inch or two smaller than its more popular cousin, and has a red band over the cere, topped with a patch of yellow.

Kakarikis do not make ideal pets, but they are a good choice for the aviary, where they will always be 'on the go'.

2.5. LOVEBIRDS *(GENUS AGAPORNIS)*

Lovebirds are small, popular parrots that are widely available. They are inexpensive to buy and to keep. There are nine species of Lovebird, all originating from Africa and Madagascar. Three species – the Peach-faced *(Agapornis roseicollis)*, Fischer's *(Agapornis fischeri)* and Masked *(Agapornis personata)* – are widely available in aviculture.

Trapping for the pet trade, drought, and changing agricultural practices, have put the Black-cheeked Lovebird *(Agapornis nigrigenis)* in danger of extinction, and this bird is now the subject of a conservation project.

2.5.1. THE PEACH-FACED LOVEBIRD *(AGAPORNIS ROSEICOLLIS)*

This is the most commonly kept of the Lovebird species. Native to the African Savannah, the Peach-faced Lovebird's diet is mainly seeding grasses. The nominate (original wild) Peach-faced Lovebird is mainly green with a blue rump and pinkish-peach face. Many attractive pastel colour mutations have now been established with extensive captive breeding. Peach-faced Lovebirds are approximately 6 inches (15 cms) in length, and can live for 10 to 15 years. The species is monomorphic, that is, the sexes cannot be distinguished visually. The dull colouring of the young birds begins to brighten into the adult plumage after two to three months.

These pretty little birds seldom learn to mimic, but, if hand-reared and carefully trained, they make affectionate and charming pets and are not noisy. Lovebirds are not generally the first choice for young children, the mature females in particular being prone to aggression when they come into breeding condition.

If two Lovebirds are kept together (and provided they get on), they will bond with each other, rather than with their keeper. Make quite sure, however, that the birds are friends before you cage them together as severe aggression can occur – they do not, unfortunately, always live up to their name!

Lovebirds will breed in a cage, but if kept outside, a frost-proof shelter is required together with a flight that gives protection from extremes of weather. These birds will nest and breed readily, either in single pairs, or as a colony. However, do not attempt to house Lovebirds with other species, again because of possible aggression.

A variety of seed makes up the main diet, plus green foods, cuttlefish, and a piece of fresh fruit or vegetable.

2.6. RING-NECKED PARAKEETS *(GENUS PSITTACULA)*

This distinctive family of parrots is native to several different parts of the world: India, Malaysia, China and Africa. Ring-necks have a distinguishing black collar around the neck (generally lacking in the female), a long tail, and mainly green feathering, variously marked with pastel pinks and blues, and other colours according to the species. The sexes are dimorphic. Size varies between 13 inches (32.5 cms) and 23 inches (57.5 cms).

Ring-necks are natural talkers, but they are not common pets due to a tendency towards lack of affection– with each other and with humans. However, there can be exceptions to this, notably the Alexandrine Parakeet. Some individuals, particularly males, which are given lots of time and attention on a regular basis by the keeper, can prove to be surprisingly affectionate. Females, however, may be more aggressive.

2.6.1. INDIAN RING-NECK (P. KRAMERI MANILLENSIS)
Probably the best known of the Ring-necked Parakeet group, the Indian is a mainly green bird, with red shoulders and a yellow undertail. Various colour mutations are available to the aviculturist.

The hardy nature of Indian Ring-necks is demonstrated by their ability to form successful feral colonies in non-indigenous countries. As they are also ready breeders and good parents, these birds can be suitable for the beginner, once a compatible pair has been established where the female accepts the male without aggression.

2.6.2. PLUM-HEADED PARAKEET (P. CYANOCEPHALA)
The Plum-headed Parakeet is distinguished by his attractive, bright-maroon head.

2.6.3. MOUSTACHED PARAKEET (P. ALEXANDRI)
The Moustached Parakeet has a black 'moustache' over the top mandible and a wide black collar extending halfway round the neck.

2.6.4. ALEXANDRINE (P. EUPATRIA)
Another notable Ring-neck, and the largest of them all at 23 inches (57.5 cms), is the Alexandrine (P. eupatria). This parakeet's colouring is similar to that of the Indian Ring-neck, but with paler, pastel shades on the nape and chest.

2.7. QUAKER PARAKEETS (MYIOPSITTA MONACHUS)
Also known as Monk Parakeets, these South American birds have unique nest-building habits. Twigs are collected and woven into a large, enclosed nest. The nests are built upon until large colonies of breeding birds are living together in one huge commune.

Like the Indian Ring-neck, Quakers are adept at surviving and breeding in feral colonies if they escape from captivity – which has become a problem in some areas of the US.

Quakers make charming pets, although they are not as common in the UK as they are in the US. Quakers are suitable for the novice birdkeeper, being loving birds that welcome physical contact. They can also be talented mimics and are full of fun – if rather noisy on occasions. These monomorphic birds have green and grey feathering, although blue and other colour mutations are now appearing on the market. They grow to approximately 11 inches (27.5 cms).

Being hardy birds, ready breeders, and attentive parents, these are suitable birds for the newcomer to aviculture, although it should be borne in mind that an aviary colony can be very noisy during the breeding season. Ideally, aviary birds should be supplied with a plentiful supply of twigs, plus a suitable wire mesh support placed high up in a corner of the flight, so that they can build natural nests. However, many pairs will also raise young in a wooden nest box.

2.8. LORIES AND LORIKEETS
Several factors set apart this charming group of psittacines:
• Vivid, gleaming plumage, in every colour of the rainbow
• A brush-like tip to the tongue, for extracting pollen and nectar from flowers
• Lively, 'jumping' action, rather than the usual, slower parrot walk
• Specialist needs in captivity.

Lories and Lorikeets are native to Australasia and the Far East, some species remaining widespread in their natural habitat, while others – such as the Vini Blue Lories of Tahiti and the Purple-capped (*Lorius domicellus*) – are rarely seen.

Lories come into their own in an aviary flock, if provided with plenty of space for flying. The many different and highly colourful species vary in size between 5 inches (12.5 cms) and 12 inches (30 cms). These are extremely active and playful birds, who need plenty of swings, ropes and ladders for their acrobatics, as well as the opportunity for frequent bathing. Watch out for aggression when birds come into breeding condition, and make sure a newly introduced pair are getting on well before housing them together. Noise may be a problem during this time. One of the Rainbow Lorikeets, the Green-naped (*Trichoglossus haematodus*) is a popular and readily-available species in the aviary and a good choice for the novice. These highly colourful birds are usually prolific breeders and good parents.

Lories and Lorikeets involve rather more work and commitment than other species as their fruit and nectar diet has to be provided and cleared away at regular intervals to ensure it is always fresh. Aviary cleaning is also an ongoing task, so that sticky droppings and dropped fruit are removed, bacterial build-up avoided, and unwelcome wasps and flies kept at bay. The most practical flooring for the flight is smooth concrete, which can be quickly and thoroughly hosed down. The enclosed accommodation also needs to be easily cleanable.

Despite their talent for mimicry, and their affectionate disposition, Lories and Lorikeets are seldom kept as pets. Their special diet results in very liquid droppings – which are expelled by the bird in all directions! Dry Lory food, designed to curb this problem by producing more solid droppings, is now available. However, some keepers are of the opinion that these birds should be given food as close as possible to what they would eat in the wild. Powdered nectar, to which water is added, is a convenient way of providing this. In addition, fresh fruit, vegetables, and seeding grasses are much enjoyed. A bunch of safe flowers – such as roses, nasturtiums, or pansies – make a particularly welcome and natural addition to the diet.

If you are feeding nectar and fruit, but you want to keep a pet Lory in the house, the cage will need to be enclosed around the back and sides, and will need to be easily washable. Sheets of clear, removable perspex can be fitted around the cage sides to prevent the droppings reaching furnishings, wallpaper etc. You will also want to protect surrounding walls and floor with clear plastic sheeting. On a fine day, your pet Lory will appreciate the freedom of a garden aviary. Most importantly, give your pet Lory or Lorikeet plenty of space and toys for the fun and games that will make up a large part of his day.

3. AUSTRALIAN AVIARY PARAKEETS
Following are some of the main families of Australian Parakeets that make good aviary subjects. Some are suitable for the novice bird keeper, while others require the keeper to have a degree of knowledge and experience before attempting to keep and to breed them.

3.1. ROSELLAS *(GENUS PLATYCERCUS)*
These are vividly coloured parakeets, with all eight species easily distinguished by scalloped black feathering on their back and wings. Size varies from 10 to 14 inches (25 to 35 cms).

The natural habitat of wild Rosellas is distributed throughout the continent of Australia. In the wild, Rosellas – also known as 'broadtails' – are active birds, and, when kept in captivity, they appreciate as much flying room as can be provided. They are ideal for an aviary in which a large flight can be provided.

Rosellas are hardy birds, with the notable exception of the Brown's, but they can be noisy if several pairs are kept. Their basic diet consists of a good seed mix and regular supplies of green foods.

The various Rosella species can be found in varying numbers in aviculture. Individuals of the more commonly available species can be purchased at modest cost. Although Rosellas are hardy, prolific aviary birds, generally, they do not make good pets. The males of some species, such as the Yellow, the Mealy and the Adelaide, can become aggressive during the breeding season, either to their mate or to the young birds, and no Rosella species should be housed in close proximity to another.

3.1.1. TASMANIAN (GREEN) ROSELLA
The Tasmanian (or Green) Rosella is quieter than his cousins, but he tends to be overlooked by many bird keepers, perhaps because of his colouring, which is rather muted.

3.1.2. STANLEY (WESTERN) ROSELLA
The Stanley (or Western) is seen less commonly in aviculture than others of the genus as the species is less prolific. However, to compensate for this, the Stanley has a more amenable disposition than other Rosella species, bonding readily with his human keeper. The sexes of the Stanley Rosella can easily be distinguished, the male being more brightly coloured than the female.

3.1.3. BROWN'S ROSELLA
The Brown's Rosella is rarely seen and requires experience on the part of the bird keeper. This is a difficult species to keep and to breed, requiring a heated shelter during the winter months.

3.1.4. GOLDEN-MANTLED AND CRIMSON (PENNANT'S) ROSELLAS
Newcomers to the hobby might choose to start with the Golden-mantled and Crimson (or Pennant's) Rosellas. Both are prolific breeders and are readily available. Various colour mutations have been established for both species.

DID YOU KNOW?
There is the danger, when breeding Rosellas or other parrots, of producing hybrids by pairing individuals of different subspecies. To protect the purity of the species, responsible bird keepers should guard against this.

3.2. GENUS POLYTELIS
Three distinct species make up this group of Australian parakeets, which are better suited to aviary life than as pets. Polytelis are not generally recommended for the newcomer to parrot keeping, although, in general, these parakeets are calm and friendly birds. They are readily available through specialist breeders. Their diet consists of a seed mix, green foods, and fruit.

3.2.1. BARRABAND OR SUPERB PARROT (POLYTELIS SWAINSONII)
The female of this species is green, while the male has the addition of yellow colouring on the forehead and throat, with a band of red at the upper chest. Young birds have dark irides, but otherwise resemble the female. These parakeets grow to 16 inches (40 cms).

The Barraband, also known as the Superb Parrot, is a sociable bird that breeds most successfully when several pairs are housed in adjacent aviaries, or even together if sufficient space is provided. They appreciate plenty of flying space.

3.2.2. PRINCESS OF WALES' PARAKEET (POLYTELIS ALEXANDRAE)
A tame and confiding bird, although rather noisy at times, the Princess of Wales' Parakeet is an attractive mixture of greens, blue and pink (the female being identified by her more muted plumage). Blue and Lutino colour mutations have also been established. Young birds resemble the female. These birds grow to 18 inches (45 cms) and are distinguished by their particularly long, striped tail feathers.

3.2.3. ROCK PEBBLER (POLYTELIS ANTHOPEPLUS)

These parakeets, also known as Regent Parrots, are predominantly yellow and green. Youngsters and females, as with other members of the genus, are more muted in their colouration and lack the red wing flash of the male bird. Rock Pebblers grow to approximately 16 inches (40 cms).

3.3. GRASS PARAKEETS (GENUS NEOPHEMA)

The five species of Neophema are a good choice for the newcomer to bird keeping, as they nest and breed readily in both indoor and outdoor housing. They are hardy, quiet aviary birds, and are straightforward to feed. They measure an average of 8 inches (20 cms) in length, maturing at about one year old, and, generally, they are not aggressive.

The species can be sexed visually. Attractive colour mutations are being developed, such as the Bourke's Parakeet (N. bourkii), a pretty, pastel-coloured bird from which several mutations have been bred – notably the popular Rosa Bourke mutation, which accentuates the natural pink colouring. The Turquoisine (N. pulchella) and the Splendid Parakeet (N. splendida) are strikingly colourful, although it should be noted that the Turquoisine can be more aggressive than others of the genus. The colouring of the Elegant (N. elegans) and the Blue-winged Parakeet (N. chrysostama) is more muted, although these birds are willing breeders and should provide an encouraging introduction to the hobby.

Pairs of Grass Parakeets should be housed separately, to avoid aggression, a suggested flight size being 6 feet x 6 feet x 3 feet (183 cms x 183 cms x 92 cms). Ask your avian vet for advice on worming.

3.4. RED-RUMPED PARAKEET (PSEPHOTUS HAEMATONOTUS)

This Australian parakeet is the most frequently kept of the six Psephotus species. The sexes are dimorphic; the female's colouring being greyish-green, while the male has green, blue and yellow plumage, highlighted by a scarlet rump. Red-rumps grow to approximately 10 to 11 inches (25 to 27.5 cms) in length, and various colour mutations are available.

The Red-rump is a hardy and productive aviary bird, suitable for the beginner. However, Psephotus can become aggressive, so different species should not be housed in close proximity to each other unless there is a double thickness of wire between the flights. The Yellow-vented (P. haematogaster haematogaster) and Red-vented Blue Bonnet (P. h. haematorrhous) are particularly aggressive.

DID YOU KNOW?
Australia has banned all exports of its native psittacines.

---

4. PARROTS

It can be good sense to start off with one of the smaller psittacines before taking the plunge and buying that pet Grey or Cockatoo you have always wanted. However, be careful you don't end up with a bird you don't really want because you were trying to be sensible.

If you want a Macaw and have thought long and hard about the reality of keeping one of these birds, if you have read up on the subject, talked to other pet Macaw keepers or breeders, and you still really want one, then that is the bird for you. By taking on a smaller parrot first, you may just be giving yourself unnecessary problems when you realise later you have not got the time, space, energy or money for more than one bird and that the Macaw you want would not be compatible with your first bird anyway.

Remember, even the smaller species are a long-term commitment, so do not rush into buying a parrot, only to realise later that you have made a mistake. The future welfare of any bird you take on should be the first consideration.

4.1. AFRICAN GREYS (*PSITTACUS ERITHACUS*)

The African Grey's unique talent for mimicry is no doubt the reason for his unrivalled popularity as a pet parrot. Added to this is the loyalty and affection a bonded Grey will give his keeper.

Wild Greys live in the wooded areas of equatorial Africa. They congregate in large flocks to fly in search of palm nuts, seeds, fruits and other available foods.

The African Grey's basic colouring is, of course, shades of grey, with a white face, red tail feathers, and yellow-ringed eyes (immature birds' eyes remain black until the bird is about two years old).

African Greys are particularly intelligent and sensitive parrots – and this can have its drawbacks as well as its advantages. Greys can sometimes appear standoffish, and have a tendency to be nervous, being particularly prone to stress when there is a change to their routine or environment. If left alone for long periods with nothing to do, these birds will often resort to pulling out their feathers in frustration. The keeper needs to be prepared to carefully socialize, train and discipline a pet Grey throughout his lifespan.

It is important to buy a captive-bred, hand-reared Grey rather than one that has been wild-caught, as these nervous birds rarely adapt fully to domestic life. The more popular Congo Grey costs a little more than the Timneh, but is easier to obtain.

DNA testing is needed to be sure of the gender, although some long-established breeders claim to be able to detect the subtle differences between male and female. Captive Greys live for approximately 50 years.

DID YOU KNOW?

The most famous African Grey alive today is Alex, owned and trained by Irene Pepperburg. Alex has been taught to verbally identify various items, foods, colours and shapes, proving that some species of parrot can link words with their meanings, rather than mimicking sounds without understanding.

Greys make rewarding and responsive pets, given plenty of attention, stimulation and training. Many individuals can learn a wide vocabulary of words and phrases, a repertoire of whistles and songs, as well as all kinds of everyday sounds. Young birds may be quiet for several months, but they are listening all the time – and once they start talking, they can be hard to stop!

These birds may not be the best choice for the first-time parrot breeder. Greys need special care and conditions for breeding success, and without previous experience with one of the easier species, the newcomer to bird keeping may be disappointed *(see page 117)*.

4.1.1. CONGO GREY (PSITTACUS ERITHACUS ERITHACUS)
The Congo Grey is the largest of the three African Grey species, and he is the most popular. The Congo grows to about 13 inches (32.5 cms). His tail feathers are bright scarlet, and he has a black beak and grey feet.

4.1.2. TIMNEH GREY (PSITTACUS ERITHACUS TIMNEH)
The Timneh Grey has darker grey plumage, and a duller, maroon-red tail. He is slightly smaller than the Congo. The upper bill is horn-coloured, with a black tip. Pet Timnehs are not as widely kept as the Congo Grey, even though they tend to have a more relaxed personality and are equally good mimics. The reason for their lack of popularity is probably their less striking colouring.

4.1.3. GHANA GREY (PSITTACUS ERITHACUS PRINCEPS)
The Ghana Grey is very similar to the Congo Grey. He differs slightly in size, being an inch or two shorter, and he has darker colouring.

4.2. AMAZONS (GENUS AMAZONA)
In their natural habitat, Amazons are found in the rainforests of South America. They are medium-sized parrots, quite stocky in appearance, with size ranging from 10 to 18 inches (25 to 45 cms) in length, depending on the species. The Amazon's colouring is basically green, with the different species having a variety of additional markings. Some captive individuals have been known to reach about 100 years of age, and 50 to 75 years is not uncommon.

Amazons are widely kept as pet parrots. The appeal of Amazons is undoubtedly their friendly, laid-back characters and their considerable ability for mimicry – although they cannot match the accuracy or repertoire of the African Grey at talking. Amazons love to play and will bond closely with their keeper. Their plumage has a distinctive, slightly musty but not unpleasant, smell.

Of the many pet species available, the most popular include the Yellow-naped, the Blue-fronted, the Double-yellow-headed, and the Orange-winged. Amazons usually have strong characters and some individuals may show unexpected bouts of aggression as they mature. As they can bond very closely with one person, it is important to accustom them to being handled by that person's spouse or partner, to avoid jealous behaviour later on. With early discipline and training, these birds can make delightful and very affectionate pets. A correct diet (with plenty of fresh fruit) is important, as Amazons have a tendency to become obese if too many seeds and nuts are given.

Amazons enjoy being included in whatever is going on, but will also amuse themselves with their toys in the cage when you are busy.

Previous experience with an easier species is advisable before attempting to breed Amazons. Some knowledge and care is needed when pairing, housing, and feeding the breeding birds, to ensure success.

UNUSUAL PARROTS

- *There is a rare, flightless parrot, native to New Zealand, called the Kakapo (Strigops habroptilus). The future of these birds – also known as 'owl-parrots' because of their round face and heavy build – is under severe threat. They prefer their own company for much of the time and breed only occasionally, the male then issuing a booming mating cry that can be heard for miles. Rats and other predators are a danger, both to adult birds and any eggs or young in the ground-level nest. However, conservation efforts are under way to try and save the few remaining individuals in the wild. At the end of the 1990s, the total was just 62 – a slight increase on the previous years.*
- *Another unusual parrot is the Vasa (Coracopsis vasa), a dark-bluish-grey bird with a pale pink beak. This bird is believed to be the oldest parrot-like species. Vasas prefer their own company during the day, living in the shadows of the forest floor and only meeting up to fly with their flock at dusk. Their favourite food is rice, and for this reason they are persecuted by the local crop growers who share their native Madagascan rainforest.*
- *The Hawk-headed Parrot (Deroptyus accipitrinus) can raise his head and neck feathers in a spectacular display when excited or alarmed, or to act as a warning.*
- *The Lesser Patagonian Conure (Cyanoliseus patagonus patagonus) will tunnel several feet into soft, sandstone cliff face before making a nest.*

4.3. CAIQUES *(GENUS PIONITES)*

If you want a fairly small, fun-loving and lively pet parrot, you could not do much better than a member of the Caique family. With firm discipline from the keeper, these are charming little characters. They are highly entertaining as they perform acrobatics from their swings and ladders and beat up their toys. Not noted for their clear mimicry, some individuals may, however, copy a few words in their distinct shrill voice.

In the wild, Caiques are flock birds, living in the northerly regions of the South American forest canopy. Caiques are well suited to aviary life if they are provided with plenty of flying room, and plenty of ropes and swings to work off their high energy levels. Unusually for a parrot, a tame and bonded Caique will often continue to respond affectionately to the keeper even when paired with a mate in the aviary.

Of the five species (all of which have the distinctive white breast and orange/yellow and green feathering), three are becoming increasingly rare in aviculture: the White-bellied *(P. leucogaster)*, the Yellow-tailed *(P. l. xanthumus)* and the Yellow-thighed *(P. l. xanthomeria)*.

4.3.1. BLACK-HEADED CAIQUE (PIONITES MELANOCEPHALA)

The most commonly kept pet of the Caique genus is the Black-headed Caique (*Pionites melanocephala*, the similar-looking subspecies being the Pallid Caique (*P. m. pallida*).

Measuring about 9 inches (22.5 cms) in length, the Black-headed Caique has green, orange, and white body colouring, with a distinctive black head and beak. In captivity, these birds may live to 40 years of age or more.

4.4. POICEPHALUS PARROTS

The three members of this African family of parrots most frequently seen in captivity are the Senegal *(Poicephalus Senegalus)*, Meyer's *(P. meyeri)* and Jardine's *(P. gulielmi)* Parrots.

4.4.1. SENEGALS

If you want one of the smaller species of parrot as a pet or aviary bird, the Senegal has much to be recommended. These are attractive little characters, with their distinctive green, yellow and grey plumage. Senegals grow to approximately 9 inches (23 cms), and live for up to 30 years. Some individuals will learn to perform tricks and can be taught to say a few words, but otherwise, Senegals are quiet birds by nature. Hand-reared birds make the best pets. However, even tame, captive-bred birds require careful training, or they may develop a tendency to nip as they reach adolescence.

4.5. PIONUS PARROTS

These quiet and gentle birds originate from Central and South America, as well as some of the Caribbean islands. Each of the eight species has distinctive red feathering under the tail. In view of their attractive looks and affectionate natures, it is surprising that they are not kept more widely in captivity.

Pionus are similar in size and shape to the Amazon parrot, being fairly robust-looking birds, with short tails. Also like the Amazon, Pionus can be prone to obesity, which can be guarded against by giving a diet high in fresh fruits and limited in seeds and nuts.

Pionus can be rewarding aviary birds. They will readily nest, breed, and successfully raise young, given a suitable diet and environment. Care is needed at the weaning stage, when some chicks may quickly lose weight and decline. Some individuals will remain tame towards their keeper after being paired with an aviary mate.

As pets, the recommended species include the Blue-headed Pionus *(Pionus menstruus)*, the White-crowned Pionus *(P. senilis)* and the Maximillian or Scaley-headed Pionus *(P. maximiliani)*.

4.5.1. BLUE-HEADED PIONUS (PIONUS MENSTRUUS)

The Blue-headed Pionus is one of the most common Pionus species seen in captivity. This bird measures about 11 inches (27.5 cms) and will live up to 25 years of age. The body colouring is green, apart from the head and neck, which are a distinctive and attractive blue. The undertail feathers are red.

Blue-headeds can make excellent family pets, particularly if yours is a busy household and you want a laid-back parrot that is peaceable, good with (responsible) children, enjoys being handled, but is not too demanding of your attention. Pionus also tend to be less destructive chewers than many other parrots. However, they are not noted for their mimicry, so if your heart is set on having a talking bird, this is probably not the best choice.

4.6. ECLECTUS (ECLECTUS RORATUS)

These exceptionally beautiful, striking-looking parrots from Australasia are unusual in several ways. The male and female can immediately be identified by their different colouration – the male being green with an orange/yellow beak, while the female is red and violet with a black beak. The feathers on the head and chest have a unique hair-like texture and the beak is softer than that of other parrots, having evolved for eating soft foods such as fruit and greenstuffs.

In the wild, these birds pair up only during the breeding season, the males and females showing no interest in each other for the rest of the year. Aggression from the female towards her mate can be a problem when attempting to breed this species in an aviary. Likewise, pet Eclectus can be rather reserved and unreceptive to physical affection from their keeper, unless they have been consistently handled and talked to as babies. They are, however, generally good-natured as pets and will enjoy playing, hiding, and sleeping in a cardboard box if one is provided. Some individuals will learn to speak quite well and all enjoy lots of different foods.

There are seven subspecies of Eclectus, the Red-sided Eclectus (or *Vosmaeri*) being the most common in captivity. Most species of Eclectus parrots grow to about 14 inches (35 cms).

4.7. CONURES

There are numerous species and subspecies of Conure, their stunning colouration varying as much as their size – from 9 inches (22.5 cms) to more than double this length for the largest species. These are intelligent and sociable birds that can be readily tamed and trained. The body shape is slim, with a long and tapering tail.

Originating in Central and South America, as well as some of the Caribbean islands, most Conure species are divided into two main genera: *Pyrrhura* (the smallest members of the Conure family, numbering 16 different species) and *Aratinga* (larger in size than *Pyrrhura*, this genus comprises about 20 species and 50 subspecies).

Infrequently seen in aviculture, perhaps because of their unusually thin upper mandible, are the *Enicognathus* genus, comprising the Slender-billed and Austral Conure.

The Nanday Conure (*Nandayus nenday*) and the Greater and Lesser Patagonian Conures (genus *Cyanoliseus patagonus*) complete the main Conure groupings.

Conures are generally hardy birds and ready breeders, so they can be a good choice for the new aviary keeper. However, some species – such as the Mitred

Conure *(A. mitrata)* and Jendaya Conure *(A. jendaya)* – can be particularly noisy and destructive. This should be kept in mind when siting and constructing the aviary. Supply plenty of natural branches and wooden toys to keep beaks busy and save damage to the frame.

Conures make lively and entertaining pets, which enjoy having fun and learning tricks. The smaller *Pyrrhura* species may only learn a word or two, but these little birds are full of fun and are not over-noisy, although they can be nippy on occasion. Of this group, the Maroon-bellied *(P. frontalis)* and Green-cheeked *(P. molinae)* are readily available on the market and make friendly family pets.

Some of the *Aratinga* Conures may learn to talk reasonably well, although the drawback with many of these birds is that they are noisy. The beautiful Sun Conure *(A. solstitialis)* can make a tame and confident pet, as well as a rewarding aviary bird – despite his raucous calls. Measuring 12 inches (30 cms) in length, this is an average-sized parrot that will live for up to 20 years.

4.8. COCKATOOS

Australia and the islands of Indonesia are the natural home of Cockatoos. Some species, such as the Galah (or Roseate) Cockatoo *(Eolophus roseicapillus)*, may congregate in huge flocks, where they are regarded as a serious pest and are subsequently culled by crop-growing farmers in Australia. By contrast, species such as the Red-vented *(Cacatua haematuropygia)* are becoming seriously endangered due to habitat destruction.

Perhaps more than any other parrot, the Cockatoo welcomes close physical affection from his keeper. 'Cuddly' is a word often associated with these beautiful and popular parrots, particularly the Moluccan, which has also been described as the 'Velcro parrot' because of his strong desire always to be attached to some part of his beloved human keeper!

The most commonly kept pet species include the Greater Sulphur-crested *(Cacatua galerita galerita)*, the Lesser Sulphur-crested *(C. sulphurea)*, the Moluccan *(C. moluccensis)*, the Umbrella *(C. alba)* and the Goffins *(C. goffini)* Cockatoos.

Size varies according to the species, from about 12 inches (30 cms) for smaller Cockatoos, such as the Lesser Sulphur-crested, to more than twice this size for larger species such as the Moluccan. The distinguishing crest on the head also varies in size, according to the different species. One feature of the Cockatoo is that he constantly produces a dusty 'powder down' from his feathers, a factor that should be considered before acquiring one of these birds, if you are particularly houseproud.

The so-called White Cockatoos include those with yellow crests as well as the pink-feathered Moluccans, Galahs and the rarer Leadbeaters or Major Mitchell's *(Cacatua leadbeateri)*. There are also several species of black Cockatoo, including the very striking-looking Palm Cockatoo *(Probosciger aterrimus)* and the Red-tailed Black Cockatoo *(Calyptorhynchus magnificus)*. As Australia no longer exports its parrots, some of the species commonly seen in the wild habitat can be a rare sight in captivity outside their native country.

Cockatoos are very long-lived, some individuals reaching more than 100 years of age. They may learn a few words, although these birds are not the most talented of mimics.

The affectionate and closely-bonding nature of Cockatoos can lead to problems if babies are over-indulged. They may then grow up into noisy, screaming adults, continuing to demand the high level of attention they have become used to. Careful discipline is also needed to avoid the possibility of aggressive behaviour when the bird reaches sexual maturity.

Cockatoos make charming and loving pets for anyone with enough time and energy to provide the interaction and mental stimulation they need. If left alone in their cage for long periods, they will probably resort to feather-plucking. Games, and trick-training with the keeper, as well as plenty of tough, wooden toys to chew on, will keep your Cockatoo happy.

4.9. MACAWS

"However much space we give our birds, it can never be enough" – Mike Reynolds, World Parrot Trust.

The Macaws' native habitat is South America, where they once flew in large, colourful flocks. There are more than 20 species and subspecies of these popular parrots. Some are regularly seen in captivity, while others are rare in aviculture, and close to becoming extinct in the wild. Deforestation, with the consequent loss of nesting sites and food sources, is now posing a serious threat to these birds. Nest robbing, and trapping for the pet trade, is further reducing their numbers in the wild, and Macaws are killed by indigenous people as a source of food and head-dress feathers. Several species are now under threat of extinction, notably the Lear's *(Anodorhynchus leari)*, Buffon's *(Ara ambigua)*, Blue-throated *(Ara glaucogularis)* and Illiger's *(Ara maracana)*. It is estimated that only 3,000 Hyacinth Macaws remain in the wild, and that captive breeding may be their only chance of survival.

DID YOU KNOW?

The rarest Macaw in the world is the Spix's (Cyanopsitta spixii), of which only one solitary male remains in its native Brazil. A painstaking conservation project was undertaken in recent years, in which a captive-bred female Spix's Macaw was rehabilitated and released into the vicinity of the lone male. The released bird was monitored for a while, but the hoped-for pairing did not take place and the female has since been found dead.

The male Spix's has paired up with a female Illiger's Macaw, although no young have been produced. A recent plan was to smuggle captive-produced Spix's eggs into their nest, in the hope that these would be hatched and fostered.

Most of us associate the word 'Macaw' with the large, highly colourful species such as the Scarlet Macaw or the Blue and Gold Macaw. However, adult Macaws range in size from the tiny Hahn's *(Diopsittaca nobilis nobilis)*, which is just 12 inches (30 cms) long, to the giant Hyacinth *(Anodorhynchus hyacinthinus)*, which is 40 inches (100 cms) long and the largest of them all.

4.9.1. PET MACAWS

Captive-bred, hand-reared Macaws are available from specialist breeders. You can expect to pay in excess of £1,000 ($1,600) for a tame, baby Macaw of the larger and popular species. Macaws are monomorphic, so DNA testing will be needed if you want to establish the gender of your bird. It should also be kept in mind that Macaws are very long-lived, often surviving their human keeper and being taken on by the next generation.

Macaws should never be given to children as a pet, because of their powerful and potentially dangerous beaks. The adult keeper needs to be fully in control. Early and consistent training is important to curb any aggressive behaviour that might occur as the bird matures and reaches breeding condition.

If you have your heart set on a pet Macaw, and you are prepared for the considerable work and commitment involved with these largest of parrots, your bird will repay your time and care with affection, loyalty and companionship. Macaws are very intelligent birds that can be taught intricate tricks and skills – cycling and roller-skating for example. Macaws will also, given the opportunity, enjoy practising their carving skills on any available wooden furniture, window sills, and skirting boards, etc. The other thing Macaws are noted for is making an exceptional amount of noise, especially at the beginning and end of each day.

It follows that, to keep one of these beautiful birds as a pet, you will need:
- Plenty of time for the training and attention your Macaw will need
- Enough room for a very large cage
- Facilities for your bird to fly about freely (under supervision)
- A regular supply of good-sized natural branches, for perching and chewing
- Tolerant neighbours (if living close by).

Large Macaws, because of their size, are particularly suited to a spacious outdoor aviary, where they are free to fly and to perform acrobatics. However, Blue and Gold Macaws *(Ara ararauna)* and Green-winged Macaws *(Ara chloroptera)* make particularly gentle, good-natured companion birds if sufficient space and time can be devoted to them. If you keep a pet Macaw, you will need a sturdy cage with a beak-proof catch, as these birds are adept at finding any weakness in the construction of their home.

The Scarlet Macaw *(Ara macao)* and the Military Macaw *(Ara militaris)* are both slightly smaller than the Blue and Gold and the Green-wing. The Scarlet is generally less trustworthy in temperament, so he would not be the best choice for a first-time Macaw keeper. However, he is valued for his stunning red, yellow, green, and blue plumage, and his special talent for mimicry. The Military Macaw has a distinctive red 'noseband', and, although less strikingly coloured than some of his cousins, he can make an excellent pet, full of fun and character.

CHAPTER 3

PET PARROTS

1. INTRODUCTION

If you are planning to keep a pet parrot, perhaps more than one, careful thought and research, before going ahead, will be time well spent. Taking on any pet is a commitment, and none more so than a parrot. A good imagination is useful here. If we put ourselves in the position of the bird, we can start to understand its feelings and needs and then work out how best to meet these.

2. CAGE OR AVIARY?

You may want a single house pet, perhaps adding one or two more in the future. Or, you may be planning to breed parrots in an outside aviary. From the list of species in Chapter Two, you will see which birds are most suitable as pets and which ones take less readily to humans, preferring the company of their own kind and the freedom of an outdoor flight. A parrot used to living indoors with a human family may never take to aviary life. Likewise, a parakeet that has always lived and bred in an aviary colony would be miserable housed in a cage in the living room.

3. HOME ALONE

Parrots are highly intelligent, sensitive and sociable creatures. In the absence of others of their own kind, they depend entirely on the

31

attention and affection of their keeper. They crave activity and interaction with others. In the case of a captive bird, this means you and your family. To leave a bird shut in his cage for hours is cruel.

Please do not buy a parrot if there is no one at home during the day. This is not only a bleak existence for the bird, it is pointless for you, as you won't have enough energy or time to give to your parrot when you come home tired from work.

If you are at home at least for most of the day, your parrot can become a valued companion. These bright little characters can be great company as you go about the daily chores, and, with plenty of freedom from the cage, your parrot is far less likely to resort to the behavioural problems of screaming or feather-plucking (*see pages 88, 93 and 183*).

4. WILL MY BIRD TALK?

It is a good idea to ask yourself what you expect from your parrot. Are you expecting a bird that talks and performs tricks, one that will fly to you on command and be a loving companion? Many parrots become just such pets, but not without time, attention and training from the keeper. Have you got the time and interest to bring the best out in your bird?

For many people, the attraction of parrots is their ability to mimic. Many species will learn at least a few words or phrases, some household sounds, and whistles. Some, notably African Greys, can develop an excellent repertoire. If, however, your reason for wanting a parrot is simply that you like the idea of a talking pet, it is worth considering the following points:

- Not all parrots (even some Greys) are good talkers
- Your bird may learn a couple of words and whistles only, then continually repeat these
- If you keep two or more parrots, they may be quite happy just chatting to each other in their own, natural language, rather than responding to you in yours
- You may take on a bird that has been taught to swear.

Remember, parrots have far more to offer as pets than mimicry. If you buy a bird just because you want him to talk, you may end up disappointed.

> ### DID YOU KNOW?
> *Pet parrots often prefer humans of the opposite sex – and once their minds are made up about someone, they seldom change it.*

5. HOW LONG DO THEY LIVE?

Many people do not consider the long-term (perhaps lifetime) commitment of keeping a parrot. Some parakeets can live for more than 20 years, while large Macaws and Cockatoos have been known to reach 100 years of age. Do you have family members who are willing and able to take on your bird should he outlive you? It is a sad fact that many bonded pet parrots are sold on to strangers and to an unknown fate. Good rescue homes offering a permanent refuge for unwanted birds are few and far between – and usually full. The best plan, therefore, is to think ahead and make arrangements for your parrot's future. Ensure that, if you are leaving the bird to a friend or relative, that person is in full agreement and will be able to care for your pet properly.

> **DID YOU KNOW?**
> *In the UK, it is illegal to keep a bird in a cage that prevents full extension of both wings without them touching the sides.*

6. COSTS

If you have always dreamt of keeping a large parrot, such as a Blue and Gold Macaw or a Moluccan Cockatoo, cost is a consideration. The price of a hand-reared baby can be in the region of £1,000 ($1600). An African Grey will cost you £500 ($800) or more. However, some of the smaller parakeets are inexpensive, with Budgerigars, Cockatiels, and Lovebirds available for a very modest outlay.

A good, strong, and roomy cage is the second major expenditure. Price will depend on the species being kept, but a rough guide is £350 ($560) for a cage suitable for a Grey or Amazon and £500 ($800) for a Macaw-sized cage.

Playstands, for the times your bird is out of his cage, range in price from £50 ($80) for a small, table-top stand, to £250 ($400) for a large, free-standing frame.

> **DID YOU KNOW?**
> *Some (although not all) Conure species can make good pets. The Maroon-bellied (Pyrrhura frontalis) and Peach-fronted (Aratinga aurea) Conures do not cost a fortune to buy and can make excellent pets. Remember, though, that Conures can be noisy.*

7. CLEANING UP

Even well-behaved parrots chuck their food around from time to time, or drop seed husks through the cage bars. Feathers and feather dust are also a reality when you keep a bird in your living room. With daily cage cleaning and a quick dust and vacuum round, mess need not be a big problem, although this will depend on how house-proud you are.

8. NOISE

If you enjoy peace and quiet, and you do not want to fall out with your neighbours, choose your species of parrot with care. Large Macaws, Cockatoos and some Conures (such as the Sun and Nanday Conure) can be very vocal at times. Amazons have their noisy times and African Greys will call and whistle, but tend not to be too raucous. Blue-headed Pionus, Senegals, and Peach-faced Lovebirds are some of the quieter species.

9. TRAINING

The importance of proper training cannot be over-emphasised. Even a tame, hand-reared young bird will need to be shown what is expected of him and to have his behaviour boundaries firmly established. This means a consistent, patient approach from you while your bird is learning. The end result will be a relaxed, confident and amenable pet, which makes it well worth the effort. Your parrot's future behaviour will largely depend on you and the time you are able to devote in the early days.

DID YOU KNOW?
Dimorphic is the term used for parrots whose sex is easily identifiable. For example, the male Eclectus is green, the female red. Male and female monomorphic parrots, such as the African Grey, look identical, or at least very similar. Gender can only be established for monomorphic birds by means of a feather or blood DNA test, or via surgical sexing.

---

10. HOLIDAYS

Many people take their pet parrots with them on holiday. Some hotels accept caged birds, and parrots will often happily accompany their keepers in the car, camping or caravanning. However, when you cannot take your bird with you, it is worth making arrangements in advance with another parrot keeper to look after him for you. A reciprocal arrangement of this kind can work well. Some birds become stressed when they are moved, in which case it is best for the carer to feed your pet in his own home. Having a trusted parrot lover you can call on is also invaluable in times of crisis – a stay in hospital for example.

11. FAMILY AND OTHER PETS

Is the whole family keen on having a parrot? Will your bird be safe around other pets? If there are young children in the house, is it really a good plan to buy that Scarlet Macaw, or would a smaller bird (with a smaller beak!) be a safer option? These are important considerations.

12. GOOD REASONS FOR KEEPING A PARROT

A tame and bonded pet parrot makes a charming and affectionate companion and will more than repay the care and attention you give him. The more integrated your bird becomes within the family, the more fun for everyone. Each individual has his own special talents and idiosyncrasies, and these can be brought out as you teach your bird to mimic, to play and to perform tricks.

34

You've thought about all the possible drawbacks of keeping a parrot, but you still have your heart set on keeping one and are looking forward to adding this new member to your family. At this stage, do not opt for economy or convenient travelling distances. If a little extra cost and a long car journey mean you get the healthy, tame bird you want, be prepared for this. After all, he will hopefully be with you for many years to come and any small sacrifices you made to get the right bird will be time and money very well spent.

CHAPTER 4

BUYING THE RIGHT BIRD

1. INTRODUCTION

You can find the names of parrot breeders by contacting your local bird society or looking in the classified sections of parrot magazines. Knowledgeable pet stores may also be able to help. Find an established and experienced breeder who can give good advice on the species that interest you.

If possible, visit a parrot or bird show. Here you will find a wealth of information on the birds themselves, the latest diets, health care products, cages, and other equipment. Breed societies, such as The Amazona Society UK (for those interested in buying an Amazon parrot), will be able to answer your questions and perhaps put you in touch with someone local who keeps or breeds the species. Sharing your interest, and increasing your knowledge, adds greatly to the fun of parrot keeping.

2. WHICH BIRD?

From the different species of parrot and parakeet described in Chapter Two, you may by now have a good idea of the one that would best suit you, your family, and your circumstances. You may have to wait a while to find the right bird, especially if you want a hand-reared baby. A good parrot breeder will let you choose a youngster and even become involved at the weaning stage, until your new pet is old enough to come home with you.

3. CAPTIVE-BRED BIRDS

It may be tempting to save money and buy what seems like a bargain bird, but 'inexpensive' parrots are usually anything but that. If a bird is low-priced, the reason may be that he is wild-caught, ill, aggressive, or stolen. You will have read in Chapter One about the cruelty involved in taking parrots from the wild, and no responsible pet bird keeper would want to be involved in this trade. The stress of capture and export can often lead to serious disease, which may not become apparent until some time after the bird has been sold on. Parrots with health or behavioural problems, or stolen birds, often end up at bird auctions, where there is usually no comeback for the unsuspecting buyer.

A documented, captive-bred parrot, particularly a hand-reared baby, will cost more, but is well worth waiting and perhaps saving up for. Proof of captive-breeding is a closed identification ring on the leg. This can only be fitted when the bird is very young, after which time the foot grows and the ring would be unable to pass over it. A baby parrot that has been carefully handled and properly weaned will be confident with humans and responsive to affection and training from the new keeper.

4. HEALTH CHECKS

If the bird you are buying does not come with a recent vet's certificate of health, it is a good idea to arrange this for yourself, before parting with your money. Obvious signs of ill-health include:

- A sleepy, fluffed-up appearance
- Droopy wings and tail
- Closed or dull eyes
- Underweight (prominent breast bone)
- Crouching low on the perch, or sitting on the cage floor
- Discharge from eyes or nostrils
- Messy undertail area
- Laboured breathing
- Sneezing
- Constant feather chewing
- Not eating.

Note: Untidy feathering is not necessarily a sign of illness. The bird may be moulting, or tail feathers may have become slightly damaged in the cage.

5. BEHAVIOUR CHECKS

Inexperienced buyers sometimes make the mistake of not asking to handle the parrot out of the cage. The fact that the seller has difficulty catching the parrot and putting him in a travelling box should ring alarm bells at once. Do not wait until you have arrived home before trying to handle your new bird – only to discover that he is terrified of humans. The reason may be that he has been taken from the wild, he is an aviary-bred bird that has never been handled, or he may be an untrained pet that has been discarded because he bites.

If you are not prepared for the lengthy process of taming a frightened bird, avoid disappointment for both of you and ensure the bird you are buying is friendly and confident around humans. Having said this, it should be pointed out that gaining the trust of a non-tame parrot, if you feel you can give the undertaking of time and patience required, is extremely rewarding *(See Chapter Eight)*.

When trying to decide on which parrot to choose, you may find that the bird chooses you! Parrots quickly make up their minds about who they like, and your prospective pet will show his approval by coming up to the cage bars and looking you in the eye. It is also important to know that female parrots often prefer men, while male parrots often prefer women. Some keepers are heard to complain that the bird they have bought only tolerates them and much prefers their human partner. Unless the sex of the species you are buying can easily be identified, you may want to arrange for a DNA test via a feather or drop of blood. This can be done by an avian vet, and parrot magazines also carry advertisements for this service.

If the bird you like also seems to like you, if he is bright and healthy-looking and will step readily onto your hand, you are off to a good start.

6. BUYING A BABY PARROT

Before he leaves his original home, a baby parrot should be fully weaned. This means that he can readily crack and eat seeds and is not still dependent on hand-rearing formula. If he is handled carefully by his first keeper, the bird will be friendly and confident with humans.

7. ASKING THE RIGHT QUESTIONS

Any responsible breeder or pet store will be happy to answer all your queries, to give you the history of the bird you want to buy, to advise on care and management, and to offer you a back-up service in case of any future difficulties. They will be able to tell you about the bird's current diet, his routine, and his preferences. Ask for a receipt that gives a full description of the parrot, as well as a health guarantee.

8. TAKING ON A RESCUE PARROT

Many parrots end up being passed from home to home, through no fault of their own. The reason may be genuine – if the keeper has died, for example. More often, however, the reason is that the parrot has been bought on a whim, then sold again when the novelty wears off or the keeper finds he does not have the time his pet needs. If left for long periods without attention, parrots make take to screaming or biting, and are consequently sold on to the next unsuspecting buyer.

There are certainly more unwanted or problem parrots than the available rescue centres can cope with, and good, permanent homes for these birds are in short supply. Taking on a rescue bird, if he is psychologically damaged, may involve months of patient effort. The reward is gaining the trust of a previously frightened or aggressive bird, and seeing him develop confidence and a sense of fun.

9. INSURANCE

Parrots can be costly, so insurance makes sense. Parrots tend to hide signs of illness until they are very poorly. By this stage, for the veterinarian to have the best chance of saving the bird's life, it may be necessary to perform a series of potentially highly expensive tests. Insurance to cover veterinary bills will avoid any hesitation you may have in seeking full and expert assistance if your bird becomes sick. Insurance can also cover theft and death, etc. Look in the classified section of avian magazines for specialist insurers.

CHAPTER 5

FITTING IN WITH THE FAMILY

1. Bringing home your parrot
2. Positioning the cage
3. Settling in
4. Early training
5. Hand-reared youngsters
6. Adding to the flock
7. Hazards in the home

1. BRINGING HOME YOUR PARROT

The safest way to bring your parrot home is in a purpose-made carrier, available from avian suppliers. Made from strong plastic, with a low perch and a front grill, this will be useful in the future if you ever need to transport your bird to the veterinary surgery or when you are going on holiday. If you have a long journey back home, your parrot will need food and water.

2. POSITIONING THE CAGE

Before collecting your new parrot, the cage needs to be equipped and placed in situ. Psittacines are sociable creatures and like to be where the action is, so house your bird where he will be with the family. Kitchens can be dangerous places for birds, so don't be tempted to site the cage there. The fumes from over-heated non-stick pans are deadly to parrots, and, when the bird is out of his cage, there are the obvious dangers of hot cooker tops and boiling liquids.

The living room is usually the best place to house your pet. Position the cage away from radiators, television, draughts, and direct sunlight. Do not put it near electrical wiring, curtains, wallpaper, wooden shelving, or anything else accessible to a beak. Chewing is a favourite parrot hobby and nothing will be sacred as far as your bird is concerned! However, your parrot will feel vulnerable and unable to relax if the cage is situated in the middle of the room, with people and pets moving past on all sides. Instead, place it in a quiet corner or at least close to a wall, where your bird can see everything going on but where he also feels secure.

DID YOU KNOW?

A parrot's beak can inflict serious damage to the face, or even remove a finger. Therefore, children should always be carefully supervised around parrots, especially the larger species. Teaching mutual respect and trust is important for both child and parrot.

---

3. SETTLING IN

Your house, family and other pets will all be new to your parrot at first, a factor that is often forgotten in the excitement of bringing your bird home. Take things slowly, and move quietly around your parrot until he is confident in his new environment. Give him plenty of time to settle into his cage, and to get used to you and the rest of the family, before you try to handle him. If you have taken on a semi-tame or very timid bird, it may be several days, or even weeks, before he will trust your hand in the cage. A patient, gentle approach is important at all times, so that your bird learns to regard you as a friend.

Even if your parrot's previous diet was less than ideal (*see Chapter Six* for advice on healthy foods), it is usually best to continue offering familiar foods at this stage, to make sure your parrot is at least eating something. Even if he only goes to the food bowl when there is no one around, you will be able to check this from droppings on the cage floor.

4. EARLY TRAINING

You will read about taming and training a pet parrot later in this book. However, right from the start, your bird will be watching and learning from what is going on around him. Establishing a routine is important, so that the parrot automatically accepts being put back in his cage after playtime and learns to amuse himself quietly when you are busy. He needs to understand from the beginning that you are 'leader of the flock', that biting is unacceptable, and that screaming does not get him what he wants. This approach will be understood by your parrot, as in the wild there is always a flock leader who is deferred to by the other members of the group. Without clear guidelines as to how he should behave, your bird will be confused and unhappy.

5. HAND-REARED YOUNGSTERS

If you take on a tame, weaned baby parrot the temptation may be to cuddle and indulge your new pet all day long. This can bring about problems that become apparent later on. If he is used to constant attention, your parrot will not understand when this is not forthcoming, or when you need him to spend longer periods in the cage.

Decide at the beginning on a workable routine, discourage nipping and, if your baby yells for attention, ignore him until he is quiet. This approach will pay dividends in future, particularly at the adolescent stage when even the most well-behaved parrot can turn into a typical rebellious teenager!

6. ADDING TO THE FLOCK

Parrots can be addictive, and you may want to take on a second or third pet bird. Having several parrots in the household can be great fun for all concerned, as long as careful thought has gone into it first.

Before you take the plunge, be realistic about the amount of time you can devote to your birds – the extra work, expense (cage, food, vet's bills etc.), mess, noise, and potential damage to furniture and furnishings that will be involved. In addition, consider the additional input needed to give time to each individual bird for interaction, training and playing.

If you decide to take on another bird, remember there is a risk of introducing disease to your existing flock, even if the new bird appears in perfect health. It is important to arrange a check-up with your avian vet, and to keep the newcomer in a separate part of the house, away from other parrots, for at least four weeks. This may seem excessive, but disease can take some time to reveal itself. In the wild, a sick bird would quickly fall victim to a predator. As a result, birds have developed an instinct to hide any signs of illness for as long as possible.

Mixing different species (and sizes) of parrots can be risky. There is always the possibility of serious injury, or even death, when a larger bird turns on a smaller one. For this reason also, do not attempt mixing parrots with other (non-psittacine) types of birds, such as canaries or finches. Depending on the individual natures of the parrots, even same-species birds may fight, or at least bicker and avoid each other. This can be disappointing to the keeper, but it is very difficult to change a parrot's mind once it is made up!

6.1. INTRODUCING A NEW BIRD

When you are ready to introduce a new bird, do so in gradual stages. Keep both parrots in separate cages where they can see each other but have no access. Move the cages closer if there is no sign of trouble. You should be able to tell from their body language if the birds are likely to get along.

Jealousy can lead to aggression, so make sure your first bird gets as much attention as the new one. If you fear a jealous reaction, you can take measures against this before bringing the new bird into the room. Bring his cage in first for a few days and let your bird see you opening the door, attending to food bowls, hanging up toys, etc. Follow this by making a fuss of your original bird. In this way, he should already be used to the idea when the second cage has an occupant.

When you are as confident as you can be that the birds are going to get along, let them out together under close supervision. Intervene at any sign of aggression. Do not leave the birds out together when you are not around until you are sure they have accepted each other. As parrots mature, unexpected aggression may also suddenly occur between previously friendly birds.

Of course, many parrots get on well together and are glad of the company of their own kind, particularly if the human keeper needs to be out of the house for several hours at a time. If you find you have become a parrot addict and keep adding to your collection, you may want to build a parrot 'tree' in the room where your birds live. This is a larger version of the natural-branch playstand, where your birds can choose from a variety of perching, eating, and playing places. Room size and your creative skills are the only limitations on creating fun environments of this kind.

7. HAZARDS IN THE HOME

As parrots can get up to all sorts of mischief, they should never be left unattended out of their cage.

7.1. TOXIC SUBSTANCES
Parrots like testing everything with their beak, to see if it is edible or worth chewing. Remember that many plants are poisonous to parrots. Toxic houseplants include Daffodils and Hyacinths. Bowls of pot pourri, tin foil, and chocolates can also be hazardous and should be kept out of reach.

It has already been mentioned that parrots should be kept out of the kitchen, in case of inhaling dangerous fumes. Non-stick cookware (e.g. Teflon) is a particular hazard (see page 222). Cigarette smoke, too, is very harmful to a bird's respiratory system. Never smoke near your bird.

Several parrot keepers in recent years have reported poisoning of their bird by fabric freshener sprays. Avoid using any chemical sprays, air fresheners or carpet freshening powders in the room where your bird lives, as many manufacturers are unable to give definite proof of their product's safety around parrots. Beware of any product that you think may give off fumes or that has a strong scent. Remove your birds if you are having new carpets laid or the room painted, because of the danger of toxic fumes. Also, beware of glues and other DIY products. Do not light incense or scented candles in the vicinity of your bird and avoid aromatherapy oil burners – tea tree oil, when heated, can be particularly toxic. Also avoid insecticidal houseplant sprays.

7.2. WINDOWS AND DOORS
Keep an eye open for possible dangers when your parrot is out of his cage – flying into glass doors, into open fires or up chimneys, or falling into a fish tank or lavatory bowl, may all be possibilities. Teach your pet to avoid flying into glass by taking him to windows and glass-panelled doors and lightly touching the obstacle with his beak. Another alternative is to fix stickers or mobiles against clear glass. Perching on top of an open door is also potentially dangerous if the door is inadvertently shut.

Windows or outside doors left open are the most obvious hazard of all, and parrots are easily lost in this fashion.

7.3. OTHER PETS

Pet cats and dogs can live amicably with parrots, but use extreme caution before allowing them to mix. Birds are the natural prey of carnivores, and accidents have happened where a seemingly benign cat or dog has suddenly attacked a pet bird. Wing-clipped parrots walking about the floor are in obvious danger from human feet, as well as pets.

7.4. SAFETY FIRST

From the above, you will see that a parrot is safer left in his cage during those times when there is a lot of coming and going, and rushing about in the household. When your parrot is out of his cage, make sure everyone in the household is aware of this fact and takes the appropriate care.

CHAPTER 6

FEEDING YOUR PARROT

1. INTRODUCTION

Food plays an important part in our lives, and this applies equally to the captive parrot. By keeping a bird as a pet, we are denying him the freedom of choice he would have in the wild to feed on a wide variety of fresh, natural, seasonal foods. Nibbling and chewing, cracking open seeds and nuts, and foraging amongst greenery, is also an activity that takes up much of the wild bird's day.

Compare the above with the fate of a caged bird that has nothing more interesting than a bowl of seed to occupy him, and you will see how important it is to give a healthy, varied diet. Correct feeding need not be complicated or expensive, but it will make all the difference to your parrot's health, behaviour, and his enjoyment of life.

DID YOU KNOW?

Parrots have a highly developed sense of colour. This can help in getting a reluctant bird interested in fresh, healthy foods by including as many brightly coloured fruits and vegetables as possible. Give red, yellow, and orange peppers, green leaf vegetables, peas and beans, yellow corn, slices of green and red apple, segments of orange citrus fruits, purple grapes, red cherries, blackberries, blueberries, pink-fleshed watermelon, peaches and apricots.

---

2. MATCHING THE NATURAL DIET

First, consider the species you are keeping, and, as far as possible, give the type of food your parrot would be eating in his natural habitat. For example, Budgerigars would feed on small seeds and grasses in their native Australia, while forest-dwelling Amazons and Macaws would seek out nuts, fruits, and sometimes protein in the form of insects and grubs. You can substitute the latter with the occasional cooked chicken bone with a little meat left on it, or a small cube of cheese.

FOODS FROM THE COUNTRYSIDE

In his wild habitat, your parrot would be nibbling on a wide variety of seasonal foods. You can provide enjoyable occupation and dietary interest with wild foods from woods and hedgerows – and, of course, they will cost you nothing.

It is extremely important that you never gather food from near roadsides, or in areas that may have been sprayed with agricultural chemicals. Wash all foodstuffs carefully in case of contamination from fumes, sprays or wild bird droppings.

The following are safe to give your parrot:

- *Blackberry flowers and berries*
- *Chickweed*
- *Dandelion leaves and flowers*
- *Elderberry flowers and berries*
- *Evening Primrose*
- *Hawthorn berries*
- *Honeysuckle flowers and berries*

- *Milk thistle*
- *Red clover*
- *Roses and rosehips*
- *Rowan berries*
- *Seeding grasses*
- *Violets*
- *Yarrow.*

Some keepers pick and freeze wild berries when in season, then thaw them during the winter months as a special treat for their birds.

Many wild plants and flowers are poisonous to parrots. Here are just a few:

- *Buttercup*
- *Daffodil*

- *Foxglove*
- *Iris*

- *Periwinkle*
- *Rhododendron.*

If in doubt about any wild foods, play safe and don't give them to your bird.

DID YOU KNOW?

The natural Bach Flower Remedies, available from pharmacies and health food shops, have been found by some keepers to be successful in treating various parrot ailments, both physical and psychological. Ask your avian vet for advice.

---

3. THE DAILY DIET

There should be at least two food bowls in your bird's cage, one for fresh foods and one for the dry mix. Give a varied choice of foods and be prepared for a change of preference from time to time.

As a basic guide, most hookbills do best on a diet of $2/3$ fresh fruit and vegetables, and $1/3$ grains, nuts, seeds and pulses (preferably sprouted – see below).

3.1. MAKE IT FUN

Caged birds need something to do, and food can play an important part in providing interest and activity. As long as your parrot is not one of those individuals stressed by new items in the cage, you can try lots of different ways of presenting foods. Here are just a few:
• Bunches of greens hanging from the cage roof
• Peanuts hidden in toys or tucked into rope swings
• A stick of green-topped celery or a piece of dry toast pegged beside a perch
• Budding twigs to nibble and strip
• A chicken bone to hold and crack open to get at the marrow
• Colour and interest with a spray of nasturtiums, carnations, pansies, roses, or hibiscus (as always, make sure flowers are clean and free of any chemical sprays)
• Attach a bunch of herb blossoms to the cage wire. Your parrot will enjoy borage, camomile, chives, sage, basil, fennel and garlic
• Thread chunks of vegetables and fruit on to a safely secured wire
• Give a piece of corn-on-the cob or millet spray, which will take time to pick at and eat
• Hang up a threaded string of monkey nuts.

Bright colours and different textures will add to the bird's interest, as will a change of flavour and smell. Be creative and think up your own ideas as you go along, so that there is always fresh stimulation for your bird.

3.2. COMPLETE DIETS

A complete pelleted food, or a good-quality parrot mix, will provide an excellent basis for your bird's diet and is very convenient for the busy keeper. Species-specific mixes can be purchased, to ensure your bird is getting the most appropriate formula.

Particularly good are the new organic pellets, which, although not brightly coloured like other manufactured diets, provide excellent basic nutrition and are free from agricultural chemicals. Vets have reported promising results in some cases where organic pellets have been fed to seed-addicts or feather-pluckers. However, although they are advertised as a carefully balanced diet for your bird, pellets should not be fed exclusively.

Food needs to provide constant interest with a variety of tastes, textures and colours, which cannot be provided by giving just pellets. Furthermore, pellets are no substitute for fresh fruits and vegetables, which are the natural foods your pet would seek out in the wild.

Rather than simply buying a bag of 'parrot mix' and hoping for the best, a better option is to research the seeds, farmed crops, etc., your particular species would be eating in his wild habitat, then make a suitably proportioned mix of your own.

Change the bowl of dry food every day, to make sure your parrot is eating enough. As many of the seed husks are dropped back into the bowl, it may seem full when there is actually nothing left to eat.

DID YOU KNOW?
Parrot seed mixes can eventually go stale or mouldy and this can be dangerous to your bird's health. Only buy parrot food from a supplier who has a quick turnover, and make sure the food is really fresh.

3.3. FRESH FOODS

When you consider what a parrot would eat in the wild, it follows that the main portion of his daily food should consist of raw fruits and vegetables. Sprouted seeds, grains and pulses are also an excellent way of providing live, fresh food that is particularly high in essential vitamins and minerals.

If you can obtain organic, seasonal produce, so much the better. Offer as many different foods as possible and you will get to know which ones your bird prefers. The wider the range your bird will eat, the more vitamins and minerals will be available to him.

Colour is important to a bird and can also be a guide for the keeper. For example, yellow, orange, and green fruits and vegetables – particularly dark, leafy greens – when included on a regular basis, will ensure your bird is receiving a good supply of vitamin A.

Freshly cut, home-grown wheat grass makes a really healthy treat for your bird to nibble on. It is packed with essential vitamins and minerals and is a good source of calcium.

As an alternative, or when fresh foods are in short supply, you can give thawed, frozen vegetables, and soaked, dried fruit (the unsulphured variety).

DID YOU KNOW?
Unlike humans, a parrot's mouth is unaffected by the stinging effect of hot peppers.

Here are some of the fruits and vegetables you can safely offer your parrot:
- **Fruit**: such as oranges and tangerines, apples, pears, plums, bananas, cranberries, grapes (the seeded varieties are best), peaches, apricots, nectarines, strawberries, raspberries, blackberries, cherries, melon, watermelon, pineapple, and papaya.
- **Vegetables**: such as cooked potato, sweet potato or swede, onions (cooked or raw), peas (can be given in the pod), green beans, carrot (and carrot greens), peppers (both hot and sweet), cucumber, cauliflower, courgettes (and their flowers), chicory, bok choy, Brussel sprouts, spinach, broccoli, kale, cos lettuce, Swiss chard, watercress, celery, beetroot, sweetcorn and okra.

4. FOODS TO AVOID

There are a few common household foods that are harmful or positively poisonous to parrots. Never give:
- Avocado
- Chocolate

SETTING UP HOME

Your pet parrot will depend on you to provide a secure, spacious and interesting environment.

The cage should be large and appropriately furnished.

Parrot playstands are a great way to entertain your parrot outside his cage.

Most parrots will greatly appreciate colourful new toys to play with.

A BALANCED DIET

Don't let your parrot become a sunflower-seed junkie!

Species-specific seed mixes are a good basic element in a diet. Lots of fresh fruit and veg should also be given.

Hawk-headed Parrot: parrots enjoy the occasional 'human' treat, such as a biscuit, or chips.

For interest and occupation, peanuts in their shells are a great favourite. Also provide fresh foods that take time to find, open, or chew.
Pictured: Illiger's Macaw (left) and Black-headed Caique (right).

HANDLING PARROTS

Your time and patience will be rewarded with a relaxed and bonded pet.

Great Western Vasa: most parrots adore a tickle on the back of their heads. The more gentle handling and attention your bird receives, the tamer he will become.

This Macaw has been trained to sit on a shoulder – but it is inadvisable unless you are an experienced handler.

Black-headed Caique: teach your parrot to step on to your hand when you want to take him out of his cage.

GROOMING

If unsure about any aspect of grooming, consult your avian veterinarian.

Spraying helps to keep your parrot's feathers in good condition, and is also a way of recreating the rain showers that your parrot would experience in his natural habitat. Pictured: Black-headed Caiques.

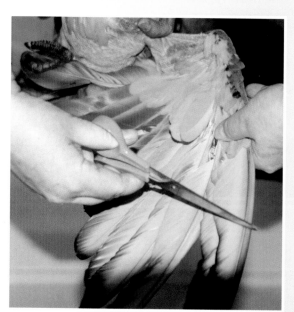

Wing clipping can severely curtail a parrot's ability to fly, so should only be carried out by an expert.

BEHAVIOUR AND TRAINING

Staying in charge of your bird's behaviour at all
times will give him a sense of security.

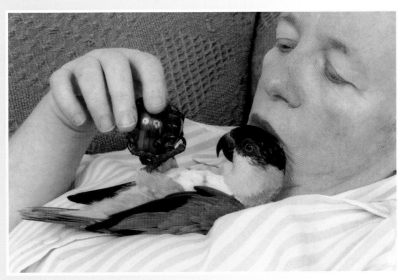

Your parrot will enjoy learning new tricks, such as picking
up a ball (above). Placing objects in a dish (below) is a favourite pastime, but
coins should be avoided – they contain zinc (particularly high in American
dimes), which is toxic to birds (see page 241).
Pictured: Black-headed Caique (above) and Spectacled Amazon (below).

BREEDING AND REARING

Think carefully before undertaking this time-consuming hobby. Seek advice from experienced keepers to get you off to a good start.

If you plan to breed parrots, you may need an incubator if problems arise in the nest-box.

After hatching from an incubator, or if you need to remove young birds from the nest, they will need to be kept warm in a suitable container. Pictured: African Grey chick.

BREEDING AND REARING

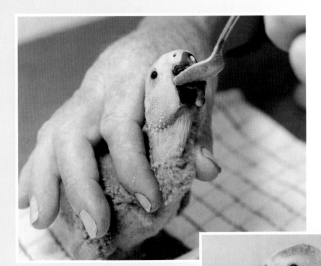

Hand-feeding an African Grey from a teaspoon.

Note the crop before (right) and after (below) feeding.

HEALTH CARE

Birds are good at hiding signs of ill-health,
so keep a careful eye on your pet.

Feather plucking may be a symptom of unhappiness. Pictured: Green-winged Macaw.

Lesser Sulphur-crested Cockatoo: it is easier to administer medicine if the bird is wrapped in a towel.

African Grey: broken wings can be healed with the aid of a splint (left), while a collar (right) will prevent your bird from trying to remove the splint.

- Rhubarb
- Cabbage
- Mushrooms.

Spinach and broccoli are fine in small amounts, but do not overfeed with these vegetables, particularly in the case of African Greys, as calcium absorption may be affected. Doubt has also been expressed over parsley, although some keepers feed small amounts of this herb to their birds without any problems.

Your bird may want to share your salted crisps, cup of tea or coffee, sweet biscuit, or glass of beer. However, salt, fat, caffeine, sugar, and alcohol are hazardous to a bird's health, so you will not be doing your pet any favours by indulging him in this way. Keep a supply of unsalted nuts or plain biscuits for giving as treats. You can also give puffed wheat and rice cereals.

5. PROTEIN

Although most of a bird's protein requirements are met by providing whole grains, pulses, nuts and seeds, wild parrots are also known to occasionally eat grubs and other insects. Some birds will pull off strips of bark to find the insects hiding underneath, or eat the insects they come across while nibbling on flowers and buds.

Extra protein can be given by the keeper, in the form of a small piece of meat or cheese, scrambled egg, or yogurt. Breeding birds in particular need additional sources of protein.

6. SPROUTED SEEDS, GRAINS, AND PULSES

Some of the healthiest foods you can give your parrot are freshly sprouted seeds, grains and pulses. Sprouts are living foods that will enhance the health,  condition and well-being of your bird. They are quick, easy and cheap to produce at home, and contain far higher levels of vitamins and minerals than the original, unsprouted versions. They are equally good for humans!

These energy-packed foods are readily digested by parrots, who will usually welcome such a fresh treat, instinctively knowing what is good for them. The best time to feed sprouts to your birds is when the growing tip first appears.

Bags of mung bean sprouts can sometimes be bought in supermarkets, but at a stage of growth when they are well past their best. A far greater variety of really fresh produce can be grown at home at less cost.

6.1. GROWING SPROUTS

A purpose-made sprouter can be purchased from health food stores, or you can just as successfully use ordinary kitchen equipment – a bowl or wide-topped glass jar. Remember, once sprouted, the seeds increase dramatically in volume, so allow plenty of growing room in the container. If you are not using a purpose-made sprouter, which has a slotted lid for rinsing and a base to catch the water, rinsing can be done in a sieve or colander.

Soak the seeds overnight in plenty of water, as they will absorb a good deal. Some will need a longer time than others to soak, depending on the type and size. Alfalfa is so tiny it does not need to be pre-soaked. Different types of seeds that take roughly the same amount of time to germinate (for instance sunflower and mung beans) can be soaked and grown together.

After soaking, rinse well under the cold tap. Put a shallow layer of seeds or beans in a sprouter, bowl or glass jar (allowing for the free circulation of air, to avoid the crop going sour) then leave in a dark place to germinate. A warm environment will speed the growing process. It is vitally important to keep the crop fresh, which can be achieved by continued thorough rinsing, at least twice a day, until the sprouts appear. This will take two to five days, depending on what you are growing. Rinse and drain well, and the sprouts are now ready to feed to your parrot.

Keep surplus sprouts in a covered container or bag in the refrigerator, where they will stay fresh for a few days. Remember, however, that they are best eaten as soon as they are ready, and that nutritional benefits will reduce after a few days.

6.1.1. A SAFETY WARNING

To avoid danger from harmful bacteria, germinating sprouts must be rinsed regularly and thoroughly. Sprouting equipment should be kept spotlessly clean by washing it carefully each time you use it. Never use sprouts that smell 'off' or where there is any evidence of mould – this can be the result of insufficient rinsing and ventilation. Also remember to wash the food dish in the cage regularly if sprouts are being fed. Remove uneaten sprouts on a regular basis.

Despite the above warning, growing your own sprouts is actually a very quick and straightforward task. The problems mentioned can be easily avoided by following the guidelines on rinsing and hygiene.

> **DID YOU KNOW?**
> *Red kidney beans can be toxic if eaten raw, so they should always be cooked before giving them to your parrot.*

6.2. TYPES TO TRY

Easy sprouts to start with are sunflower seeds and mung beans, which can be bought in supermarkets or health food stores. By sprouting sunflower seeds, harmful fats are reduced, making them a healthier alternative to the dry seed. You will get to know which fresh sprouts your bird prefers, but remember that split lentils, rolled oats, etc. will not germinate – they need to be whole.

Also try aduki beans, chick peas, lentils, millet, oats, brown rice, wheat, popping corn, alfalfa, fenugreek, pumpkin, and radish. Buy organic whenever possible.

7. HOME-GROWN WHEAT GRASS

You do not need a garden to provide your bird with fresh organic greens. Wheat grass can be grown indoors, in seed trays of potting compost, to provide a source of highly nutritious green food.

Sprinkle wheat grains (soaked overnight) over the tray of soil, water, and then cover loosely with a plastic bag, allowing the air to circulate. Continue watering lightly once a day for several days, before exposing the growing shoots to the light, so that they turn green. After about a week, when the wheat grass is several inches high, trim the top growth and give to your parrot. Continue to water the plants for further cropping.

8. SPECIAL DIETS
Lories and Lorikeets have evolved brush-like papillae at the tip of their long tongues so that they can probe for and extract nectar and pollen from flowers. These birds need a special diet of nectar, fruit, and fresh flowers, which can be given in the form of a proprietary nectar mix to which water is added.

Even more convenient are the dry food mixes now available to the Lory keeper, although it is considered by many that fresh, natural foods are best for these birds. One potential problem is the large amount of water Lories need to drink if given dry foods. Lories seem to enjoy nothing better than a bunch of fresh flowers or a dish of over-ripe bananas to feed on.

9. SEASONAL DIETS
It is worth remembering that a wild parrot would not be eating the same selection of foods all year round, but rather what is fresh and in season. Also, these intelligent birds will often instinctively eat what their bodies need. The best policy is always to offer as wide a range of suitable foods as possible and be prepared for changes in your pet's preferences.

10. CUTTING DOWN ON FAT
A bird's digestive system quickly metabolises food and eliminates waste, so the parrot keeper should ensure there is always food and fresh water available in the cage.

Birds tend to nibble throughout the day, and, given the choice, many pet parrots (like the rest of us!) will go for fatty foods, such as nuts, sunflower seeds, and, if offered, crisps, chips, or sugary biscuits. There are two dangers here:
• Pet birds do not get the opportunity to fly and exercise as extensively as their wild counterparts
• High-fat foods can become addictive, so that the parrot refuses to eat healthier items such as raw fruit and vegetables.

Amazons in particular can be prone to obesity, so it is important to limit nuts and other fatty foods in their diet. A diet high in fresh fruits is best for Amazons. However, whichever species you keep, it is advisable to keep an eye on your bird's weight and keep peanuts and fatty 'human' foods as occasional treats, rather than everyday meals.

The commonly fed sunflower seed can be a dietary disaster for some parrots, notably African Greys, who may get in the habit of eating this one food to the exclusion of everything else. Sunflower seeds are high in fat and low in essential vitamins and minerals. Rickets in young birds, chronic feather plucking, and vitamin A and calcium deficiencies are the serious health problems that can eventually result when the diet consists mainly of sunflower seeds, with few fresh fruits or vegetables. Veterinary advice and medication will be needed in these cases.

11. CONVERTING THE FUSSY EATER

In the wild, parent birds introduce their young to the foods that are tasty and healthy to eat. A captive parrot also needs to be shown which foods are safe to try, or he may grow up being suspicious of anything unfamiliar. A bird that has been introduced to a wide variety of fresh foods from the weaning stage will usually readily accept these items as part of a normal diet. Adult Cockatoos can be particularly fussy if good habits have not been established early on, but this problem can apply to any parrot.

As we all know, bad eating habits are hard to break! However, we also know how much better we feel – and look – once we give up the junk food and substitute it with such things as fruit, salads, fresh vegetables, sprouted seeds and whole grains. On the whole, what is good for us humans is also good for parrots. The problem, however, is how to persuade our sunflower-seed junkie or nutaholic to eat and enjoy sprouted seeds or green foods instead of the old, addictive diet.

It may be tempting not to persevere if your parrot resolutely ignores every tempting piece of fruit or vegetable you give him. However, for his health and happiness it is essential to persist. When introducing new and healthier foods, make sure they are not flung out of the bowl in favour of the familiar seeds and nuts.

Rather than present your fussy bird with a big chunk of carrot or segment of orange (which he will most likely drop to the floor in disgust), you need to be devious. Add tiny pieces of fruit or raw vegetable, peas, or individual kernels of sweetcorn to the parrot's normal food. Although much of this will probably be thrown out of the bowl as your bird sorts through to find the food he prefers, at least some of it will be inadvertently eaten. You could also try squeezing a little orange or carrot juice over the usual food to introduce the idea of a new flavour.

Parrots enjoy the taste of cayenne, so a sprinkling of this pepper over a dish of food containing new items may tempt him to try them. It will supply useful vitamins and minerals too.

Get your parrot interested in new foods by introducing as many different colours, textures, shapes and sizes as possible. Hang bunches of leaves by the perch your bird favours, to encourage experimental nibbling. Offer a clove of garlic with the skin left on – he will enjoy peeling it off and may then be interested enough to try this healthy titbit. Hide pieces of fruit or vegetable around the cage, so that your parrot is intrigued enough to prise them out. If all raw foods are refused, offer cooked peas, beans, sweetcorn, etc. instead, as these may be more readily accepted. Let your bird see you eating – and obviously enjoying – a piece of apple, a grape, or a stick of carrot, so that he is encouraged to try the food himself. Wait until he looks really interested and hopeful, then offer a piece to him.

DID YOU KNOW?
A reluctant fruit and veg eater may be persuaded to try healthier foods if he sees another bird eating them.

Of course, many parrots are happy to try new items, but some will starve rather than give in. It is, therefore, important to keep a close eye on your bird while you are making the change. If he is not eating, or eating very little, either cut down on the proportion of new food or go back to the original diet for a while. You can try again later with very small amounts of the new foods, gradually increasing these when you are sure your pet is not going hungry.

It may take weeks or even months before your parrot has accepted a healthier diet, but keep thinking up new ways to tempt him. Whatever you do – do not give up!

12. SUPPLEMENTS

A balanced, varied diet normally provides everything a bird needs for health. Vitamin and mineral supplements should not be used in the place of fresh foods. Over-supplementing can actually cause toxicity and serious health problems in parrots.

However, nutritionally depleted parrots, or those proving difficult to convert away from a seed-only diet, may need a vitamin or mineral supplement, at least for the time being. Your avian vet will be able to advise on this. Supplements can be sprinkled on food or added to drinking water. Some birds enjoying nibbling at mineral blocks, which are attached to the cage wire.

Calcium deficiency, which can particularly affect African Greys, Cockatiels and Cockatoos, can be treated by your vet with vitamin D_3 or a calcium supplement. However, the parrot keeper can also provide extra calcium in the diet in the form of oyster shell, almonds, small amounts of cheese, a cooked chicken bone, or some crushed eggshell in a little scrambled egg. A piece of cuttlefish is traditionally given as a calcium supplement, but this will not be enough to cure an existing problem. Remember that a varied diet, high in fresh fruit and vegetables, is the best way to avoid nutritional deficiencies and disease.

13. EATING WITH THE FAMILY

Many people let their parrot join in at family mealtimes. This can be fun for everyone, but be careful what you give your bird. If you always offer chips, roast meat or chocolate cake, this is what he will come to expect – and he will make a fuss if it is not forthcoming! Pasta, rice and potato are all healthy foods that your parrot can share with you, provided they are not accompanied by fatty, salty sauces. Alternatively, you can offer items from the salad bowl, a wholemeal toast crust, a little cottage cheese, or a small rib with a few shreds of meat left on it.

Remember, parrots enjoy being included in the activity of their human 'flock' and mealtimes are an ideal opportunity for this. However, keep it on your terms, not the bird's!

CHAPTER 7

CARE AND MANAGEMENT

1. GENERAL CARE PRINCIPLES

It is good practice to remember the natural origins of your pet parrot and do whatever you can to bring a little of the wild into his life. This involves researching the types of food he would be eating in his natural habitat, and developing an awareness of the temperature and humidity levels he would be exposed to (e.g. desert scrub or rainforest). Living wild, your bird would be constantly active, flying in search of food, interacting with his flock, and climbing or chewing on branches.

What the keeper can provide are:
- Regular periods of freedom from the cage
- The chance to bathe
- An outside flight or aviary, for warm days
- Natural foods and branches to nibble on
- Social interaction
- Toys and games for occupation and mental stimulation.

2. FIRST AID

Not every veterinary surgery has an expert in bird care, so it is important to track down and register with your nearest avian vet before you purchase your parrot. Keep the telephone number handy in case of an emergency. You will also need a suitable carrier for transporting your bird.

Being with your parrot every day, you will get to know his normal, healthy behaviour, so you will quickly notice if anything is wrong. A happy, healthy bird is alert and vocal, he will enjoy his food, and he will have clear, bright eyes. If your pet is unusually ruffled, quiet and lethargic, if there is a change in the appearance of his droppings or the sound of his breathing, or if his feet feel unusually cold, these are signs that something is wrong. Birds can hide their illness for some time, so never delay contacting your vet.

When nursing a sick bird overnight, make sure he is warm and leave a light on to encourage him to eat and drink. Warmth is essential to an ill or injured bird. Your bird should be nursed in a room where the temperature falls between 29.5 to 32.5 degrees Celsius (85 to 90 degrees Fahrenheit). For a quick source of heat, you could tuck your bird into your jumper. The room in which you nurse your bird should also be quiet and peaceful, to keep stress to a minimum.

Until expert attention can be given, place the bird in a hospital cage or another suitable enclosure (e.g. a small box) where your pet is comfortable, warm, and secure. Encourage him to drink, but do not leave him with an open water bowl, which may spill and reduce his body heat. Tempt your bird to eat by offering soft foods you know he likes, such as baby rice pudding from a jar.

If your bird has an injury from which he is bleeding, you can help to stem the flow by applying cornflour or styptic powder to the wound. If you suspect a broken wing, this can be gently bound in place, or the bird can be placed in a loose-fitting sock, to prevent further injury while you transport your pet to the veterinary surgery. In the case of broken wings or bones, do not let the bird attempt to perch, or further damage could be caused. Keep him confined securely and comfortably, instead.

Most importantly, do not hesitate to call the vet if you even suspect a problem. The 'wait and see' approach may lead to tragedy.

2.1. FIRST-AID KIT

Your avian vet will be able to advise on stocking a first-aid kit for your parrot, but basic essentials are:
• Heat pad or hot water bottle
• Hospital cage
• First-aid manual
• Avian antiseptic
• Antibiotic ointment
• Gauze bandage
• Scissors
• Tweezers
• Cotton buds
• Towel
• Styptic powder or cornflour (to stem bleeding)
• Magnifying glass
• Emergency nutrient formula
• Electrolyte solution (to prevent dehydration)
• Glucose (give in water from a syringe as a quick source of energy).

It is a good idea to keep a supply of first-aid nutrients to hand. These are special emergency formulas for birds that have stopped eating and drinking, and can provide essential interim care before medical help is available.

> **DID YOU KNOW?**
> *Parrots respond well to some homoeopathic and herbal remedies. These can be used successfully as complements to prescribed medication. Ask your vet for advice before treating the bird yourself.*

3. THE CAGE AS A SANCTUARY

The cage should be as large as possible. Your bird should be able to fly freely in the cage, and have plenty of room for climbing, perching, feeding, and playing on ropes and swings. Width, as well as height, is important, so that your bird can move about in all directions. Think 'horizontal' when choosing a cage – birds don't fly up and down, but forwards.

The best way to provide a welcoming home for your parrot is to imagine living in it yourself. Is it big enough? Warm enough? Too hot? Too draughty, exposed, boring or lonely? Hopefully, it is located in a quiet, cosy corner, in a room frequented by the rest of the family. The cage should feel spacious, with lots of interesting food and toys, fresh air, and a view through the window, bunches of greens to nibble on, and lots of opportunity to come outside to play.

Some species, such as African Greys and Cockatoos, like to scratch around on the ground (or in this case, the cage floor). These birds are happier in cages with a solid bottom, rather than walking about on mesh bases, designed for easier cleaning.

3.1. SIZE AND CONSTRUCTION

The size of your bird is not necessarily a guide to the size of cage you will need. Smaller parrots and parakeets tend to flit and dart about more often and more swiftly than the larger birds. Greys, for example, often choose to clamber about rather than to fly.

A strong, non-coated stainless steel cage is ideal. Poor-quality cages should always be avoided, as in some cases the production process can leave residues of zinc on the wire mesh. Likewise, if the cage wire is painted, ensure that the paint used is lead-free. Both zinc and lead are poisonous to parrots.

Check the construction – is it strong enough for your bird, with sufficiently narrow bar spacing (to prevent the head becoming trapped) and no sharp edges that could injure your pet?

Make sure the cage door catch cannot be undone from the inside – any weakness will soon be discovered by that strong beak, and parrots are ingenious when it comes to escaping.

Some cages come complete with an anti-scatter base that catches flung seed, feathers, and other mess before it hits the floor. A pull-out litter tray makes cleaning the cage quicker and easier.

If you choose a cage on castors, you will be able to move it about more easily, e.g. into the garden on a fine day.

An opening top and overhead perch allows freedom to come and go during supervised playtimes, as well as encouraging the bird to perch (and therefore also poop!) over the newspaper in the base of the cage.

3.2. CAGE ACCESSORIES

You should arrange the cage layout – perches, swings, ladders and dishes – so that your bird has the opportunity to exercise in a variety of ways, using all his muscles and acrobatic skills in the process.

3.2.1. BASE-LINING MATERIALS

Several materials have been tried by bird keepers as a means of lining the cage floor and collecting droppings, spilt water, and discarded food. However, paper is the most satisfactory for both safety and convenience.

Pine shavings can be used, although their consistency means it will be difficult to keep a close check on your bird's health via his droppings. Also, shavings need to be changed frequently to avoid the build-up of bacteria. Never use cat litter, as this is dangerous if ingested by the bird.

Newspaper is safe, readily available, cheap, quick and easy to change each day, and allows for the monitoring of droppings. Simply lay several sheets of newspaper on the cage floor and then remove them as necessary. Some parrots enjoy hiding under the newspaper or ripping it up, so it is important to keep it fresh.

3.2.2. FOOD AND WATER DISHES

Stainless steel bowls are beak-proof and hygienic, so they are the best choice for parrots. If the dishes are fitted to a swing-out holder, they can be removed, cleaned, and refilled, without the risk of escape or the need to put a hand inside the cage. This is ideal for nervous birds, or if someone unused to parrots is caring for your pet temporarily.

As well as a water bowl, you will need one for dry foods, and one for fruit and vegetables. Buy dishes a size or two larger than you think you need, so that you do not need to fill them right to the top – this will save spillage as the parrot picks through his food. Make sure you position bowls beside the topmost perches, so that food and water does not become contaminated by droppings from above.

Food and water should be changed every day. The dishes should be thoroughly rinsed with each change, to prevent the build-up of mould or bacteria. Some parrots enjoy dipping their food in the water dish before eating it, so everything needs to be kept clean to avoid the growth of harmful bacteria.

Another way of ensuring the water supply remains fresh is to provide it in a plastic bottle with a drop feeder – the kind used by small, caged animals, such as guinea pigs and mice. However, make sure your parrot is happily drinking from a bottle before substituting this for the usual water bowl.

3.2.3. PERCHES

Avoid plastic or smooth dowel perches. These provide no exercise for the parrot's feet or natural wear for his toenails. You can buy special abrasive perches that are designed to wear down toenails. However, these have been found to cause sore feet with some birds.

Natural branches, in a variety of shapes and thicknesses, make the best perches. Always wash the branches carefully, to remove any chemical spray residue or possible contamination from wild birds.

Rough branches with the bark left on will provide exercise for feet and legs, and your parrot will enjoy chewing on the wood. Just two or three perches, of varying thickness and suitably placed, are sufficient, allowing as much free space as possible in the cage. Position them so that when your bird is perching he is not soiling the branch beneath.

Parrots like to roost high up. Provide a comfortable, forked branch towards the top of the cage where your bird can feel secure while sleeping.

SAFE WOODS TO USE

• *Apple*	• *Guava*
• *Ash*	• *Hawthorn*
• *Aspen*	• *Hazlenut*
• *Beech*	• *Larch*
• *Birch*	• *Manzanita*
• *Citrus*	• *Maple*
(orange, lemon, etc.)	• *Pine*
• *Elm*	• *Poplar*
• *Eucalyptus*	• *Sycamore*
• *Fir*	• *Willow*

Unsafe woods include horse chestnut, yew, laburnum and those of the Prunus family (e.g. apricot, cherry, and peach). Although some keepers give oak, this is not considered safe by all.

Some parrots particularly enjoy chewing wood and stripping off the bark, in which case the perches will need replacing at regular intervals. If you do not have a garden, ask friends and neighbours for off-cuts whenever they are trimming their trees.

In the case of nervous birds – notably African Greys – you may need to leave replacement perches outside the cage for a few days before changing them for the old ones, so that your bird can get used to them beforehand.

3.2.4. TOYS

These are vital to a caged bird *(see page 69)*.

3.2.5. PRIVACY

We all need a bit of peace and quiet from time to time and some parrots appreciate the refuge of a small box where they can retreat. This can be attached to the side of the cage, with access from a perch, or placed on the base. If your parrot is one that likes to hide under the newspaper on the cage floor, he may enjoy the privacy of a bolthole of this kind. A wooden nesting box is ideal. However, problems may arise if your bird is a mature female, as the provision of an enclosed space like this may encourage her to come into breeding condition, resulting in aggressive nesting behaviour and chronic egg laying.

3.2.6. HYGIENE
Washing the cage once a week to remove droppings and discarded food will keep it hygienic. Use household detergent and rinse carefully.

Special avian disinfectants are available for thorough cleaning, which should be done every few weeks. Do not forget to wash the perches too, as these can build up a layer of grime and grease which makes perching uncomfortable for the parrot.

4. A BUSY PARROT IS A HAPPY PARROT
It has been said that keeping a pet parrot is like living with a toddler that never grows up. Full of curiosity, into everything, noisy and messy, continually demanding attention – the comparison is a good one. Just like young children, parrots love to explore and to play, and so they need careful supervision, as well as the opportunity for learning and self-expression.

4.1. HUMAN COMPANY
It has already been stressed that no parrot should be left alone all day or confined to a cage for long periods. Your bird will look to you for companionship, and he will be miserable if neglected. Building up a close relationship brings great rewards for both the parrot and his keeper, and it is surely the only good reason to keep a pet parrot. Every time you speak or whistle to your bird he is listening. Soon he will be greeting you as you walk into the room. Behaviour training, and teaching your bird to play *(see Chapter Eight)* will also strengthen the trust and friendship between you.

As far as your parrot is concerned, you are his mate as well as his flock leader. He will look to you for guidance and company, always waiting patiently until you reappear. We all rush about in our busy lives, dashing to work, the shops, to drop the children off to school, etc. However, we must not forget the strong bond our pet bird feels for us, and his dependence on our physical presence. Establishing a consistent routine is a good idea, setting a time each day when your parrot knows you will be there to give him your attention. This way he will play happily alone at those times when you are busy. Parrots pester for attention when they are unsure if or when they will receive any.

Whenever possible, let your parrot join in with what you are doing, whether it is watching television, writing letters, or having a cup of tea with a friend. The more he is with you and involved in your everyday life, the more relaxed and confident he will be. Teaching what is, and what is not, acceptable behaviour can be a natural part of this daily interaction with you, and it will increase the mental well-being of your bird as he gets to know he can rely on you for both company and guidance.

4.2. TOYS

Parrots really enjoy investigating, beating up, swinging from, or chewing on a toy. Toys provide invaluable mental stimulation for captive birds – whether home is a cage or an outside aviary – and you will soon get to know which ones your own pet particularly enjoys.

Intricate, colourful toys will challenge and intrigue your parrot, and he will also enjoy shredding up items intended for destruction, such as pieces of wood or card. Rawhide dog chews will be held and gnawed by the larger parrots.

There is a huge range these days of every kind of parrot toy. Just visit any parrot show or store and you will be spoilt for choice. Commercially produced toys include brightly coloured ropes, swings, bells, and wooden blocks for your bird to chew on or to practise his acrobatics. Remember to buy toys large and strong enough to withstand your bird's beak, however, or they will fall apart very quickly and may not be safe.

4.2.1. MAKING YOUR OWN TOYS

If funds are limited, you can easily make your own parrot toys from objects found around the home. They will cost you nothing and your parrot will be just as delighted as if you had bought them.

Always consider the size of your bird and the strength of his beak when giving any toy, and avoid items that could get caught round a leg, beak, or wing, or be swallowed.

A larger parrot will have fun with a tough, squeaky dog toy, or you could put large, brightly coloured beads or buttons into a clear plastic bottle for him to investigate. Hang bottle tops, wooden balls, spools, rings etc. from leather bootlaces. Plait lengths of rope, or non-fraying fabric, and hang toys or food treats from these. Your parrot will enjoy the challenge. An old paperback book or telephone directory makes ideal shredding material for a bored bird – smaller species may prefer to rip up knotted paper tissues or paper bags. Some parrots will welcome a soft toy secured beside a favourite perch. A bundle of clean feathers for picking at (you could use a natural feather duster) has been known to distract birds from pulling out their own feathers.

Many parrots will enjoy chewing on a tough, plastic baby's teething ring or building block (children's toys can sometimes be bought very cheaply from charity shops), ripping up the cardboard tubes from kitchen or bathroom paper, or testing their strength on plastic containers such as margarine tubs or yoghurt pots. Just a small cardboard box or a few sheets of newspaper to hide under and rip up can make ideal toys. Off-cuts of wood for chewing, or a length of thick rope for a swing – you will be able to think up your own parrot toys. Remember to use only durable, non-toxic materials. Keep it colourful, and watch your bird have fun.

Parrots love a challenge, so make toys even more interesting by hiding small food treats inside. Use favourite toys to make up shared games with your parrot, or to teach him tricks. This is a great way to strengthen the friendship and trust between you.

DID YOU KNOW?
Rubber can be poisonous to parrots if swallowed. Give tough plastic toys instead.

4.2.2. KEEPING IT SAFE

Whether you give your parrot shop-bought or home-made toys, ensure they are made from strong, non-toxic materials, with no hidden dangers. Hooks or unwelded chain links could get caught on a beak; lengths of thread might tangle around a wing. Keep a close eye on your bird when giving a new toy – parrots are experts at getting themselves into trouble if they can!

Check bells for strength and safety – parrots are adept at prising off and possibly swallowing any moving parts. Check that metal toys do not contain lead or zinc and that vegetable dyes only have been used. Choose the size of toy recommended by the manufacturer for your particular species. Parrots quickly panic if something goes wrong, so look carefully at any potential plaything before giving it to your bird.

JEWELLERY
If you allow your bird to sit on your shoulder (not generally recommended, especially with larger birds), there is a potential danger from earrings, brooches and chains getting caught round a beak or foot. This is not only hazardous to your bird, but also puts you in danger of being bitten in the ensuing panic. Anticipate possible problems and avoid accidents.

Some, but not all, children's toys may be suitable for a parrot. They should be of strong, durable plastic or wood, with no moving or removable parts.

Make sure you leave enough room in the cage for flying and climbing. Too many toys are as bad as too few! Give one or two playthings at a time and change them at regular intervals.

Finally, toys can become sticky, and may possibly harbour bacteria, so wash them regularly, along with the cage, perches and food bowls.

AFRICAN GREYS AND TOYS
African Greys, in particular can be nervous of anything new in their cage. If your Grey is the sensitive type, introduce new toys, perches, etc., with care, or he might panic. Try leaving the new toy outside the cage for a while, moving it nearer each day until your bird has overcome his suspicion. When you first put the toy in the cage, leave it on the floor as this is the least threatening place. You can move it higher up later on.

4.3. PLAYSTANDS

A special base for your bird when he is out of his cage is an advantage for both of you. Your parrot will have somewhere to perch, eat, chew and play. Droppings will be mainly confined to the tray beneath and there will be less wear and tear to furniture and fittings.

Avian suppliers offer a wide range of excellent playstands, in a variety of sizes and with any number of perches, swings, ladders and toys. Small, simple stands can be put on table tops for parakeets and other small species, while the bigger playstands – suitable for larger birds – are free-standing on legs or castors.

With a few basic materials, however, you can make your own. You will need a base tray to catch droppings and spilt food, strong, natural branches for perching and climbing and for supporting toys, ropes, ladders and swings, as well as food and water bowls on the top perch. Make sure there are no exposed screws or nails that could injure your bird.

Playstands provide an interesting and stimulating place to play and climb and a change of environment. Change the toys regularly and give rawhide strips or other items for chewing and destroying.

4.4. FOOD FOR THOUGHT

Another way to provide occupation for your bird is with certain food items. Some foods take time and ingenuity to eat and parrots enjoy the challenge.

Picking the individual seeds out of half a pomegranate is fun for a bird, as is extricating pieces of nut from a halved walnut or the peas from a pod. The beak of a large Macaw can crack open even the tough shell of a Brazil nut, while smaller parrots will enjoy prising raw peanuts out of their shells.

Millet sprays, bunches of budding twigs, flowers and green foods, hung from the cage top, are much enjoyed for their freshness and variety and the time taken to nibble at them. Give seeding grasses, chickweed and wild berries (remembering to wash carefully anything gathered from hedgerows or verges). Try a bunch of marigolds or nasturtiums from the garden, or fresh green broccoli. By offering a variety of these foods, you will find some that your parrot particularly enjoys. As with introducing a new toy, offer unfamiliar foods with care if your parrot is the suspicious type!

4.5. THE NEED TO CHEW

Parrots need to chew, and there are good reasons for this. If not worn down naturally, by chewing on rough perching, the beak can become overgrown. This is uncomfortable for the parrot, and you will need to take him to the vet, to have his beak trimmed. You can avoid the need for trimming by providing materials on which your parrot is able to chew regularly, e.g. natural wood branches. Stripping bark, and nibbling at leaf shoots and stems, provides natural stimulus and occupation. This is particularly important for a captive bird, who can easily become bored.

5. EXERCISE

Birds need to stretch their wings. The bigger the parrot, the more
space he will need to get sufficient exercise. Give regular,
supervised playtimes out of the cage when your bird can clamber
and fly about freely.

When the weather is warm, moving your pet to an outdoor flight
in the garden will give an ideal opportunity for flying. Avoid sudden
extremes of temperature when taking your bird outside, and make sure there is
a covered area where he can shelter if the sun is particularly hot or if there is a
cold wind. Some parrots will welcome the opportunity of bathing if there is a
shower of rain. Provide perches, rope swings, logs and other toys, and do not
forget food and water. Safe plants for growing in or around an outdoor flight
include clematis, honeysuckle, pyracantha, hazel, hibiscus, elder, and willow.

6. GROOMING

6.1. BATHING

Regular bathing or misting is essential for healthy feather condition. It will
also help to prevent a build-up of the dusty powder produced by some species
that can result in skin irritation and subsequent feather picking. If possible,
birds should have the chance to bathe about twice a week, more often in hot,
dry weather. Room humidifiers will ensure the environment is not too dry for
your parrot. Placing a bowl of water over a radiator will also help in this
respect.

Parrots have their own ideas about getting wet – some love it, while others
try to avoid it at all costs. However, remember that getting wet is natural for
wild birds, particularly those dwelling in rainforests, where they would be
subjected to a humid atmosphere and regular downpours of rain. The best idea
is to get your parrot used to the idea of bathing at an early age. Even if you
keep a reluctant, older bird, teach him that this is a part of the regular routine.

Some birds will try to bathe in their water bowl, but refuse to go anywhere
near a bath of water on the cage floor. If your bird enjoys a good soaking,
provide a shallow bowl of water in which he can splash about (to avoid the
danger of drowning, never give a deep bath of water). Alternatively, put an
inch of water in the kitchen sink or bathroom washbasin for him to bathe in.
Another good way to ensure your parrot has the chance to bathe is to take him
with you into the shower. Warm, summer showers of rain give an ideal
opportunity to bathe if your bird enjoys this. If you do not have an outdoor
flight, but the cage is on castors, this can be wheeled outside.

If your bird is exceptionally dirty, you may want to use a purpose-made
parrot shampoo, suitable for the species you keep. Normally, however, plain
water is best.

6.1.1. MISTING

Reluctant bathers can be introduced to the idea of water with mistings from a
sprayer. The water will need to be quite warm to start with, as it cools quickly

once sprayed into the air. Test it on your own hand first. If the water temperature is pleasantly warm, your bird won't be so reluctant. If your pet is really nervous or suspicious of water, start with just a very light misting, spraying into the air above the bird rather than aiming the sprayer directly at him. You will know when he starts to enjoy the sensation, as he will spread his wings to catch the moisture. If you are going to spray your parrot in his cage, remember to remove food bowls first and let him out afterwards to shake and flap himself dry in a warm environment.

Morning baths or showers are best, so that the feathers can dry completely before the bird settles down for the night.

6.2. NAIL AND BEAK CLIPPING

If your parrot is clambering about all day on rough wood perching, he may not need extra nail or beak trimming. This is obviously the ideal situation and avoids the stress to your bird of catching him up for grooming.

6.2.1. NAIL CLIPPING

Nails will need to be clipped if they become too long. Your avian vet can do this for you and will also be able to show you the correct procedure so that you can do it at home once you are confident.

- Get someone to help you, so that the job can be done as quickly and smoothly as possible, with minimum upset to the parrot. If necessary, do the trimming in several stages of a minute or two each, rather than stress your bird with a long grooming session.
- Unless your bird is unusually calm and obliging, you will need to carefully wrap him in a towel. Speak to him gently, to reassure him.
- While one person holds the confined parrot, the other takes each foot in turn, and, with nail clippers (those used for small dogs or cats are suitable), removes just the very tip of each nail. Until you are sure, cut too little rather than too much, or you will cause bleeding from the blood vessel that runs part way down the nail. The longer the nails have been allowed to grow, the greater care will be needed. With regular clipping, however, the blood vessel will shrink back so that the job becomes easier.
- If bleeding is inadvertently caused, you can stop the flow by applying styptic powder, cornflour, or soap.

If you have a young parrot, accustom him to being handled for grooming before he learns to fear it. When you are sitting relaxing together, try taking one of his feet and just gently file the tips of the nails for a few seconds, so that he gets used to the idea. You will then be able to progress to clipping, if it becomes necessary, with the minimum of fuss.

6.2.2. BEAKS

It is advisable to seek veterinary expertise if your parrot's beak has become overgrown. Only attempt to trim your parrot's beak yourself once you are confident of the correct procedure. As with the nails, the beak contains blood vessels and you will hurt your bird if the trimming is over-severe. Beak trimming should not be needed if your bird is young and healthy and has plenty of chewing material available.

7. REST AND SLEEP

Parrots need a lot of sleep – more than many people realise – a fact that needs to be kept in mind in those households where the human occupants stay up late. After a busy day with lots of coming and going, your bird will want up to 12 hours' peace and quiet. Too little sleep, and no refuge from bright lights and noise, will be stressful to him. If you are planning a late-night party, move the cage to a more peaceful place in the house.

By fitting a dimmer switch, you can gradually fade the electric light to imitate the natural setting of the sun. This will enable your bird to settle down gradually for the night, as he would when roosting in the wild – rather than going suddenly from bright light to darkness.

8. IS MY PARROT LONELY?

Having taken on one parrot, many people then wonder if they should buy another bird. The reason may be that they enjoy the company of parrots, or that they feel their single bird might be lonely when they are out of the house, or that they are considering breeding from their pet in an outside aviary *(see Chapter Nine)*.

Your pet may well be glad of the company of another bird, but before going ahead, the following points should be considered:

• The new bird needs to be of a species, size and temperament compatible with your existing pet. Jealousy and aggression can be a danger.
• Despite your best efforts, the birds may simply not get on, which may mean they cannot be let out of their cages together.
• The new bird will need to be quarantined for a month in a separate part of the house, in case of any possible disease that could be passed on.
• Have you got room for another cage? Unless you are sure the birds are getting on really well, and there is no chance of aggression, it is safer to house them separately.
• Are you prepared for double the noise, mess, and expense?

It may happen that two birds will chat to each other through the cage bars and never show actual aggression, but nevertheless prefer to keep apart when free in the room together. A distinct advantage of keeping more than one bird is that the company and interaction can distract an individual from such habits as feather plucking and screaming for attention.

Of course, if you keep birds of different sexes, they may eventually want to breed. If they are showing breeding behaviour – preening and feeding each other, tearing up newspaper in the cage to make a nest, etc., you may decide to let them raise young. A breeding cage in a quiet room in the house can be suitable for some species, while others will thrive better given the space and privacy of an outdoor aviary.

Be prepared, when letting your pet birds pair and breed, for the fact that they will probably lose their close bond with you in the process. However, although some may become aggressive towards the keeper once allowed to breed, others – if particularly tame and bonded – will continue to accept human intervention when nest inspection is needed.

8.1. BIRD ROOMS

If you have a spare room or conservatory and want to keep several (non-breeding) birds, you can create a bird room where they can live and fly freely.

First, you need to be sure that the birds will get on well together and be happy in this environment, but they will still need careful watching in case of squabbling or possible accidents. It is important that you continue in your position as 'head of the flock' so that the birds will come to you when required.

Maintaining a clean, hygienic, safe environment is the next consideration. The floor and walls need to be easily cleanable, and mesh at the windows will allow fresh air to enter without the possibility of a bird escaping. Ensure there are no toxic materials, dangerous fittings, or electrical wires that your birds could chew.

Now you can get creative! Paint the walls in colours that a parrot would see in the wild – blue, green, and sunshine yellow. Build 'trees' from large, natural branches, with lots of different places to perch and roost. Hang thick lengths of rope vertically and horizontally, to act as perches, swings and ladders. Include a shallow 'pool' for bathing. Create different feeding areas, give bundles of edible twigs in bud, or provide some favourite flowers. Remember to include a constant supply of chewable, destructible materials, and other, durable toys. A dimmer fitted to the light switch will quieten the birds at night, and individual cages will give them security when they are sleeping.

As long as they get on well together, keeping more than one pet bird can be great fun for them and for you. They will enjoy playing and chattering together, as well as the opportunity for mutual preening – all natural activities for members of a flock.

9. WING CLIPPING

Wing clipping is a subject currently provoking strong debate among parrot keepers. Many feel it is the only way to keep their pet bird safe and under control, while others feel it robs the bird of his natural birthright of free flight.

Performed correctly, wing clipping will curtail a parrot's flight, but it will not completely rob him of the ability to fly. It means that your bird will not be able to obtain full height or speed when flying about, and you will have more control over him.

Ideally, repeated clipping will not be needed once the parrot has become tame and socialised – and therefore under control.

9.1. PROS OF CLIPPING

Even if you do not like the idea of wing clipping, a temporary clip may be the best way to calm an aggressive bird, so that the balance of power is changed and you are able to approach him more easily to begin training.

Male breeding birds in the aviary can be very aggressive towards their mate. Clipping their wings slows them down and gives the female a chance to escape from the harassment.

A temporary clip is also helpful with nervous pet birds that dash about the room in a panic and put themselves in danger of flying into something. Do not risk your bird breaking his neck by flying at speed into clear glass or a moving ceiling fan. Training is impossible with the frightened (or just plain stubborn) individual that flies up on to the curtain rail every time you ask him to sit on your hand. The flight feathers will eventually grow back again, but, in the meantime, socialising and training your bird should prove an easier task.

Another obvious advantage to clipping a bird's wings is that this will substantially reduce his chance of escape, although even with clipped wings, birds have been known to fly away. How high and how far they can go depends on the severity of the clip. Birds can also escape if the keeper forgets that the flight feathers will grow back again.

9.2. CONS OF CLIPPING

"If you don't want a pet that flies, get a dog" – Rosemary Low. If you decide to keep your parrot fully flighted, you will need to be aware at all times of the possible dangers this poses whenever the bird is out of his cage. Despite our best intentions, accidents can and do happen – a window or door is left open and in seconds your pet has vanished. Glass panels can be flown into at speed, or the bird may land on a hotplate that has only just been turned off, or even drown in an open-top fish tank. Set against this is the fact that your bird will be free to fly as nature intended.

Teach your parrot where the hazards are – take him up to windows and glass-panelled doors and gently touch his beak on them. Repeat this until he is aware of the obstacle. Train him to come to you on command. Use a set word or whistle and practise this constantly. If your bird escapes outside, he will be confused at suddenly finding himself in an alien world. However, if he hears the familiar recall command, he may fly back to you instinctively.

If your bird is fully flighted, a parrot harness will allow you to take him out and about with you. An older or nervous bird may not like the idea of wearing a harness, in which case you will need to introduce it in careful stages, until he has accepted the idea. Once he has got used to the look of it, let him pick it up and toss it about. Take time and care when attempting to fit the harness, so that your bird does not suddenly panic. Stop and try again later, rather than frighten him by forcing the issue.

Leg chains may seem a simpler solution, but these can be extremely dangerous and may break your bird's leg if he suddenly takes fright and tries to fly away.

9.3. BABY BIRDS

Parrots need to learn to balance, manoeuvre, fly, and land in every kind of situation. It is, therefore, wrong to clip a young bird's wings before he has had the chance to develop flight muscles and practise flying and manoeuvring skills. Many breeders still automatically clip the wings of their young stock before selling them on, so if you are buying a baby, ask for him to be left fully flighted.

9.4. ASK THE EXPERTS

A veterinary surgeon specialising in birds, or an experienced keeper, will be able to clip your bird's wings and show you how to safely go about it yourself in the future. Never trust this procedure to anyone unless you are confident in the clipper's ability. Over-severe clips can cause long-term stress or even permanent disability to the bird. Feather re-growth from a bad wing clip can be problematic and lead to chronic feather picking. Curbing flight completely is like putting a bird in a straightjacket, with the real danger of a fall and serious injury. If only one wing is clipped, the bird will be unbalanced, which can also give rise to accidents.

If you decide a wing-clip is the best option for your bird, remember that both wings should be clipped gently and evenly, and preferably in gradual stages. This will allow your bird to continue to move and fly about while he gets used to the change, and will not suddenly curtail his mobility.

10. RECOVERING A LOST PARROT

If your parrot flies off through an open window or door and over the garden fence, he will quickly become disorientated in the unfamiliar surroundings. What this means is that, although he almost certainly wants to get back to you and the security of home, he does not know how to go about it.

Obviously, windows and doors should never be left open when the parrot is out of his cage. To let fresh air into the room during hot weather, fit framed, wire mesh grills securely over open windows. However, accidents do happen. For example, it only takes a moment, as you answer the front door bell, for the parrot on your shoulder to take fright or be caught in a sudden gust of wind. You had forgotten he was there and now he has disappeared over the rooftops. He has never left your side before, you meant to get his wings re-clipped and you didn't know he could fly that far or that fast!

10.1. WHAT CAN I DO?

Of course, some escaped parrots are never retrieved by their keepers, but most do not travel very far once they are free, so there is a good chance of getting your bird back if you try the following tips:

- Make a careful note of the direction your escaping bird is taking and watch him for as long as possible.
- Head for where you last saw him and search the area for possible landing places. Remember, if your bird is not used to flying, he will soon get tired and want to perch.

- Call to your parrot, using familiar words or whistles. If you have already taught him to fly to you on command, this could really pay off now.
- Get the bird's favourite family members to join you in the search, armed with bowls of tempting titbits, toys, etc. The important thing is that you, the food, and the toys will be the only familiar objects in the new, frightening environment your bird has found himself in, so keep calling and whistling. He may well be able to see or at least hear you, but be too confused to move from his perch.
- Keep searching for your bird, while your helpers call on nearby residents to ask them to keep a lookout. If he is not quickly found, photocopy a good quantity of leaflets and distribute these door-to-door. Stick up posters and ask shops to put them in their windows. You could offer a reward for the safe return of your bird – this will encourage people to look out for him and also deter anyone thinking of keeping him. Contact the local police, veterinary surgeons, rescue centres, newspapers, radio and TV. Parrots usually create interest, so your story may well be published and broadcast by the local media.
- Check local papers in case someone has found your parrot and is looking for the keeper.
- Be patient – it may be many hours before you, or someone else, finds your parrot. Dusk and dawn are the times you are most likely to hear your bird's distinctive voice, so keep searching and listening.
- After all the waiting and worrying, you hear that familiar whistle. Your parrot is high up in a tree, out of sight. At this stage you don't want to frighten him away again, so proceed with care. Although the fire brigade have suitable equipment for such emergencies, they would almost certainly scare your bird away while trying to retrieve him. Instead, keep calling to him, rattling his food bowl or favourite toy, or bringing his cage – with the door left open and food and water inside – within sight. This may just give your parrot the confidence to fly down to you.
- If necessary – and if possible – climb up slowly towards your bird, talking gently to him all the time. Offer food treats as you approach. A trained parrot may step on to your hand or arm once you reach him, but don't make a sudden grab for your bird.
- Secure your parrot inside a jumper or jacket, or, if he is used to it, fit a harness so that you can bring him down without further mishap.
- Give your pet plenty of time to rest, drink, and eat in peace in his cage.

It may be some days, of course, before there is a sighting of your bird, so keep up the search. Leave his open cage in the garden in case he is nearby. If there is food and water inside, he may just fly down to this familiar sanctuary.

11. PARROT THIEVES
Parrots, particularly rare species and larger, popular birds, such as Greys, Cockatoos and Macaws, are a valuable commercial commodity,

and they are increasingly becoming the target of thieves. Some may be stolen to order.

Get your avian vet to microchip your bird. The identifying number will settle any dispute over ownership, should your bird be stolen and subsequently turn up elsewhere. A pet parrot clearly visible from the street is potentially in danger, so situate your bird's cage away from the public eye. Outdoor aviaries should also be well hidden from view, and secured with padlocks. Keep all doors and gates locked at all times and install alarms, electric fencing, and security lights – whatever you can afford. Make your property as inaccessible as possible, with high fences or hedges. Do not leave catching nets or carrying cages handy for the thieves to use.

Do not broadcast the fact that you keep birds, in case word gets round the criminal fraternity. If you run a parrot-related business from your home, have an anonymous Post Office Box address for your mail. If you breed birds, check out potential buyers or sellers carefully before you give them your address. Make it as difficult as possible for thieves to hear about your birds and to gain access to them.

If your bird is stolen, let the police, pet shops, veterinary surgeries, rescue homes, etc., know. Get local papers to print pictures and details of your missing bird and offer a reward for his safe return. Visit bird auctions, which are sometimes a marketplace for stolen parrots.

DID YOU KNOW?
In the UK, it is illegal to set free a non-indigenous bird or animal.

---

12. SECURING THE FUTURE

All being well, your parrot will be with you for many years to come. Even a small parakeet can live for a quarter of a century, and your large Macaw or Cockatoo could well be around for the rest of your life – and longer.

It is important for your birds' sake that you make provision for their future care. This means that if you die, or, for whatever reason, you can no longer look after your pet, he will go to a caring home and not simply be sold on to a stranger. Good, permanent parrot sanctuaries are scarce – and usually full – so do not rely on this option unless you have made prior arrangements with the sanctuary owners.

If you are planning to bequeath your parrot to a relative, friend or neighbour, make quite sure that that person is willing and able to take on the task. You also need to know that they will be able to pass the bird to another responsible person if ever they themselves cannot look after him.

Discuss your plans with the potential new keeper and ensure that he or she likes and understands your bird and is prepared for the daily care and expense involved. It is also important to the success of the arrangement that your bird is well disposed towards his new keeper.

You are now in a position to make your wishes known in your will and perhaps leave a bequest to help cover expenses.

You may decide to set up a trust fund, whereby funds are regularly made available from your estate for the care and upkeep of your bird. For this, you will need a trusted and responsible person willing to take on the task of trustee, plus a back-up trustee in case the first is unable to carry on.

Detail your exact wishes as to how trust funds are to be used, and, to help ensure the continuing welfare of your bird, include remuneration for the trustee. A solicitor will be able to help with the wording of any legal document to make sure you have covered everything.

Finally, it is a good idea to make notes about your parrot's daily routine and diet, particular likes and dislikes, habits, medical history, etc. If this is available to the new keeper, it will help to smooth the changeover period.

CHAPTER 8

BEHAVIOUR AND TRAINING

1. INTRODUCTION

You will have read earlier in this book about the distinct advantages of buying a captive-bred, carefully weaned, tame bird. Socialising and training is usually straightforward with a parrot that has grown up with caring humans and has learnt to trust them. The same cannot be said for wild-caught parrots. These birds have no reason at all to trust us and they will be frightened and confused by their alien surroundings. Some wild-caught birds will eventually respond and become tame, although not all. Some parent-reared, aviary birds can also be extremely nervous of people, although a gentle, patient approach will get results in the end.

2. MUTUAL TRUST

Whichever bird you have taken on, the important thing is to spend time with him each day until he learns to see you as a friend.

If you have taken on a tame bird, you will probably have no trouble persuading him to come out of his cage on your hand and be put on to a playstand to amuse himself. A nervous bird, however, will require time and patience from you until he learns to relax. Growling, hissing, or fluttering madly about the cage, are clear signs of fear and should be respected.

The cage is the bird's only sanctuary at this time, and he will be reluctant to leave it. Move slowly and quietly around the cage, and keep pets and boisterous children away, at least for the time being. Do not try taking your bird out of his cage until he seems calm and confident. In the meantime, talk and whistle encouragingly to him throughout the day, drop little food treats into the cage as you pass, and establish a routine for feeding and cleaning out the litter tray.

Do not be tempted to put a hand in to make a grab for the bird. This will undo all your good work and you may get bitten. Remember, your bird is constantly watching and listening and taking in everything around him. He has a long memory, and he will not forget any harsh or impatient treatment.

Chasing the bird all round his cage or wearing gloves to catch him up, then wrapping him in a towel to calm him down are commonly used methods. However, they only add to the bird's fear of his keeper. A gloved hand can look very alarming, and to be confined and unable to move when wrapped in a towel must feel to the bird like being trapped by a predator. Far better is to do only those things that will make your bird like you, however long this takes. Once the bird chooses to come to you because he knows you are fun to be with, and that you give him nice things to eat and fun things with which to play, your relationship is off to the best possible start.

When you first put your hand in the cage, do this very slowly and smoothly, talking softly to your bird to put him at ease. He may be tempted by a small food treat held in your fingers, or allow you to tickle his chest feathers. A nervous bird may still be suspicious of your hand after several attempts, so patience is the key here. The next step is teaching your bird to step on to your finger or hand *(see page 86)*.

DID YOU KNOW?
Feather plucking is a condition of captivity and does not occur in the wild.

---

3. BODY LANGUAGE
With a little experience, you will be able to interpret your parrot's different vocal sounds, eye movements, head or wing position, and other body posturing, which tell you how he is feeling or what he wants. This is important knowledge when it comes to understanding and training a bird. Here are some of the common actions and stances of a parrot and what they mean:

3.1 WHISTLING AND CHATTERING
Your bird is happy and relaxed – and has probably just woken you up at 5 o'clock in the morning!

3.2. GROWLING
This sound shows that the bird is fearful or angry and may bite if he is approached. This is common in nervous or wild-caught African Greys.

3.3. WING SPREADING
Parrots may spread their wings out and puff themselves up to intimidate another bird.

3.4. FOOD REGURGITATION
This is natural behaviour between bonded birds – or sometimes by a pet parrot to his human 'mate', or even a mirror or toy. Try to remember that your bird's regurgitated breakfast is a sign of his love and devotion! When your parrot starts to bob his head up and down, he may be about to give you a tasty morsel.

3.5. HEAD LOWERING
When a parrot lowers his head, looks down and fluffs out the feathers on the back of his head, he is usually asking for a tickle. However, think twice if the bird clicks his beak, spreads his tail feathers, raises his shoulders, and is looking at you as he lowers his head – he may be about to bite.

3.6. DISPLAYING
When in breeding condition, parrots will perform ritual movements to attract their mate. This 'displaying' varies between the species, but includes strutting, wing trembling, pupil dilation, head bobbing or swaying, and tail and wing spreading.

3.7. LYING ON HIS BACK
Very tame birds can be taught the trick of 'playing dead' by rolling on to their backs, feet in the air. However, this requires great trust as, in nature, it would be a bird's last resort when overwhelmed by predators. A pet bird may lie on his back when extremely frightened.

3.8. FLASHING EYES
This can mean several things. The parrot may be very pleased or excited about something, he may be displaying to his mate, or he may be warning you or another person or pet to keep away. If he stands up tall as his eyes dilate, it shows the bird is afraid and may bite if approached. By his accompanying body language, you will soon be able to tell the different meanings for this behaviour.

3.9. YAWNING
Your bird is tired!

4. SOCIALISATION
In the wild, there is always a hierarchy or 'pecking order' among birds. In your home, it is vital that your bird understands that you are the flock leader, and that he must always look to you for any important decision making. This starts with the basic decisions of when he comes out of, or goes back to, his cage; and when he steps on

to, or down from, your hand – either on to another surface or on to a family member's hand or arm, etc. From this, the training can be extended to include such things as teaching him to defecate in convenient places designated by you, as well as playing games and performing tricks.

With gentle, consistent socialisation, discipline and training, you will be building up your bird's confidence and sense of security. By knowing that you are in control, he can relax. A bird that has never been taught his place in the family will be unhappy and confused – the human household is far removed from a parrot's natural habitat, so the bird cannot be expected to know how to behave unless he is shown what to do by the keeper. Aggressive, noisy behaviour results when an undisciplined parrot tries to establish himself as leader.

5. TRAINING

5.1. BABY PARROTS

Like human babies and puppies, baby parrots have a lot of learning to do. How they behave as adults will depend on how they are treated as youngsters. If you let your young bird nibble at your fingers, this will progress to nipping, then biting. Stop any unwanted behaviour right from the start, by saying, "No!" very firmly, glaring fiercely (parrots watch our facial expressions closely), and giving no further attention to your bird until he has stopped the behaviour. Then reward him with praise. Be consistent. Never hit your bird, and do not leave him for prolonged periods in the cage as a punishment, which he will not understand.

Establish a routine so that your baby parrot gets used to the idea of playing with his toys in the cage, or at least not having your undivided attention all the time. Alternate this with playtime out of the cage and short training sessions. If you incorporate basic commands as you go about the daily routine – such as "Up", "Down", "Come here", "No", and "Good bird", these will quickly become accepted.

Some young parrots are less confident than others. If yours cries for you constantly, this may not be a demand for attention, but rather the need for reassurance. He will learn to accept your absences if you keep these very short at first, gradually leaving him for longer periods as he gets used to the idea.

Encourage handling of your baby parrot by responsible family members and friends. Get him used to lots of different foods, new objects in the cage, and a parrot harness for trips out. A parrot that has had early socialisation will be far more adaptable to new situations in the future.

Keep a close eye on your baby as he investigates everything around him. Finally, remember to allow your young bird plenty of time to rest and sleep.

5.2. BASIC TRAINING

Specific training times do not require more than a few minutes here and there during the day. In fact, lengthy training periods are inappropriate as you will probably not be able to hold your bird's full attention beyond 10 minutes.

Training lessons can be reinforced as you go about the daily routine of feeding, cleaning out and talking to your parrot.

Clear, consistent boundaries are essential. By giving in when your parrot disobeys a command, you are giving him the message that he is in charge. This is not only confusing to the parrot, it also puts him in potential danger. In an emergency, you need to know that your bird will fly to you at once when asked. It is also much easier to deal with a sick or injured bird if he can be quickly caught up and he is relaxed in human hands.

How much and how quickly the parrot learns will depend on his species, age, status (captive-bred, parent-reared, or wild-caught), and individual temperament. A young, hand-reared Green-wing Macaw, for example, is likely to be calmer and more responsive to training than a small, aviary-bred parakeet. However, with time and patience, most pet birds can be taught the basic essentials of stepping on and off the hand on command. One exception to this is the nervous wild-caught parrot that may only ever progress to stepping on to a hand-held perch. As you get to know your parrot, you will be able to judge his potential. Make a friend of him and give positive reinforcement every time he does something even half right.

5.3. DO'S AND DON'TS OF TRAINING
Once your new parrot is relaxed and responding to you, allocate a few minutes a couple of times a day for whatever training you want to do – obedience, speech training, or trick training. The best time for this is when the house is quiet and there are as few distractions as possible. Choose a time of day when your bird is lively and attentive, and keep the lessons short and fun.

5.3.1. DO
- Be patient and go at your pet's own pace – what seems a simple command to you is totally new to him.
- Praise the desired response from your bird and simply ignore everything else.
- Stop the session and try again later if your parrot does not appear to be in a responsive mood.
- End on a high note at the end of every training session – even if it is only a very modest success.
- Use the same praise word or phrase each time any progress is made.
- Use a positive, encouraging facial expression.
- If it helps, give a peanut, sunflower seed or other favourite food as a reward.
- Whatever food treat you give, make it something that can be eaten quickly so that you can get on with the training without delay. If the bird has not recently eaten before a training session, the food will be more eagerly sought.
- Use a consistent closing word or phrase at the end of each session – such as "All done".

5.3.2. DON'T
- Go on too long – your parrot will get bored and cross if you do.

- Try to train more than one bird at a time – they will distract each other.
- Rush the pace, get irritated, shout, or worse, hit your bird for not doing what you want him to.

5.4. STEPPING ON TO YOUR HAND

When your pet parrot is stepping on to your finger, hand or arm every time you ask him to, you have achieved the most important basic of his training. Once he has got used to you, and he is confidently taking food from your hand in the cage, your parrot is ready to be taught to step up.

If your bird is still a little nervous of hands, or if you are afraid of being bitten (particularly if you own a large parrot), start with a wooden, hand-held perch (or whatever surface he will accept) to teach the stepping up command. If you carry out this – or any other training procedure – just before feeding time, your bird will be eager for the food rewards on offer and should therefore respond more readily.

To get your parrot to step on to your hand from his cage perch:

- Gently introduce your hand into the cage
- Touch your flat hand against the bird's lower chest
- Slightly increase the pressure
- Give the command ("Up", "Step Up" or whatever you have chosen)
- Give your chosen praise word, such as "Good Bird" as he steps on to your hand (he will do this automatically, to regain his balance as you push back gently against him).

Repeat this lesson at regular intervals – whenever you are attending to food and water dishes for example, cleaning out the cage, or when your parrot is on his playstand. Teach him to step up as soon as you give the command – and that he has absolutely no choice in the matter!

Of course, before taking your bird out of the cage, you will need to ensure your sitting room is secure and free of hazards.

Even once he is stepping on to your hand, your bird may not be confident enough to stay on it long enough for you to lift him out of the cage. If this is the case, resist the temptation to simply give up and leave the cage door open until he decides to come out on his own. Instead, be patient and continue to reassure your bird as you repeat the exercise. Hold a piece of cheese or biscuit in the free hand as a bribe if necessary. Once he has finally been persuaded to come out, show him what a nice, safe place he has come to, with favourite foods on offer, interesting playthings, etc. Remember, your parrot needs to know that it is you, not he, who dictates his actions.

5.5. STEPPING DOWN

Stepping down is not quite as easy an action for a bird as stepping up, and you may need to persuade your pet to do this by holding a small piece of tasty food just out of reach. To get your bird to step down:

- Hold your hand (arm, hand-held stick or whatever) just below your bird's perch

- Give the chosen command ("Down", "Step Down", etc.)
- Praise success.

A parrot's beak acts as a third foot, and your bird may grasp your hand quite firmly with his beak as he tests it out, steadies himself, and gets a grip before stepping up or down. Do not mistake this for biting and pull away, as this will only confuse the bird and make him nervous. Keep your hand steady and secure – your own show of confidence will reassure him.

Get your parrot used to stepping on to, or from, all kinds of perches – playstand, chair backs, cage top, etc. It is important that he is also taught to step on to (or down from) other family members. This will act as a reminder of his place in the household pecking order and will help curb over-bonding with you and any possible jealousy towards others in the future.

5.6. "COME HERE!"
When the parrot is out of his cage but some distance away from you, hold out your arm and give the command in an upbeat, encouraging voice. A tame and bonded parrot will soon learn what is required and be happy to oblige. A less responsive bird may be tempted if you hold a food treat in your free hand when calling him to you.

It is important, when teaching your bird to fly to you, that he has also learnt to step down from you when you ask him to – or you may find your devoted bird permanently attached to some part of your anatomy!

5.7. "NO!"
Just like a pet dog, parrots can soon learn the word "No!" – and will know if you really mean it. "No!" must result in your bird stopping whatever he is doing at that very moment. If he nips, screams, or starts a bit of furtive feather plucking, say "No!" as sternly as possible, really mean what you say, and give your parrot the fiercest look you can manage.

> **DID YOU KNOW?**
> *Taming and training a difficult parrot can sometimes be easier if the bird's cage is kept below eye level. This reinforces the idea that the keeper is at the top of the 'pecking order' and that the parrot must look up to him or her for orders.*

5.8. CUDDLING UP
It may take a while to get your parrot used to being touched by you, let alone stroked and cuddled – particularly if he is not a hand-reared bird. Being enclosed and held by a human hand is naturally threatening. He may enjoy you ruffling his head and neck feathers through the cage wire, but object to you touching his back or wings.

However, it is fun and very rewarding to have a bird that welcomes a cuddle or that will happily burrow into your jumper for a snooze. Some species will be more amenable than others to physical affection, but, with many birds, trust can be built up in stages.

A good time to develop it is in the evening when your bird is playing out of his cage and you are relaxing with a book or watching the TV. Let him come to you, sit on your lap, and clamber about. Get him used to your hands and to being gently stroked. If you keep everything on the bird's own terms he will lose any fear of being touched and you should, in time, have an affectionate and confident pet.

5.9. HOUSE-TRAINING
It may seem unlikely, but many parrots can be trained to defecate in a specific place – for example, on a specially designated perch or playstand, where newspaper on the base tray can be quickly and easily replaced. Certainly, the time and effort spent in house-training your bird will be more than repaid by all the cleaning up you will be able to avoid in the future.

Watch your parrot and learn to recognise the body language that tells you he is about to produce a dropping. When you can see he is about to defecate, swiftly lift him up and place him on the allocated 'poo perch'. As always, use a consistent word or phrase of command, followed by lots of praise when you get the desired result.

6. PROBLEM BEHAVIOUR
Behavioural problems in a captive-bred bird can set in if one or more of the following factors apply:
- Insufficient care with handling and/or weaning of the baby bird
- Over-indulgence of the young bird
- Lack of early discipline and training
- Being passed from home to home
- Boredom and loneliness
- Adolescence
- Sexual frustration
- Inadequate diet.

There is much the keeper can do to remedy an unwanted behaviour. All that is usually needed is an understanding of the problem and a commitment to putting things right.

Please do not be tempted to sell your bird on because you are disappointed with him, or because his behaviour is becoming troublesome. Too many parrots are passed from home to home, which is highly stressful to them and only increases their unsocial behaviour.

If, after trying out the advice given below, you feel you need extra help with a persistent problem, a parrot behaviourist may well be able to offer you a new insight and some practical advice. Bird publications sometimes carry advertisements for these specialists in their classified section. Alternatively, ask your avian vet, contact your local parrot club, or look on the Internet. The behaviourist may want to see you and your bird together to assess the situation, or, if the problem seems straightforward, advice can often be given over the telephone *(see Appendix)*.

6.1. BITING

The first thing to remember, if your bird habitually bites, is that this is not usual behaviour between parrots in the wild. Aggression is more likely to be shown by means of threatening body language, and the pecking order established in this way so that physical violence does not become necessary. Parrots will beak-wrestle with each other for fun, but consistent, aggressive biting means that something is wrong – and biting is the only way your pet can communicate this to you. One or more of the following may apply:

- A baby bird's exploratory nipping has been allowed to progress into actual biting
- A wild-caught or aviary-reared bird has never overcome his fear of humans
- Emotional unbalance, caused by past abuse or neglect from a keeper
- A wing-clipped parrot is badly frightened, cannot fly away, and bites in panic
- The keeper has not established himself or herself as boss and the bird – even though he doesn't enjoy the situation – has been forced into a power struggle
- Strong dislike of a particular person
- Insecurity, caused by the keeper's (or recipient's) fear of being bitten
- The bird has reached adolescence and, like any other teenager, is feeling stroppy
- He has come into breeding condition and is showing natural, aggressive behaviour
- A game or training session has gone on too long and the bird is over-excited and needs a break
- He is jealous of the keeper's wife/husband
- Children or visitors are pestering or frightening the bird
- He is over-territorial about his cage or playstand
- He is tired, ill, or in pain.

The good news is that this least-pleasant parrot behaviour can be stopped. Curb biting in its early stages, and, above all, resist the temptation to simply leave an aggressive parrot in his cage because you are afraid of his beak. This situation is a pity for both of you and need not continue. What is needed is time, patience and determination on your part to turn things round.

6.1.1. STAYING IN CONTROL

A parrot that is allowed to perch above his keeper's eye level is being given the message that he is superior. He will then want to protect this position and may try to keep control by biting, whenever he is challenged. When your bird is perched on you, keep your hand or arm at chest level or below. Many keepers allow their parrot to perch on their shoulder and it can be tempting to encourage this habit with a small, tame bird. However, there is always the danger of a bite to the eye or face – and with one of the larger parrots, such as a Cockatoo or Macaw, this could be very serious indeed.

6.1.2. BABY BIRDS

Prevention is better than cure, so by discouraging playful nipping from a young bird, telling him, very firmly, "No!", and giving him a really fierce look, he will soon learn that biting is not acceptable at any time.

6.1.3. OVERCOMING FEAR

Establish a training routine as soon as you take on a new bird, leaving him in no doubt that you are in charge and that if he bites he will simply be left on his own for a while in the cage and ignored (which he will hate!). As with any problem behaviour, if no reward is forthcoming, your parrot will have no reason to continue with it. By rewarding good behaviour with praise, and ignoring the bad (in this case, biting), you will instill confidence in a nervous parrot. As he learns that he can trust you in all things, biting from fear or insecurity will no longer be an issue.

If your bird tends to nip or bite when you lift your hand towards him, it may be because, in the past, he has learnt to associate the human hand with rough treatment. In this case, when he is out of his cage, try letting him come to you to accept a piece of tasty food from your fingers, but without making any move to touch him. Keep doing this and he should gradually lose his fear, until he is automatically stepping up on to your hand or arm.

6.1.4. TEMPORARY AGGRESSION

Adolescence and breeding cycles are temporary states, and you may have no option but to put up with some uncharacteristic aggression during these times. Do not put yourself or anyone else in danger, and, if the bird is likely to attack, leave him in his cage until he is calmer.

6.1.5. JEALOUSY

If the parrot has learnt to socialise with all members of the family and be handled by them, aggression towards your partner should not be an issue – even if he or she is never going to be your bird's favourite person! People's lives have been made a misery by a parrot that swoops and bites the moment the perceived enemy comes into the room, but you can curb this situation before it gets serious. Teach your bird to go from your hand or arm to your partner's and back again. Let him know that he is below you both in the pecking order – and that aggressive jealousy will only get him put back in his cage and ignored. Tell him what a good bird he is whenever he is behaving as you want him to.

6.1.6. PROTECTING THE CAGE

If your bird tries to bite you whenever you want to remove him from his cage, or whenever you approach him when he is sitting on the open-top perch, he is being over-protective towards his territory (the cage). Teaching him to step on or off your hand or arm on command – every time you ask and not just when he feels like doing it – will put you back in charge of both the bird and his cage.

6.1.7. A GOOD REASON FOR BITING

Like the rest of us, parrots get tired and there are times when they just want to be left alone. A warning nip may tell you your pet wants a bit of peace and quiet. Likewise, sickness or pain may drive the bird to give an unexpected bite. If you suspect your bird may be ill, do not delay in consulting an avian vet.

6.1.8. REACTING TO BITING

If your parrot bites, it is a natural reaction to jump, yell and maybe even hit back. First, though, never hit him if he bites – even though he has taken you by surprise and you feel you did not deserve it! Hitting back will create fear, insecurity, and mistrust, and may also injure your pet. You are much bigger than him and hitting is never justified. Never shake or pull a parrot by the beak, either, as this will hurt him.

If at all possible, try not to show any reaction. Parrots love to get a response and if you shout at your bird for biting, this will only encourage him to do it again! Stay cool, say "No!" very firmly, give the bird a really cross stare, then put him in his cage without fuss and go out of the room. From this, he will learn that he can't get the better of you and that biting will only get him 20 minutes' solitary confinement.

Remember, ignoring your parrot for a while is a good way to stop unwanted behaviour.

6.2. SCREAMING

If you like a quiet life, it may be that a parrot is not the ideal pet for you! All psittacines enjoy having a good shout and scream at times, especially at dawn and dusk, and two or more birds will encourage each other to yell all the louder. A single African Grey, Senegal, Eclectus or Pionus may be fairly peaceable, whereas a collection of Cockatoos or Macaws can be deafening.

You are more likely to have a quiet parrot if you:
- Choose one of the quieter species, preferably a young bird that has been hand-reared in a quiet atmosphere where he has not learnt noisy habits.
- Keep only one bird, or mix different (compatible) species if you want to keep more than one. Parrots of the same type often encourage each other to make proportionately more noise than they would if kept singly or with different species. Remember, also, that a previously quiet bird may copy the yells of a noisy newcomer.
- Always maintain a quiet atmosphere around your bird.
- Speak to him in a quiet, soft voice.
- Ignore him when he is being noisy, and give him attention only when he becomes quiet again.
- Situate the cage where your parrot feels safe. The sudden appearance of a cat or other predator at the window will produce loud shrieks of alarm.
- Draw the curtains at night and cover the cage with a cloth, so that your pet does not start shouting at first light and wake you up.

Pet parrots take their lead from what is going on around them. If yours is a busy, noisy home, with TVs, radios and stereos playing in different parts of the house, telephones always ringing, people arguing, and dogs barking, your bird will simply try to copy and compete.

6.2.1 CAUSES OF SCREAMING
If screaming is becoming a problem, the causes may be:
- A problem with the cage or environment. Is the cage too small? Too crowded with toys and perches? In direct sunlight? In a vulnerable position where passing dogs, cats or visitors are perceived as a threat?
- Attention-seeking from an over-indulged bird. If you spoilt your bird as a baby, cuddling him all day long and indulging his every whim, you cannot blame him for expecting this treatment for the rest of his life. Maybe the novelty has worn off, you have got busier with work, or there is a new human baby or pet in the household. Your bird will not understand why you are no longer spending so much time with him, and he will scream to regain your attention.
- Lack of discipline and training. A parrot that has not been taught his proper place in the pecking order – below that of his keeper and the rest of the human family – will scream in an attempt to impose his authority.
- Boredom from over-long periods in the cage. You would scream, too, if you spent as long as some parrots do in their cages, especially if they are alone a lot of the time and there are no toys to play with.
- Seasonal breeding condition can trigger aggressive screaming in a bird. Reducing the amount of protein in the diet (pulses, nuts, seeds, cheese, etc.) may reduce the noise levels at this time. In most cases, uncharacteristic noise and aggression will cease as hormone levels return to normal. However, if screaming and other unsociable breeding behaviour is an ongoing problem, you may want to consider letting your parrot have a mate.
- Confined in his cage, unable to retreat from the surrounding activity and noise of the family, your bird may be suffering from fatigue. If the light and television are left on late into the night, or if your bird is over-stimulated and seldom left in peace, he will become very tired. One way he can let you know how he feels is to start screaming. Parrots need lots of sleep and your evening routine will need to take this into account.

6.2.2. PREVENTING SCREAMING
Try to work out the reasons for the screaming and take whatever practical measures are needed to put things right. Perhaps cats or other predators outside the window are causing alarm calls, in which case move the cage out of sight. If your bird dislikes the food you are giving him, he may scream in protest – change it for something new and tasty. If he is bored with his toys, offer him new, more challenging ones.

If you have eliminated all the obvious, practical causes for the screaming, but it is still continuing, some behaviour re-training is probably needed. Screaming and shouting for the keeper becomes a habit once the parrot discovers it brings the reward of attention. By dashing back into the room to see what's wrong, or yelling back at the bird to keep quiet, you are giving your bird every reason to carry on with the behaviour. He will have learnt that the more noise he makes, the quicker and more dramatic your response will be – and parrots love nothing better than a good shouting match!

Cockatoos that have been spoilt as babies can be particularly demanding as adults. These birds bond closely with their keepers and their screams for attention can be ear-splitting! You can avoid this situation by establishing a routine early on and sticking to it. Accustom your pet to the idea that there are times when he plays alone with his toys in the cage or on the stand, and times when you are with him and will give him your attention.

However difficult it may be to ignore a screaming parrot, this is what you need to do. Pretend that you are unable to hear a thing – walk out of the room if you can't bear the noise. If your pet screams when you are in another part of the house, do not go to him until he is quiet. Once the noise stops, go back in immediately, praising him for being a good parrot. Let him out of his cage to play or give a food treat as added rewards. In time he will learn that screaming gets him ignored, while quiet behaviour gets results.

6.3. FEATHER PLUCKING

Feather plucking and chewing is a condition of captive parrots only. It can occur as the result of a medical or an environmental cause.

If your bird is losing his feathers, it is generally easy to see whether this is caused by plucking or a normal moult. Moulting occurs naturally, usually once a year. Old feathers are gradually lost as new pin feathers start to appear. During this time the bird may look somewhat tatty. However, in the case of a parrot that is pulling out his feathers, rather than moulting, tell-tale isolated downy or bald patches will start appearing, particularly on the chest and legs.

You will read in more detail, in the veterinary section of this book, about the various medical reasons for feather plucking. If your parrot has begun to pull out his feathers (not to be confused with normal preening), the first thing to do is to consult an avian vet. The cause could be dietary, where seed is the main food eaten and there is a lack of fresh fruits and vegetables. Other possibilities are mites (less likely in pet birds), an allergy, an infection, or even liver disease. Poisonous residues of lead or zinc on poor-quality cage wire, ingested by the parrot, have also been known to trigger feather plucking.

DID YOU KNOW?
Grape seeds contain a powerful antioxidant, and it is thought that the active ingredient in grape seed extract may be beneficial in curbing feather plucking. Give seeded grapes to your parrot, rather than the non-seeded variety.

Another natural remedy recommended by some keepers for feather plucking is to spray the parrot with diluted aloe vera.

Plucking is often seen in African Greys, whose sensitive, intelligent natures mean they can readily become stressed by change, or bored from inactivity.

Normal preening, if done to excess, can turn into a plucking habit. Rather like the human habit of nail-biting, once started it is hard to stop. If head feathers are being pulled out, this is obviously the work of another parrot, but all other parts of the body can be reached by the bird himself. Your pet may pluck out a few chest feathers from time to time, or he may develop a severe habit, which can eventually result in a totally bald bird, apart from the feathered head. Where the fluffy under-down has consistently been pulled out, re-growth may not be possible. The urge to pluck can become so strong in some birds that they actually tear at their flesh. It follows that, whatever the cause, this needs to be identified and eliminated as quickly as possible.

6.3.1. ENVIRONMENTAL REASONS FOR PLUCKING
• Insecurity, due to lack of consistent training from the keeper
• Boredom and frustration from over-long periods in the cage
• Loneliness
• Attention seeking
• The need to bathe
• Stress of a house move or temporary change of environment during holiday periods, etc.
• Fear of a new item in the cage or room
• Sexual frustration
• Clumsy or over-severe wing clipping
• Fatigue.

6.3.2. PREVENTING FEATHER PLUCKING
As feather plucking is only a problem with captive birds, it stands to reason that reducing the stress of captivity may help to curb a feather-plucking problem.
• Give your bird a sense of security and confidence by establishing the ground rules for his behaviour. Let him know that he can trust you as leader and care giver.
• Boredom and frustration are the most common reasons for feather plucking. A bird left in a cage for hours on end will resort to the only activity available to him – pulling out his own feathers. Give a variety of interesting toys and foods, as well as plenty of supervised free time out of the cage. If you see your bird start to pick at his feathers, distract him with a new item to chew or nibble on, or play a game with him. It is much easier to stop bad habits in the early stages.
• Parrots are highly sociable creatures and need company during the day. If you are out a lot of the time, another bird will help to ease your pet's loneliness.
• If your response to your pet's feather plucking has always been to throw your hands in the air, rush to your bird's side and shout at him to stop, this will only teach him to do it all the more – he plucks at his chest and immediately gets your attention, which is exactly what he wants. Instead, say "No!" very firmly as soon as you see him start, give him the fiercest glare

you can manage, then ignore him completely. The moment he stops, go to him and praise him, take him out of his cage or give a small food treat. In other words, he only gets the reward of your attention for not plucking out his feathers.

- A wild parrot is exposed to mist and rain, or can find water to bathe in to keep feathers in good condition. This facility is missing in the dry, warm climate of your living room, which can mean itching and discomfort for your parrot, resulting in feather plucking. Give a shallow bath of warm water or regular mistings from a spray bottle.
- A previously feather-perfect bird may suddenly pull out a large area of feathers in a short space of time. The cause may be a change of environment or circumstances, such as moving to a new house. Getting a young bird used to change – leaving him with a friend for a few days when you are away, taking him out and about with you – is the best way to prevent problems in the future.
- Another type of change is the introduction of a new item in the bird's cage or surrounding environment. African Greys in particular may start to feather-pluck from fear of the new. If gradual introduction of an unfamiliar perch or new piece of furniture in the room does not help in reducing the parrot's stress, you may have to remove the offending item altogether.
- A bird in breeding condition may pull out his feathers from frustration. If this problem continues, the best solution may be to give him a mate *(See Chapter Nine)*.

6.4. VANDALISM

If your house is full of precious antique furniture, it is a good idea to keep a close eye on your parrot when he is out of his cage – and keep him well supplied at all times with wooden items meant for chewing and destroying! Of course, the larger the bird the more damage he can do. However, even an innocent-looking parakeet can make quite an impression on a picture rail or curtain-top.

Parrots are not discriminating and will chew on anything they can get hold of – whether it is a rough piece of perching or an inlaid walnut desk, it is all the same to them. Doors, skirting boards, and window sills, as well as curtains and wallpaper, can all be the target for beaks. Teach your parrot from the start that he is not allowed to chew up the home. If he has learnt "No!", and he knows that he will be returned to his cage if he starts gnawing at the dining table, he will be more likely to stick to his toys or natural branch playstand.

6.5. OVER-BONDING

One of the main pleasures of parrot keeping is to have a pet bird that loves you and comes to you at every opportunity. It can be tempting to let him be with you every minute of the day, perched on your shoulder, sharing your lunch, or curled up with you on the sofa.

Problems may start, however, if your parrot has never learnt to amuse himself when you are busy, be left alone for a couple of hours while you go out, or go to members of the family other than yourself. A pet parrot that is fixated on one person may be aggressive to other humans, perceiving them as a threat to the relationship.

There will almost certainly be times when you need to leave your parrot with someone else – or at least have a friend or neighbour come into your home to feed your pet while you are away. An overbonded bird will fret when you are not around – and you will feel guilty at leaving him. However, this situation can be avoided.

Start as you mean to go on:
• Don't over-indulge that cuddly baby
• Get him used to the idea that you can't always be around
• Encourage handling by other responsible members of the family and visitors (*Note: take great care when letting children handle parrots*).

Your parrot's affection for you may become problematic when he (or she) comes into seasonal breeding condition. You may find your bird repeatedly offering you regurgitated dinner during this time, or, in his confusion, trying to mate while sitting on your hand or arm. The way round this temporary behaviour change is to gently remove the parrot to his playstand or cage, and to distract him with an interesting piece of food or a new toy (a simple household item like a cardboard tube or a bunch of paper tissues) that he can chew on and tear up.

7. SPEECH TRAINING

Many parrots and parakeets can be taught to mimic words and whistles – with varying degrees of success. African Greys are particularly noted for their talking skills, as well as their astonishing accuracy when imitating many of the everyday sounds they hear around them.

Young birds may not start talking for the first few months, but they are always listening. As time goes on, you may start to detect familiar sounds and expressions sprinkled in with their daily mutterings and chatter. Hand-reared youngsters used to human speech will usually start talking earlier than parent-reared birds.

If you want your bird to talk, you can teach him words or phrases by repeating these at frequent intervals during the day, using a clear, bright voice and a lively tone. By using the same greeting every time you come into the room – and a consistent expression of farewell as you leave – you will be teaching your parrot to link the word or phrase with the action. Likewise, when you are cleaning out the cage, filling the food bowls, etc., use the same expressions each time ("Chores time", "Mm, nice dinner", "Here come the kids" or whatever is going on at that moment). In this way, many parrots will learn to use speech appropriately.

7.1. SPEECH TRAINING LESSONS
Some parrots will automatically mimic frequently heard words and sounds as

time goes on. However, you may have greater success if you give your bird regular speech training lessons.

It is important to get a parrot's attention for speech training and this can be done if the bird is placed for a few minutes in an empty cage that is then covered with a cloth. Without toys or outside distractions for this short period, the bird will be concentrating entirely on the sound of the keeper's voice. Alternatively:

- Take your parrot (in or out of his cage) to a different room, where he will be more focused on you. For any kind of training, having your bird settled in his cage or on his playstand, rather than moving around where he chooses, will limit distractions and achieve quicker results.
- When you have his attention, say the word or expression you want him to learn, keeping your voice bright and lively. Repeat this a few times. Remember, he will be listening to your tone and inflexion, so keep these the same with each repetition.
- As the parrot increases his mimicry skills, you may want to teach something more complicated – a couple of lines of poetry or a verse of song. You will need to break this down into short sections, which can be taught one at a time. Next, try putting a line together, then the whole thing. In this way, a gifted parrot can learn to repeat his address or telephone number – which may help reunite him with the keeper in the event of escape or theft.

You may choose to record specific words, phrases or songs on to a tape, which can then be played to your parrot when you are out. Alternatively, there are several commercially-produced speech training tapes and CDs available from avian suppliers. However, the best results are usually obtained when there is one-to-one interaction between keeper and bird. As with all training, keep lessons short and stop while things are going well and you still have your bird's attention. In this way, it will be fun for both of you.

8. TEACHING TRICKS

Once your parrot is fully tame, disciplined and trusting, he is ready to learn to play games, and, if willing, a few simple tricks. Interactive play is highly stimulating for these intelligent birds, and, depending on the species and the parrot's individual personality, some quite challenging feats can be taught.

As with any training, choose a quiet environment away from the cage, where you will have your bird's full attention. Also, as before, reward all desirable behaviour with praise, a tickle on the back of the neck, or a small food treat – and simply disregard everything else. Do not scold your parrot for getting it wrong as this will only confuse him.

8.1. LEARNING TO PLAY

You may find at first that you need to teach your bird to play, until he gets the idea of having fun with you. Encourage him to join in with you on the sofa or carpet as you make up simple games. Find the toys and activities your bird responds to and enjoys most, and build on these. He may like to play 'Hide And Seek' under a few sheets of newspaper, play with a ping-pong ball, or retrieve a child's plastic brick thrown by you. Cut holes in an upturned cardboard box and let him run in and out. Hide sunflower seeds or peanuts in your clothing, pockets, hand, under cushions etc., and play 'Hunt The Treat'. (Note: If you are giving sunflower seeds or peanuts as rewards, avoid over-feeding your parrot by reducing the daily ration of these items accordingly.) Use a box or plastic tub to hide a few small, interesting items, food treats etc., among scrunched up paper, fabric, or bubble wrap, and let your parrot hunt through to find the goodies.

The complexity of the games – and tricks – you can teach your parrot will, of course, depend on which species you keep. The aptitude of a Budgerigar or Lovebird will be more limited than that of a Sulphur-crested Cockatoo or Blue and Gold Macaw, for example. Specialist avian toy companies now sell a variety of props, equipment and games for all levels of ability.

Start trick-training your bird with simple tasks that use his natural skills and that he will enjoy – acrobatics, flying, picking things up and throwing them down. Teach the trick in simple steps, praising each successful (or even moderately successful!) move, and giving a reward. Remember, parrots can detect different colours, so this skill could be incorporated into the trick training.

Clicker training is one method of letting your parrot know every time he has made a good move. As soon as he does something right, you press the clicker then give the reward (praise, a tickle, or a food treat). Training clickers are simple, hand-held devices that can be purchased quite cheaply in pet stores. If enjoyment, not fear, is the incentive, you will soon have success.

8.2. SIMPLE TRICKS
Simple tricks to try include:
• Chasing and retrieving a small ball (or any other small toy)
• Waving hello and goodbye
• Picking up buttons and dropping them into a cup.

9. FLYING FREE
Some bird parks allow their trained Macaws to live freely in the trees during the day, recalling them to feed and to roost in an aviary at night. With a high level of bonding and control, some pet parrots can also be trained to fly from, and return to, their keeper out of doors. However, even a very tame and devoted parrot can quickly lose his bearings, fly off in the wrong direction, and become lost. Obviously, only highly experienced and knowledgeable keepers should attempt to free-fly their bird.

CHAPTER 9

BREEDING PARROTS

1. INTRODUCTION

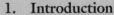

The hobby of breeding parrots and parakeets can give a lifetime's fascination and absorption. Every species has its own special characteristics and needs, and there is always something new to learn, with pleasant surprises as well as a few inevitable disappointments along the way. Even pairs of the same species can behave very differently when nesting and raising young, so the challenge is to identify particular idiosyncrasies and preferences, and adapt the diet, housing and nest boxes accordingly.

Many of today's successful aviculturists started out with just one or two pairs of the smaller parakeets, progressing on to the more demanding Amazons, Greys, Cockatoos and Macaws as their interest and expertise grew.

2. POINTS TO PONDER

If you are planning to breed parrots, perhaps hoping to make it a paying concern, the following points should be considered first:

2.1. WHICH SPECIES?

Think carefully about the type of parrot you really want to breed, rather than just buying the first one you see and then realising you would have preferred something different. You will be going to a lot of trouble and expense to build and equip an aviary, so make sure you end up with birds that please and interest you.

2.2. TIME
Feeding, watering, cleaning-out, and checking the birds, has to be done each day. The breeding season – spring and summer – can be very time consuming, particularly when chicks are being hatched and reared. Holidays away from home cannot be planned during the breeding season, in case hand-feeding becomes necessary. To avoid inter-breeding, care needs to be taken and records kept, to ensure that only unrelated birds are paired up.

2.3. A LIFETIME COMMITMENT
Psittacines can be very long-lived – a fact that should be considered before taking on the long-term commitment of a breeding aviary.

2.4. COSTS
Veterinary treatment may be needed – and the more birds, the more potential expense to the keeper. Injury from attack, egg binding, hand-feeding difficulties and splay leg in a young chick are just some of the problems that may be encountered when breeding parrots, all of which will require medical help.

2.5. NEIGHBOURS
Some species can be particularly noisy. If you have close neighbours, they may well object. Have a chat with them before starting to build the aviary, to avoid possible problems later on.

2.6. PROFITS
Not all parrot breeders make much, if any, profit from selling their young stock. Aviculture has made great leaps forward in recent years, with a consequent increase in breeding successes. The result of this is that many of the smaller, more easily bred psittacine species are widely available and fetch only very modest prices. The larger parrots, especially if hand-reared, still command a good price, but these birds also require a higher level of time, expertise, facilities, and attention from the breeder. If you plan to sell the babies from your breeding pairs, you will have a better chance of this if (a) you keep a popular species, (b) the market, particularly in your own local area, is not already flooded with these birds, and (c) you are prepared to hand-rear them if they are to be sold as pets.

2.7. UNSOLD STOCK
Responsible aviculturists ensure that their birds are only sold to homes where they will be cared for properly. This could mean that they may have to keep any unsold stock.

2.8. STARTING OUT

It is a good idea to start with one of the more easily managed, hardier species that are early maturing and will readily nest and breed. Captive-bred Budgerigars, Cockatiels and Peach-faced Lovebirds, for example, are ideal for the novice, or for children who want to take up the hobby.

2.9. BREEDING FROM PET PARROTS

Think carefully before moving your pet parrot to an outside aviary and giving him or her a mate. Although you may feel your bird would be happier having the chance to live and breed with his own kind, this is not always the case. A bonded pet, which has only ever known human company and household routine, may be stressed by the drastic change to aviary life.

However, some birds are clearly miserable at not being allowed to breed (obvious signs are obsessive nest building and egg laying, feather plucking and raucous, aggressive behaviour whenever the bird comes into breeding condition). If you have decided to move your pet bird to an aviary, make the change in gradual stages and during warm weather, so that he becomes used to the new surroundings and temperature. Choose the mate carefully, ensuring the birds get on well before putting them together. Continue to keep a close eye on them for a while, to make sure there is no bullying going on.

Parent-reared or wild-caught birds, which have never become fully tame and relaxed as pets, may be happier if allowed the freedom of an aviary and a mate of their own kind. Be aware, though, that a previously loving pet may lose interest in you, or even show aggression once bonded with a new mate.

2.10. SEXING THE BREEDING PAIR

It may sound obvious, but you will need to be sure that your pair of parrots does in fact comprise a male and a female! Buying a proven pair (one that has already produced young) from a reputable breeder can save a lot of wasted time while you wait for your two males or two females to produce eggs!

Some species are obviously dimorphic (that is, where the difference between the sexes can be readily seen), others less so. With some species, the African Grey for example, the only way to be certain is to have the birds DNA tested. This can be done surgically by your avian vet (requiring anaesthetic), or via a drop of blood or a freshly plucked feather, at a DNA testing laboratory. The latter two methods are obviously less intrusive to the bird and are also less expensive. The advantage with surgical testing is that the vet can check the bird's general health at the same time.

2.11. INTRODUCTIONS

Just like humans, there is no guarantee that a male and female bird will automatically like each other. Fortunately, if introductions are done with care, most paired birds will get along well. However, never take the risk of simply putting two birds into an aviary together until you are confident they are friends. If you introduce a new (and passive-natured) bird into the cage of a more dominant bird, attack is likely. Severe injury and even death may result.

This is a particular danger with male Cockatoos, as the male may savagely attack his mate and even kill her.

If you have bought an established breeding pair, it is important to continue to house them together, as any period of separation may result in the female being attacked by her mate when they are reunited.

When pairing parrots for breeding, introduce them with care, by placing their separate cages close to each other (but sufficiently far apart so that the birds cannot actually reach each other through the bars). Keep a close watch for the first sign of aggression.

The best way to establish a successful pair is to let unrelated birds choose each other from an aviary flock. This should avoid the possibility of aggression between two birds that have been forced together. By watching the birds over a period of time, you will know if they are getting on well when you see them constantly sitting close together, preening each other, sharing the same bowl of food, and feeding each other.

HAND-REARING
You will need to check the nest box regularly once eggs and chicks are in the nest. Even if you have decided to let the parents rear their own young, be prepared to hand-rear chicks if difficulties arise. This is a big commitment as new baby birds need feeding throughout the day and night during the first week.

2.13. SPECIAL DIETS
Leading up to and during the breeding season, your birds will need a good variety and supply of foods from which to choose. Besides the normal diet of parrot mix, green foods, fruit and vegetables, it is important to include extra protein and calcium-rich items, such as scrambled egg, nuts, beans, seed sprouts, pulses etc.

DID YOU KNOW?
A hybrid is a cross between two parrot species. With many species in decline in the wild, it is the aim of most committed aviculturists to breed only pure stock.

---

3. AVIARIES
Your breeding birds will require a roomy flight, as well as enclosed accommodation for roosting and nesting.

The more destructive the species, the stronger the construction will need to be. Think ahead before starting – if you plan to progress from, say, Lovebirds to Pionus, you may want to build a bigger, stronger aviary in the first instance, which will accommodate either species.

You may want to build the aviary from scratch yourself, or buy one ready-made. This will come in self-assembly sections from the manufacturer. Some of the smaller ones have castors, so that the aviary can be moved about and kept indoors. Kit-form aviaries are also ideal if you are planning to move house, as they can be taken down and put up again.

3.1. BUILDING AN OUTDOOR AVIARY

If you are building an outdoor aviary yourself, you will need to put in solid foundations to support the frame, plus suitable flooring that can be easily cleaned and is rodent-proof. Concrete and paving slabs are suitable materials for the aviary base. Turf and gravel are other alternatives, but these floors are more difficult to keep clean and free from bacteria.

The less destructive psittacine species can safely be housed in a wood-frame aviary. A good, safe wood preservative to use on the frame is *Cuprinol*. However, all-metal (aluminium) housing is more secure and easier to keep clean, as well as being light to handle and to move. The stronger the beak, the tougher the wire-mesh and frame will need to be. If a wood frame is being used, ensure that all the wood is securely covered with mesh – never underestimate the chewing power of parrots!

If you are building your own aviary, make sure you buy the right strength and size of galvanized, welded wire mesh. Do not use thin chicken wire, as this will not be strong enough. A specialist avian supplier will be able to advise on the correct gauge for the species you are planning to keep. Good-quality, purpose-made avian mesh should also be free of toxic lead or zinc residues from the manufacturing process. To make sure, rinse the mesh with vinegar before use, to remove any traces.

If you are building more than one aviary – or plan to do so in the future – remember that there must be a gap of a couple of inches between each flight, so that each aviary has its own separate wire mesh. This 'double-wiring' is important to prevent one bird attacking another through the aviary wire – a particular danger with some species and especially during the breeding season.

If there is a safe entry porch to the aviary, whereby one door is closed before the second (to the aviary itself) is opened, you do not run the risk of losing a bird as you enter the flight.

3.1.1. UNWELCOME VISITORS

Rats, mice, and even wild birds pose a serious threat to aviary parrots as they can spread disease. Rodents can frighten birds, and, if they get into the nest box, rats will eat the eggs and young birds. Make sure the aviary is fully secure, with a strong base, suitably sized wire mesh, and no gaps or holes where an uninvited guest could enter. Alternatively, flights can be supported on posts, so that they are well above ground level and rodents are kept at bay.

Rodents will be attracted by dropped seed and other foods, and the best way to deter them is to keep the aviary floor as clean as possible at all times. Store foodstuffs in the house, rather than in an outside shed, where they may be found and eaten. Your parrots could then be at risk from disease-carrying urine.

If you see a mouse or rat, do not be tempted to put down poisoned bait. Not only could this prove hazardous to your birds, but it is also a cruel death for the intruder. Traps are a better alternative. If you do not like the idea of killing an animal, use a humane trap, where the rodent is caught unharmed and can be released in a different location, well away from your garden and aviary.

Cats are always a potential danger. Even though they cannot enter the aviary, they may climb on the roof and cause panic and resulting injury, or attack the feet of birds sleeping on the wire sides. A secure, covered-in area of the flight, where the birds can perch and roost safely, as well as separate enclosed accommodation, will provide protection against cats, other pets and birds of prey.

3.1.2. PROTECTION AGAINST THE ELEMENTS

Give your birds protection from the elements – shade in summer, and shelter from cold winds and rain in winter. A partially covered flight will give adequate perching comfort for most of the year. However, extra protection is needed for particularly cold or wet weather. This can then be taken down when conditions improve.

Some breeders use plastic 'bubble wrap' stapled to the aviary sides to keep out the worst of the weather. However, this can easily tear in strong winds and it is rather expensive for what will be temporary use only. Removable panels of strong, clear, plastic sheeting are ideal, as these give good weather protection and also let in light.

Extra nutrition is needed in cold weather. You can provide this in the form of seeds, nuts and pulses. Water should also be checked regularly during icy spells. Some birds will want to bathe even in the coldest weather, so a shallow bath should always be available. This will need to be re-filled at regular intervals if the water freezes over.

Parrots and parakeets can injure or even lose a foot from frostbite, so make sure sleeping quarters are dry and draught-free, and that your birds can roost in comfort during the winter months. The particularly susceptible species will fare best if they are housed in an indoor aviary in cold weather.

3.1.3. POSITION

If the aviary is to be sited out of doors, it is a good idea to make sure your neighbours do not have any strong objections. Choose the most sheltered, peaceful corner of your garden, out of reach of extremes of cold, wet, wind, or hot sunshine. Ideally, it will be in a place that offers scope for further aviary building alongside in the future. It also needs to be easily accessible for feeding and daily care, as well as being close enough to the house for you to watch your birds. On cold, dark winter mornings, you will be glad you built the aviary next to a pathway or other hard standing, rather than having to trudge to the bottom of the garden across a soggy lawn to feed and check your birds! Another consideration when siting the aviary is the danger from overhanging trees. If a branch crashes down in a high wind, the roof will be damaged and you could well lose your birds.

Any surrounding plants or bushes will be nibbled at if the parrots can reach them, so ensure they are safe for birds to eat – willow, elderberry, hibiscus, lavender, honeysuckle, sunflowers, roses, apple, pear, evening primrose, nasturtiums, hawthorn and hazelnut are considered safe.

DID YOU KNOW?
Most parrots adapt well to the climate of the northern hemisphere, if properly fed and protected from extremes of weather. However, for some delicate species, heaters can be used in the aviary. Choose a safe form of heating, such as oil-filled radiators.

3.2. INDOOR AVIARIES

You may want to house your breeding parrots in an indoor aviary, perhaps having several pairs of birds in one room. This will give you more security against theft, and, unless heating is to be provided in an outdoor aviary, the more delicate parrot species will certainly be better off during the cold winter months.

Suspended breeding aviaries housed within a bird room can be successfully used for some of the more amenable species. This form of housing is more hygienic, as the open wire base cannot harbour bacteria from a build-up of droppings and rotting food.

Some breeders use a series of small, suspended cages with a nest box attached, and many have had success with breeding pairs housed in this way. However, the severely limited space allows little or no scope for flying and playing, and, although young may be produced and raised, many keepers consider this an unsatisfactory environment for a parrot. Bear in mind when positioning the housing units that some species will be aggressive towards their neighbours if given the opportunity, in which case screening between them will be needed.

Hygiene is particularly important when housing your birds indoors, so when designing your bird room, make sure it can be easily and thoroughly cleaned on a regular basis. Daylight and ventilation can be provided via large, opening windows, and an extractor fan will help to prevent the build-up of harmful fungal spores. Bathing facilities will also need to be provided. Some keepers install full-spectrum ultra-violet lighting, which mimics daylight and is beneficial in stimulating birds into breeding condition.

Hot and cold water are a useful addition, plus storage space and worktops for food preparation, etc.

3.3. NEST BOXES

The size and design of a nest box will depend on the species being bred. Parrot stores offer a wide range of boxes, or you may prefer to make your own.

3.3.1. TYPE AND CONSTRUCTION

Wood is preferable to metal, being warm, absorbent and natural, although some birds will accept metal boxes. Metal boxes last longer, because they cannot rot or be chewed, and they can also be more thoroughly cleaned.

Many parrots will accept whatever box is offered to them, although some pairs can be very fussy and may take quite a while before they will set up home inside. In this case, do not try to tempt them inside with food – some parrots will eat their own eggs, so you could be setting up bad habits.

Some birds will happily nest in hollowed-out logs placed on the aviary floor, or in a wooden beer barrel adapted for the purpose. By reading up on the particular species you want to breed, you can provide nesting facilities that most closely match those used in the natural environment.

The box needs to be of sturdy construction – up to 1 inch (2.5 cms) thick plywood – which should be attached securely to the aviary side. Heavier boxes, for Cockatoos or Macaws for example, will need extra support underneath. Make sure there are no sharp nail or screw heads exposed inside.

There should be a hinged lid, or other hatch, at a convenient and safe place for inspecting the nest, a wooden or wire mesh ladder from the entrance hole to the floor of the box, and extra pieces of thick wood affixed inside the box for the birds to chew up for extra nesting material (this is also important to prevent damage to the box itself).

Parrots that produce eggs during the cold winter months, as well as the less hardy species, will need an insulated nest box (a layer of polystyrene between an outer and inner wall can be used to provide extra warmth).

3.3.2. ENTRANCE HOLES

The entrance hole should be situated towards the top of the box. The hole should be large enough for the bird to enter, but no larger, as this will give the bird a feeling of security. If the entrance is slightly too small, the birds will happily chew it to the desired size.

If there is any danger of aggression from the male bird, a T-shaped nest box can be the best option. This has two entrance/exit holes at either end of the 'T', leading along and down to the nest below.

There should be a short dowelling perch below the entrance hole for the birds to enter, to leave, and to guard the box.

3.3.3. DARKNESS AND PRIVACY

Darkness is very important to nesting birds, so the box needs to be deep enough to allow for this. Long, rectangular boxes, where the bird has to climb down some distance, or L-shaped boxes, where the nest is built in a section away from the entrance hole, offer extra privacy and darkness and are often preferred. These boxes imitate the conditions found in the wild, where parrots would climb down into a hollow tree and dig themselves a nest in a dark, secluded hole.

Some psittacines like boxes built on the slant, so that the nest is positioned at an angle, away from the entrance hole.

Breeding birds dislike being disturbed, so it is a good idea to get your parrots used to your presence in or around the aviary, particularly near the nest box, as you will need to inspect this on a regular basis once eggs have been laid and the chicks have hatched. If you have previously established a routine of feeding and nest box inspection, the birds are less likely to be stressed by this intrusion once nesting is under way.

3.3.4. LOCATION

Consider the habits of wild birds when positioning nest boxes. Many parrots nest in trees, where they can avoid predators and extremes of weather. It makes sense, therefore, to place nest boxes high up in the aviary, in a secluded, sheltered corner away from rain and hot sun. Where more than one pair of birds is housed together, squabbling may occur over nest sites, so give extra boxes for the birds to choose from.

Position the box well away from feeding dishes, so that when you want to inspect the nest later on, you can wait until the parent birds are well out of the way, eating on the other side of the aviary.

By attaching the nest box to the outside of the aviary, the keeper can inspect the nest without disturbing the birds. When using breeding cages, this arrangement also gives the birds more room to move about.

As many parrots like to sleep in the nest boxes during the non-breeding season, you can leave them in place for this purpose. However, you will need to remove them if they stimulate your birds to continue breeding and nesting during the winter, when they should be resting and building up their reserves.

3.3.5. NESTING MATERIALS

A few inches of pinewood chips make good nesting material as these will not harbour harmful mould or bacteria. Put plenty of woodchips in – the hen will remove what she does not want. It is important for the young chicks to have plenty of support around them, to prevent their delicate legs from splaying outwards and becoming deformed.

DID YOU KNOW?

In the wild, breeding birds chew at the inside of their tree hollows to provide absorbent nesting material for the chicks. Chewing wood is an important and instinctive part of breeding behaviour, so remember to give your birds extra pieces of wood inside the nest box, as well as twigs and branches in the flight.

3.4. HOME, SWEET HOME

Once you have built your aviary and added the nest boxes, you can have fun making it an interesting and stimulating place for your birds to live.

3.4.1. PERCHES

Fit a variety of carefully washed, natural perching – whole branches with varying thicknesses of wood for your birds to chew on and to clamber about. Consider the size of your bird's feet, and ensure the perches can be comfortably gripped so that balance is not lost during mating. As a rough guide, small parrots such as Senegals and Caiques need perches of up to about 1 inch (2.5 cms) in diameter. Amazons, Greys and medium-sized Cockatoos will need branches of 1 to 1¹/₂ inches (2.5 to 3.75 cms), and the large Macaws and Cockatoos will need branches of 2 to 3 inches (5 to 7.5 cms).

Make food and water dishes accessible from a comfortable perch in a sheltered corner of the aviary.

3.4.2. TOYS
Hang ropes, swings, and ladders, so that your parrots can practise their acrobatic skills. Include toys in which pieces of food can be hidden. Chunks of sweetcorn, monkey nuts, and peas in the pod can be strung on wires from the aviary roof or a perch. Put a pile of rocks and logs on the ground, to provide hiding and playing places. You could also include parrot-safe plants in tubs – if you don't mind replacing these when they get chewed up.

3.4.3. FOOD AND WATER
Breeding birds will appreciate access to a shallow bath of water while they are hatching eggs, as they may want to add moisture to the nest.

By fitting swing feeders, which can be swung to the outside of the flight for cleaning and filling, you will not need to continually disturb your birds.

4. ROUTINE CARE

4.1. SPECIAL DIETS
Breeding birds need a special diet, to stimulate breeding activity, to keep up their strength, and to feed their babies. In addition to a good variety of the usual fresh foods, soft foods, such as scrambled egg, soaked sunflower seeds, bread and milk, cooked peas, soaked dried fruit, etc., containing plenty of calcium and protein, are important both before and during the nesting period. Some breeders add a few drops of cod liver or halibut oil to the feed during the cold winter months.

4.2. WORMING
Aviary birds, particularly if the housing has an earth floor, will need to be wormed. Ask your vet for advice.

5. BREEDING

5.1. TIMING
Nervous species or individuals may take some months to settle before they are ready to start courting and breeding. Spring is the usual time that birds nest, so if they have had the preceding autumn and winter to get used to their new quarters (and each other), they are more likely to breed in the following spring than if they were purchased in the March or April of the new year. Some parrot species will take longer than this before they produce eggs and young, while some of the small parakeets may surprise you at how quickly they settle, bond, and start nesting.

> **DID YOU KNOW?**
> *Unlike humans, parrots can perceive ultraviolet light, which enables them to distinguish whether another bird is male or female – even though, to us, the two may look identical.*

5.2. WHEN NOTHING HAPPENS

You have built your aviary, bought a male and female pair, given them a good parrot mix, bathing facilities, and a nest box, but there is no sign of breeding or nesting. Alternatively, eggs may have been laid, but they are infertile, or they have been broken or abandoned in the nest.

Remember, even the most experienced parrot breeders have problems at one time or another. The reasons for lack of success may be one or more of the following:

- The birds are not compatible (one or both are too young, too old, or unwell)
- Noise from the surrounding environment is frightening the birds
- The keeper or other human visitors are over-intrusive
- The diet lacks variety or is inadequate in some way
- The nest box shape or size is not acceptable to the pair.

Make whatever changes you think may be needed and do not despair. Your birds may just be taking a while to adjust to their surroundings and each other, and will likely breed successfully next year.

5.3. EGG LAYING

Just before she lays her eggs, the hen may show a swelling in her lower abdomen. Depending on the species, anything from two to five eggs will be laid over a period of several days, the incubation time varying from approximately three to four weeks. During this time, the cock bird will spend much of his time feeding the hen and standing guard over the nest. With some species, the male will share incubation duties, although more often only the hen sits on the eggs.

It can be alarming to note that the hen is not sitting on the eggs at the beginning and end of the hatching period. However, this is normal practice. At the beginning of the incubation period, this delay helps regulate the eventual hatching time for the eggs (which are laid a day or two apart). When incubation is nearly over, the hen sometimes instinctively moves off the eggs to trigger the start of hatching.

6. CHECKING THE NEST

If the female is spending much of her time in the nest box and the male seems to be always at the food dish and perhaps particularly aggressive, you will know that egg laying is under way. Hopefully, within a few weeks, you will start to hear the first tiny squeaks from the babies.

6.1. CLOSED-CIRCUIT TV

Once you are hooked on parrot or parakeet breeding, you will probably wish you knew more about what is going on in the aviary or nest box when you are not around. One solution is to install CCTV, with cameras in strategic positions around the aviary and nest boxes, and a monitor in the house. This will allow you to check the progress of the eggs and chicks, without upsetting the parent birds.

6.2. EGGS

You can check the fertility and progress of an egg by holding it against a halogen candling light (available from avian product specialists).

While eggs and chicks are in the nest, you will probably want to make regular checks to see that all is well, rather than just hope for the best. However, remember that this is stressful to the parents, and they may try to bite you. Keep inspections brief and proceed with care.

Broken eggs should be removed if found, or they will otherwise go bad and infect the nest. If the parent birds are alarmed or unsettled, or if their diet lacks calcium, they may resort to eating their own eggs. Eggs that never hatch may be infertile, or the embryo may have died in the shell from becoming too cold during incubation, or as a result of a viral infection.

6.3. CHICKS

Chicks may perish from cold if the parent birds are alarmed by predators such as cats or raptors and abandon the nest for an over-long period.

If a baby looks cold and lethargic, or if you suspect he is not being fed (there should be an obvious crop bulge), you may decide to remove him for hand-feeding. You will also need to remove a youngster if he has received an injury, or if he is being picked on or feather-plucked by his parents. Do not delay if you think there may be a problem, as young birds can decline very quickly.

DID YOU KNOW?
Inexperienced parrots may need to learn parenting skills. If your breeding birds do not successfully hatch and rear babies the first time round, do not despair. It may be that they need more practice, and will do better next time.

6.4. INCUBATION AND FOSTERING

In the case of parent birds that habitually lay fertile eggs but do not successfully hatch them, some breeders may want to invest in an incubator that will do the job for them. There are several purpose-made incubators on the market that will keep parrot eggs at the correct temperature and humidity levels until hatching. However, if the eggs are incubated artificially, the babies will have to be hand-fed.

An alternative to artificial incubation is to introduce the eggs into the nest of another pair of parrots – of the same or another species.

6.5. CLOSED BANDING

Closed banding is proof of captive breeding. It gives details of the bird, his age, and his breeder. Fitting a closed band around a parrot's leg can only be done within the first two weeks of his life (the exact timing will depend on the species), after which time the ring will not pass over the bird's foot. Bear in mind that serious injuries can occur if leg bands catch on aviary wire, or become crushed by a strong beak. Seek veterinary advice at once if this happens to your bird.

7. HAND-REARING

Even if you want your parrots to raise their own young (and after all, they are the ones best suited to this job), it is sometimes necessary to remove a chick for hand-rearing. If the chick has been injured, or, if the parents have started plucking the chick or are not caring for him properly, you will need to remove him. Many breeders hand-rear their parrot chicks specifically to ensure they have tame, people-friendly birds for the pet market.

Some (although certainly not all) parent birds will allow you to handle the young in the nest once they are a few weeks old. If this is done regularly, the babies will get used to human contact at an early stage, making the transition to their new home an easier one.

If your intention is to hand-rear the babies from the beginning, the ideal time to remove them from the nest is once their pin feathers are starting to appear. Although some breeders advocate taking the babies away sooner than this, they are probably no tamer as a result and have not had the advantage of the parent birds' expert care during the first few weeks.

Taking a bird from his parents and raising him in the home is a big responsibility, and it should only be undertaken with careful forethought and thorough research. Remember, once you have taken the chick, the parents are unlikely to accept him back, even if he has been gone for a few days only. It is important to take advice from an experienced hand-rearer, so that potential pitfalls can be avoided – inadequate nutrition and care in the early stages can affect the bird physically and psychologically in later life. If you have a bird club near you, there will be plenty of enthusiastic and experienced keepers only too willing to give advice and to lend a hand.

If you do not have the confidence, or indeed the time to hand-rear your baby parrots, make contact in advance with an experienced parrot keeper who is offering this service. You should be able to find a specialist hand-feeder by asking around at local bird clubs or parrot retailers, or by looking through the classified sections in avian magazines. However, check that different species are not hand-reared together at your chosen establishment, as this can transmit infectious diseases.

7.1. NESTS

A simple baby brooder (or 'nest') can be made from a suitably sized ice-cream tub – depending on the number of chicks being housed – lined with kitchen paper or soft cotton fabric that will not fray and pull on delicate toenails. You will need a good supply, so that it can be changed regularly.

Chicks benefit from being brooded together, rather than separately. Make sure they are held snugly and securely in the brooder (as they would be in a natural nest), to avoid the danger of splayed legs. Cover the top with a towel, to simulate the darkness of a natural tree hole, leaving a gap at one corner for ventilation. It will also reduce stress to the babies if the brooder is situated in a peaceful place, in dim light.

The baby parrots will huddle together quietly if they are too cold, or become pink and fretful if too hot. For the first three to four weeks, baby parrots need humidity and warmth. The temperature can be reduced gradually from about 32.5 degrees Celsius (90 degrees Fahrenheit) until, at approximately one month old, the young birds can be kept at a normal, comfortable room temperature of about 21.5 degrees Celsius (70 degrees Fahrenheit).

7.2. FEEDING

Baby parrots can be successfully hand-fed using a teaspoon with the sides bent up, a plastic pipette, or a syringe. If you use a pipette or syringe, take care not to force too much formula into the chick at one time, or to give the food too quickly. Using a spoon takes longer for the keeper, but is likely to be a more enjoyable experience for the baby parrot, giving him more control over how much food he takes and how quickly (or slowly).

Specially formulated baby foods are available, containing important bacterial cultures to aid digestion in very young parrots. However, if the chicks have been left with their parents for the first few weeks before hand-rearing, problems with digesting food are less common. With experience, you can also make your own formula. Ask an experienced hand-rearer for advice on what to give your own particular species.

Little and often is the rule to start with, when the baby's crop is tiny and can hold only minute amounts of food. The gaps between feeding times become longer as the chick gets older and can take more food each time.

The younger the baby, the more sloppy the food needs to be. You will be able to see when the crop is full and when it has emptied – which means it is feeding time again. It is important that food is digested, and the crop emptied, before giving the chick more to eat. If this does not happen, *sour crop* may develop, in which the food 'goes off' – a serious condition which needs immediate expert attention.

Follow the manufacturer's directions carefully when you are mixing the formula, ensuring that sufficient *really hot* water has been added to the mix, fully hydrating it, before it is allowed to cool to the correct temperature for feeding. If fed too dry, the food may become impacted in the crop and will be unable to pass through. The baby may also become dehydrated.

Make sure the formula is not too hot, or you risk burning the baby's crop. If you use a microwave to heat the formula, make sure you stir the mixture very thoroughly and test it for overall temperature before you offer it to the baby. Food heated in this way may feel quite cool in one place, but be burning hot in another. Never give cold food, as this will stick in the chick's crop and will not be digested.

Remember, if in doubt, consult your avian vet at once. Crop burns or infection need proper medical attention.

7.3. WEANING

Switching from soft foods to seed, fruit, and vegetables varies according to the different species – eight weeks for Greys, for example. You may get a signal that the youngster is ready to wean when he starts refusing or regurgitating formula, and seems more interested in nibbling and testing things with his beak.

This is the time when future good eating habits can be established, so you should encourage your parrot to eat a wide range of foods. To tempt the youngster to try something other than formula, start him on soft items, such as cooked peas, sweetcorn, tiny pieces of fruit, soaked seed, etc., as well as baby pellets. At the same time, provide a bowl of water. Continue offering the formula when the birds want it, but gradually replace this with 'adult' food. Once the baby is happily nibbling on a variety of soft vegetables and pellets, you can start to offer seeds and a few nuts. A parrot is properly weaned when he is cracking and eating seed without problem, and he is no longer asking to be fed by hand.

Keep an eye on the weaning babies, to make sure they are all eating properly – some will make quicker progress than others. If an individual seems slow to feed himself, give more feeds until he has caught up with his siblings, but continue to encourage him to eat the new foods. Some reluctant weaners will copy the feeding habits of an older bird. If a youngster will not wean, despite your best efforts, consult your vet.

The weaning stage is also the time to introduce the young bird to his first cage and the idea of perching and drinking from a water dish. Initially, young birds can be put together in the same cage for short periods, to accustom them to the idea. Later, you should give each bird his own cage. Fit perches low down at first, with food and water bowls accessible.

8. SELLING YOUNG STOCK

Advertise young stock well in advance of the date by which you expect them to be fully weaned. This applies particularly if you are planning to advertise in an avian magazine, which may only be published six or twelve times a year, and which will require copy well in advance of the date of issue. Other outlets for baby birds are the pets-for-sale section in the local newspaper, bird stores, garden centres that sell birds, and, for a much wider audience, the Internet.

Do not pass on your carefully raised baby bird to a stranger until you have (tactfully) asked a few relevant questions:
• Have they kept birds before – and what happened to them?
• What does the buyer expect from a pet bird? Do they simply want a pet that 'talks'?
• If buying the bird as a pet, is there someone at home during the day?

- If the bird is intended as a child's pet, how old is the child? Is the species suitable?
- Is the buyer aware of the amount of attention and training a parrot needs?
- Do they have room for the size of cage required?
- Are there any smokers in the family?

If the prospective keeper is new to parrots, the responsible seller will point out the possible lifespan of the bird, as well as the noise, mess, and damage parrots can create in the home. A detailed diet and care sheet should accompany the baby bird to his new home, together with the seller's telephone number in case any difficulties or queries arise in the future.

Although it may appear as though you are trying to 'put off' the prospective owner, a new keeper who is committed will be interested to know exactly what to expect, and should have additional questions of his own to ask. If someone is discouraged when they learn, for example, that the parrot may nip or that something a lot bigger than a budgie cage is required for this breed of parrot, parrot keeping is not for them.

9. BREEDING COCKATIELS

Many newcomers to parrot breeding choose to keep Cockatiels as their first birds. These charming parakeets make an excellent introduction to the hobby, and, given good basic care, they should thrive and breed readily. There are many attractive colour mutations, and breeding for colour varieties adds extra interest and challenge.

As with any aviary birds, if your newly purchased Cockatiels were previously housed indoors, do not put them straight outside in cold weather. Move them to their permanent home in gradual stages, until they have become acclimatised. You could move them to and from the aviary in temporary cages for a while, until the final transition is made and they are released into the flight. After this, as long as enclosed accommodation and a partly covered flight are provided, these birds will happily adapt to the winter climate in many different countries. Indoor aviaries are an alternative.

9.1. HOUSING WITH OTHER SPECIES

As Cockatiels are gentle, non-aggressive birds, they should not be housed with other psittacine species, which might bully them. In a dispute over nest boxes or food dishes, the amenable little Cockatiel is likely to come off worse.

9.2. HOW MANY BREEDING PAIRS?

A single pair of Cockatiels will appreciate having the whole aviary to themselves, but more than one pair can be kept together, provided there is plenty of room for the birds to get away from each other, there are lots of food dishes available, and a choice of nesting boxes – with more boxes than pairs of birds, to prevent arguments. Allowance should also be made for the extra birds that will be sharing the aviary once the chicks have fledged.

Ideally, put all the birds into the aviary at the same time, to avoid the possibility of squabbling. Once established, Cockatiels will breed successfully in a colony and some will even feed another pair's chicks. Of course, if you want to be sure of the chicks' parentage, or if you wish to breed for specific colour mutations, you will need to house each pair in a separate flight.

Any unpaired birds should be removed once the breeding season is under way, to avoid any trouble.

9.3. AVIARY

As Cockatiels are active flyers, a single pair will need a flight of 8 to 12 feet (2.45 to 3.65 metres) long, 3 to 4 feet (0.9 to 1.2 metres) deep, and 6 to 8 feet (1.8 to 2.45 metres) high, or larger if this is possible. Although these birds have been known to breed in much smaller enclosures indoors, they will fare better given plenty of space and an outdoor environment. While they are breeding, you will notice that your birds do not fly about so much, but for the rest of the year they will appreciate a good sized flight. As birds fly horizontally rather than vertically, the length of the flight is the most critical dimension.

9.3.1. CONSTRUCTION AND FITTING OUT

A wooden frame (treated with a suitable preservative) is adequate for Cockatiels, as they are not destructive chewers. Wire mesh of 19 (or 16 for extra strength) gauge, $^1/_2$ inch by $^1/_2$ inch (1.25 by 1.25 cms) is a suitable size for these birds and will keep out rodents.

Go over the completed construction carefully, making sure there are no exposed wire ends anywhere that could catch on a foot or tongue and cause injury.

Include a safety porch in the design, to prevent one of your Cockatiels dashing past you as you open the door. To provide shelter from the elements, cover a good portion of the roof and sides with strong, transparent corrugated plastic. Fit stainless steel food and water dishes alongside the perches in this weather-proof corner of the aviary, leaving just a perch or two in the open area, so that the birds can fly about freely as well as bathe in a shower of rain.

Flooring can be earth, turf or concrete, etc. For indoor aviaries, newspaper can be laid on the floor for ease of cleaning.

Fit a variety of perches, bearing in mind the Cockatiel's small feet and allowing for comfortable gripping. Suitably sized ropes, swings, and toys will also be needed.

9.3.2. ENCLOSED ACCOMMODATION

A snug shelter within or attached to the flight will allow protection from severe weather and provide somewhere safe to roost at night. Some breeders make use of a small garden shed fitted against the end of the flight, but the shelter can be just a few feet square and set above ground inside the flight on blocks or bricks. It needs to be of strong wood construction, with the inner surfaces lined with wire mesh to prevent damage from chewing. Fit perches inside the shelter and cut an entry hole of a few inches square, with a platform beneath to allow your birds to come in and out comfortably.

You will need to have access yourself to the enclosure, so that it can be checked and cleaned periodically. Cleaning is made easy if you put several sheets of newspaper on the floor and just remove one or two as they become soiled.

9.3.3. NEST BOXES
A simple, wooden box of about 12 inches (30 cms) square will be readily accepted by Cockatiels, with an entrance hole of 3 inches (7.5 cms) above a small perch attached to the front, towards the top of the box. You can either make your own, from $3/4$ inch (2 cms) exterior-quality plywood, or you can buy the box ready made, or ready for self-assembly.

An interior ladder leading down from the entrance hole will allow the adult birds to enter and leave easily, and the chicks to eventually leave the nest. This will not be chewed to pieces if made of wire mesh rather than wood. The nest box will need an overlapping and backward-sloping roof, so that rain can run off, as well as an inspection hatch so that you can keep an eye on what is going on inside.

In early spring, attach the nest boxes securely within the sheltered area of the flight, allowing at least one box per pair of birds. Remember to fix them so that they are accessible for inspection, whether inside or outside the flight.

A suitable nesting material is a couple of inches of soft, crumbled-up rotten wood, which would be found in the natural nesting holes in dead trees in the wild.

As Cockatiels will often go on breeding and laying eggs all year round – even during the winter if allowed to do so – you can make sure they rest and recuperate by removing the nest boxes after they have produced one, or, at the most, two broods. Remember, though, to put the boxes back in place in plenty of time for the spring breeding season.

9.4. EGGS AND CHICKS
The breeding pair will need to keep their strength up for the busy season ahead. In addition to their usual seed and green food diet, give plenty of soft foods such as wholemeal bread and milk, eggfood, and sprouted seeds.

Cockatiels usually nest and breed without hesitation, often successfully raising two or even three clutches of four or more eggs. Some males will share incubation duties with their mate.

The incubation period is about three weeks, after which time the eggs will start to hatch. The chicks are ready to leave the nest at about five weeks of age.

Some Cockatiels that have been hand-reared can be reluctant to wean from soft food on to solids. Start with tiny pieces of fruit, soaked seed, and cooked rice and peas, mixed in with formula, and encourage the youngsters to pick up small seeds such as millet. Gradually increase the periods between offering soft foods, until the chicks are hungry enough to try the other foods on offer. Do not let your birds starve, however, and give extra feeds if necessary.

Young Cockatiels should be cracking and eating seed, and therefore old enough to live independently of their parents, by two months of age, being fully mature by one year old.

BE PREPARED

Although some species will successfully rear a full brood of healthy chicks with little or no intervention on the part of the keeper, problems can arise when there are eggs or young in the nest. Be prepared for unforeseen difficulties by reading up as much as possible beforehand on the species you are hoping to breed, and also asking established keepers for advice and tips. Most will be glad to discuss the hobby with you and pass on the benefit of their own experience.

- *Look out for egg-binding. If the hen looks at all unwell – and the vent appears swollen – take her to a veterinarian without delay. This serious condition can occur when insufficient calcium has been provided in the diet and/or has been depleted by continual egg laying. A particularly large egg may also be the cause of binding.*
- *Parental neglect, feather picking or attack may necessitate removal of one or more of the young from the nest box. The chick will be in immediate need of warmth and hand-feeding before being returned to the parents – if they will accept him back. The chances are, however, that you will need to keep the chick in your care. It is, therefore, a good idea to equip yourself in advance with a brooder, hand-rearing formula, kitchen towels, etc... in case of an emergency.*

---

10. BREEDING AFRICAN GREYS

With a steady market for hand-reared baby Greys, and perhaps having kept one of these birds as a pet, you may want to try breeding African Greys as a hobby. Ideally, you will already have gained experience with a less demanding species before undertaking this new venture.

Allowing your male and female to choose each other from a flock is the best way of making sure you have a true and compatible pair. Remember, though, that they will need time to settle into their new accommodation and may not breed for a couple of seasons. If they are young birds, you will have to wait until they are four or five years old before they are mature enough to raise their own young.

10.1. HOUSING

African Greys are generally quiet birds, uttering melodious whistles rather than unpleasant screeches (unless alarmed), so aviary birds should not pose a noise problem with your neighbours.

Greys seem to be content in relatively confined accommodation when breeding and nesting, and may accept a flight of no more than 4 feet (1.2 metres). However, more space will be needed during the rest of the year, when the birds are more active. A 20-feet (6-metre) wide flight, at least 6 feet (1.8 metres) high and 3 feet (0.9 metres) deep, will give them scope for proper exercise. These birds will breed indoors, but an outdoor flight offers more scope for flying, as well as access to rain and sunshine.

A metal or strong wooden frame will be needed, with 14-gauge wire mesh. Make sure there is no exposed woodwork for the birds to chew through.

Weather protection as well as a draught-free enclosed shelter will be needed.

Privacy is important to Greys when they are breeding and raising young, so keep noise and other disturbance around the aviary to a minimum. Limit nest inspections to when the parents are away feeding. These birds can also be fussy about nest boxes, so offering a choice of design and location is a good idea.

L-shaped boxes, which offer more privacy and security than a standard square nest box, may be most successful. Otherwise, a nest box of 12 inches (30 cms) square and 24 inches (60 cms) deep is a suitable size. Place the box about 6 feet (1.8 metres) up and put in a good layer of pinewood shavings for nesting material.

It is good practice to thoroughly wash, disinfect, and sun-dry nest boxes between broods. Leave them up during the winter, when the pair will probably use them for roosting.

10.2. YOUNG IN THE NEST

The average clutch size for African Greys is three eggs. These are incubated by the female for 28 days, during which time she is fed by her mate. You will know when the chicks have hatched by the tiny squeaks coming from the nest box. These will become louder as the babies grow.

Baby Greys begin life with pink skin, covered in fluffy white down. The eyes are open, and grey down replaces the white, by two weeks of age, with the pin feathers growing through at four weeks. Their eyes remain dark grey until two years of age, when the outer ring of the eye turns to yellow.

Once the chicks have hatched, both parents share the task of feeding them. It is important to keep food supplies topped up during this time, with particular emphasis on extra calcium and protein from such items as scrambled egg with a little crushed-up shell left in, sprouted seeds and pulses, nuts and sweetcorn, as well as a variety of fruit and vegetables. Keep trying new foods until you find the ones your birds prefer.

Some parent birds will pass on dry seed mix or pellets to their young chicks, with disastrous consequences. In these cases, only give the parents soft food.

Nest inspections should always be done with care, especially when the babies are newly hatched, to minimise damage from the adult birds to the unhatched eggs or newborn chicks. To avoid being bitten by the brooding hen, one method is to use a piece of card or rolled-up newspaper to gently shield the bird away from your hand while you make your inspection of the eggs or young. A good time to check progress in the nesting box is when the parents are feeding. If you need to make an inspection and the birds will not come out, proceed very gently to avoid being bitten. Keep checks brief and to a minimum or the nest may be abandoned.

Fledging takes place at about three months of age, although the youngsters will start appearing at the entrance hole a few weeks before this. Soon after leaving the nest, they will be learning to crack seed and find food for themselves.

Chicks that are injured or malnourished need to be removed from the nest without delay if they are to survive. It is then the task of the keeper to hand-feed the chicks.

10.3. HAND-REARING GREYS

Baby Greys should be left with their parents for two weeks or more, so that they have the chance to establish a healthy digestive system, before being taken for hand-rearing. It is then essential to feed the correct proportions of nutrients, calcium, and protein if the chicks are to survive and develop properly – there is a 75 per cent incidence of Rickets among apparently normal, hand-reared African Grey chicks. Rickets can result from poor diet.

Choose a species-specific (that is, for baby African Greys) formula or ask an experienced breeder for advice on making your own feed – do not guess at the ingredients or amounts. Many breeders base their own recipes on powdered human baby foods, with such additions as ground-up seed. This is then mixed to a sloppy consistency with boiling water and allowed to cool until it is warm, never hot. A more solid mixture can be given as the birds get older.

Hand-feeding is a messy business, but be patient and let your chick eat at his own pace – keep plenty of kitchen paper handy for mopping up. After he has eaten, the baby should have a very noticeable bulge on his chest, which shows he has a full crop. By weighing the chicks each day, you will be able to make sure they are putting on weight.

If you are hand-feeding from day one, you will need to be permanently on call for the first week, as the babies will need food every couple of hours. They will also need to be kept comfortably warm. The periods between feeding are gradually increased until the birds are a few weeks old and can go through the night. The temperature in the brooder can gradually decrease, until the birds are weaning on to solid foods and no longer require extra heating.

10.4. WEANING

When making the transition from the formula to solid foods, begin by offering soft, tempting foods, such as cooked peas, sweetcorn, and tiny pieces of colourful fruit. Initially, the babies will pick up the food, drop it, and walk over it, as they will not know what to do. As they get the idea you can gradually introduce more items such as small, hulled seeds and different fruits and vegetables, finely chopped. Give as much variety as possible at this stage, so that the bird will accept new foods in later life. However, do not stop giving the baby formula until he is eating well on his own. By two to three months of age, the youngsters should be eating an adult diet without problem, at which stage they are ready to go to their new home.

When you first introduce your baby Grey to a cage, remember that he has not yet learnt to perch, so place food dishes on the floor. Put in a perch at floor level, then, as the baby learns what to do, raise up both the perch and dishes in gradual stages, until he is perching and eating from the dish attached to the cage side. Special free-standing training perches are available, which can be placed on the floor of the cage.

DID YOU KNOW?
During the weaning stage, young parrots will lose weight for a while. This is normal when they come off formula and become more active.

---

11. NOTES ON OTHER AVIARY PARROTS

11.1. COCKATOOS

Lesser Sulphur-crested Cockatoos *(Cacatua sulphurea)* make delightful and affectionate pets if they have been carefully weaned and trained. However, you will need some prior experience of aviary birds before attempting to breed these parrots.

The most important starting point is to ensure you have a compatible, bonded pair. Serious aggression from the male towards his mate is always a possibility with any Cockatoo species. You will also need to ensure that the female is feeding – a bullying male may prevent her from getting to the food dish, so that she eventually starves. The threat of aggression can be reduced if the breeding pair is housed in a large aviary, with refuges installed, where one bird can get away from the other if necessary. As the male bird will sometimes corner and attack the female in the nest box, an extra escape hole in the box is also advisable.

Keep a close eye on the breeding pair until you are confident they are settled and getting on well. Be prepared to separate the birds if the female is being harassed or kept away from the food dish.

Like many species of parrots, breeding pairs of Moluccan Cockatoos *(C. moluccensis)* need a peaceful, private environment with minimum disturbance from the keeper. They will spend much of the time in the nest box while breeding. Give plenty of wood to chew, to save the nest boxes and aviary framework.

One or two eggs comprises a normal clutch, with a four-week incubation period. Sometimes, the parents will neglect one chick in favour of the second, weaker one, in which case hand-rearing becomes necessary. Raising baby Moluccans is not always straightforward, as they can be picky eaters and slow to wean.

As the babies mature, the original dark-pink baby feathers turn to the luxurious creamy salmon pink of the adult plumage.

11.2. MACAWS

Good-sized, extremely robust aviaries will be needed for these birds, with swings, ropes, and branches, for occupation and chewing. The breeding pair should be fed a varied diet, including foods with a high fat content.

Military and Green-winged Macaws will often make good parents, but you will need to be prepared to hand-rear a Green-winged chick if he is being neglected by his parents.

PARROTS AND PARAKEETS

From the cheerful little Budgerigar to the mighty Macaw, parrots and parakeets have evolved in many stunning colour combinations.

◀ Budgerigar: an ideal choice for children, the newcomer to birdkeeping, or where space is limited.

▲ Cockatiel: full of character and relatively easy to keep, Cockatiels make friendly companion birds.

◀ Goldie's Lorikeet: these colourful little birds are best kept with others of their own kind in an aviary.

PARROTS AND PARAKEETS

Buy

◄African Grey Parrot: an exceptionally talented mimic, he can be more sensitive and nervous than other pet species.

Lesser Sulphur-crested Cockatoo: ► friendly, funny and noisy. Be prepared to give your pet Cockatoo lots of time, toys to play with, and things to chew.

PARROTS AND PARAKEETS

Jardine Parrot: a friendly ▶
pet if bought as a captive-
bred, hand-reared
youngster.

▲ Greater Western Vasa Parrot:
becoming endangered in their native
Madagascar, Vasas are one of the least
colourful parrot species, although
they are full of character.

Hawk-headed Parrot: this bird is ▶
often nervous and noisy, and is not a
suitable species for the beginner.

AMAZONS

Some species of Amazons, with their laid-back nature and ability to mimic speech and tunes, can make good pets, usually bonding closely with their keepe

◀ Spectacled Amazon Parrot: This small, South American parrot makes up for his diminutive size with his loud voice and the occasional nip.

Yellow-fronted Amazon: ▶ affectionate as pets, although aggressive when breeding, Yellow-fronts have personality-plus!

LOVEBIRDS

Lovebirds have been bred in a wide variety of pretty pastel colours. Buy a hand-reared baby and handle him regularly – and you will have a friendly little pet.

Lutino Peach-faced Lovebird: one of the many colour varieties that have been developed in captivity.

Peach-faced Lovebird: the most well known and widely kept of the pet species.

Masked Lovebird: like all members of this genus, he can be aggressive when breeding.

Blue-masked Lovebird: a pretty variation of the original Black-masked Lovebird.

MACAWS

Macaws can make wonderful companions for those who can offer plenty of space, time and attention to keep these birds, which are the biggest of all parrots, happy, healthy and fully occupied.

Scarlet Macaw: the dazzling red, ▶ yellow and blue plumage has sadly led to extensive poaching of this species in the wild.

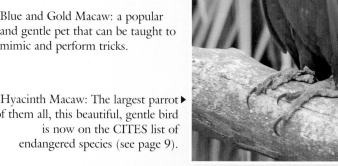

▲ Blue and Gold Macaw: a popular and gentle pet that can be taught to mimic and perform tricks.

Hyacinth Macaw: The largest parrot ▶ of them all, this beautiful, gentle bird is now on the CITES list of endangered species (see page 9).

MACAWS

◀ Illiger's Macaw: habitat destruction and capture from the wild have drastically reduced numbers in recent years.

Green-winged Macaw: ▶ a gentle giant and usually quieter than the other large Macaws, this parrot makes an affectionate and intelligent companion bird.

CAIQUES

Caiques are full of fun and energy, and make excellent pets for anyone wanting a smaller companion bird.

◀ Yellow-thighed Caique: less commonly seen in captivity than the Black-headed Caique (below), this pretty little parrot originates in South America.

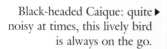

Black-headed Caique: quite ▶ noisy at times, this lively bird is always on the go.

11.3. AMAZONS

Amazons will breed from approximately three years of age onwards, and, given the right environment and diet, they make reliable parents. Plenty of fresh fruit, vegetables, bread and milk, and sprouted pulses should be given to the breeding pair, as well as extra protein – cooked chicken bones with a little meat left on will be enjoyed.

The male Amazon will be very protective of the nest, particularly when the chicks are first hatched, so take extra care when making your inspections. Baby Amazons can usually be readily hand-reared and tamed.

11.4. ALEXANDRINE PARAKEETS

A good choice for the novice, these hardy birds will start breeding and nesting in the winter months, and they are usually very good parents. Alexandrines are noisy, and they will need a good-sized flight, preferably made of metal, because these birds can be destructive to exposed woodwork.

Give a good, mixed diet with plenty of calcium before and during the breeding season, as well as lots of branches to keep those strong beaks busy. Because these birds like to scratch about on the floor of the aviary, they will need to be wormed at regular intervals.

Alexandrines will breed in a colony, although they do better kept in single pairs. They like a deep nest and will often prefer a tall, hollowed-out log to the usual nest box. Incubation takes three to four weeks. Take care around the newly fledged youngsters, which tend to be very nervous. Hand-rearing is usually straightforward.

11.5. PIONUS

Pionus will breed and rear their young successfully given a peaceful environment and plenty of variety in the diet – the emphasis being on vegetables and fruits, with the addition of sprouted seeds and pulses, rather than a fattening diet high in seeds.

Some species, such as the hawk-like Dusky Parrot *(Pionus fuscus)*, are rarely seen in captivity, due both to export restrictions from the countries of origin and also to these birds' susceptibility to fungal infections, which often prove fatal. Their natural, high-altitude climate is cool and dry, and problems arise when acclimatising to warmer, damper environments, which can harbour fungal respiratory diseases, such as aspergillosis.

In view of the clampdown on exports, the rarer species would make a worthwhile challenge for the more experienced aviculturist.

11.6. LORIES AND LORIKEETS

A good species to start with is the Green-naped Lorikeet *(Trichoglossus haematodus haematodus)*. These colourful parakeets have bright green-and-yellow feathering on the body, a blue head, and barred-red chest feathers. They are straightforward to breed, good-natured and comical. Once paired, however, they should be housed separately to avoid aggression with other pairs.

All Lories need a good-sized flight as they are active flyers. They will need a special nectar-based diet. Lories love to bathe, so a large, shallow container of fresh water should always be available in the flight.

Clutches of two eggs are laid, the incubation periods varying between 22 and 25 days. Hand-feeding and weaning of the chicks is usually straightforward, the babies becoming tame very quickly.

CHAPTER 10

PSITTACINE ANATOMY AND PHYSIOLOGY

1. Musculoskeletal system
2. Skin and feathers
3. Special senses
4. Digestive system
5. Respiratory system
6. Urinary system
7. Reproductive system

1. MUSCULOSKELETAL SYSTEM

Although the skeletal anatomy of birds varies from that of mammals, there are very close similarities. The basic differences are discussed below.

1.1. SPINE

The spine comprises a variable number of small bones called vertebrae. Most psittacine birds have 12 neck vertebrae. These are highly mobile and facilitate a great range of head and neck movements, because, while mammals move their eyes to see objects in different directions, birds are unable to move the position of their eyes. Instead, they move their whole head to obtain a better view.

As well as the 12 neck vertebrae, psittacines have 8 thoracic (chest) vertebrae, 8 lumbar (back) vertebrae, and 8 tail vertebrae. Like many other bird bones – such as the ribs, humerus (upper arm), coracoid (shoulder bone), clavicle (collar bone), sternum, pelvis, and skull – the vertebrae are pneumatised (i.e. hollow and air-filled). The bones are hollow, with a thin cortex (outer wall) and a wide medulla (central cavity), to assist in flight by keeping the bones as light as possible. However, as a result, the bones are weaker and more brittle. During flight, terrific forces are placed on the spine, so, to overcome this, many of the vertebrae are fused together to assist in maintaining flight.

THE SKELETON

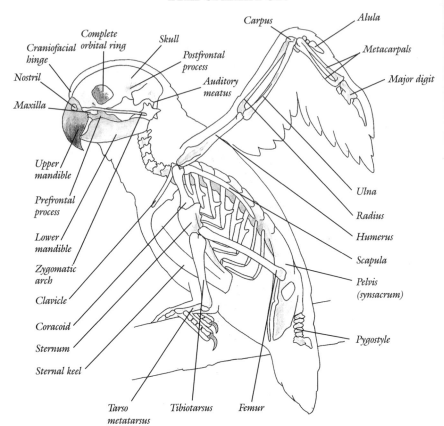

Most of the vertebrae in the thoracic region (from the shoulder to the lower back) are fused together as a single unit, termed the notarium. The last two vertebrae of the lower back, the pelvis, and first two tail vertebrae, are all joined in a unit termed the synsacrum. The last few tail vertebrae fuse to form the pygostyle. Between the notarium and the synsacrum there is one mobile vertebra, the fourth lumbar vertebra.

In view of the leverage forces acting on the spine, the mobile fourth lumbar vertebra is an inherently weak spot in the spinal column. Birds suffering minor trauma (e.g. flying into a window) can develop fractures, dislocations, or severe bruising, which can lead to abscess formation resulting in temporary or permanent paralysis of the legs. Birds suffering such an injury should always be checked over by an avian vet, even if they appear unharmed.

1.2. PELVIS
The pelvis of a bird is formed from the same bones as that of a mammal, but it is also joined to additional vertebrae in front of and behind the pelvis.

However, the floor of the pelvis is open (unlike a mammal, which has a circular ring). The open pelvic floor enables the passage of an egg, which is far larger in relation to the adult bird's size than is a foetus in a comparable adult mammal.

1.3. LIMBS

The bones of the shoulder (scapula, clavicle and coracoid), upper arm (humerus), and forearm (radius and ulna) are very similar to those of a mammal. However, an extra shoulder bone is required – the coracoid – which acts as a strut to keep the shoulders apart, counteracting the pressure of the downward beat of the wings. Unlike mammals, birds have a much simplified arrangement of bones below the wrist. Birds possess two metacarpae, on to which the primary feathers are attached.

A bird's leg starts with a hip joint, which is situated deceptively near the top side of the lower back. At the other end of the thigh (femur) bone, the knee (stifle joint) articulates the thigh with the tibiotarsus or leg bone (similar to a mammal's tibia). The tibiotarsus is connected to the tarso metatarsus by the intertarsal joint (the equivalent to our ankle, or a four-legged mammal's hock). When a bird stands, it does so on its metatarsal phalangeal joint (the equivalent to the ball of the human foot).

The toes of a parrot have what is termed a 'zygodactyl' arrangement; they have two toes pointing forwards and two toes pointing back. This is different to most species of bird, which have three toes forward and only one toe pointing backwards. This arrangement allows parrots to be far more dextrous; they can pick up objects and manipulate them with their feet, as well as being able to climb well.

The tendons in a bird's leg run down the front and back of the leg, the front tendon balancing the rear tendon, and vice versa. When a bird falls asleep, his own weight pressing downwards causes the tendons to tighten against each other. This causes the toes to clench, and so the bird can sleep standing up gripping his perch.

1.4. HOLLOW BONES

Birds need to reduce their body weight as much as possible to assist in getting airborne. The inside of mammalian bones (the marrow) is composed mainly of fatty tissue. In some major bones, birds have replaced the marrow with pockets of air sacs, which extend in many birds as far as the elbow, the knee, and even into the spine. To make up for the loss of this bone marrow, a bird's remaining bone marrow is more efficient at blood cell production.

1.5. MUSCLES

The chest area has specific adaptation for flight. The pectoral muscles, which provide the power for the downstroke of the wing, are attached to a bony plate (the sternum) – similar to a Roman gladiator's armoured breastplate. The sternum has a bony ridge (ventral spine), termed the 'keel' or carina, and it is to this ridge that the pectoral muscles attach.

A bird's general condition can be assessed by feeling the prominence of his keel, i.e. by feeling how much muscle is, or is not, covering it. In an underweight bird the keel is very prominent, while in an obese bird it is difficult to feel. It is useful to locate your own bird's keel and note the degree of prominence, checking it once a week for any changes. If the keel becomes more or less prominent (i.e. changes), it may indicate a medical problem, and the bird should be taken to your avian vet. Although condition can be assessed well using this method, it is also good practice to weigh your bird weekly. Birds should be weighed at the same time of day and a record maintained.

The power of flight requires vast energy expenditure in order to lift the bird into the air in the first place, but, once aloft, flight is a much more efficient mode of transport than walking or running. This is why birds can cover distances of hundreds of miles a day. The energy used in flight per minute is estimated at between 2 and 25 times the amount of energy used in walking. However, flight is so efficient that a bird flying a distance of one mile uses approximately one per cent of the energy used by a similar-sized mammal walking the same distance.

2. SKIN AND FEATHERS

2.1. SKIN
Bird skin has a number of key differences from mammals. It is considerably thinner and more delicate, and, for this reason, if a bird suffers a cat bite, a fractured bone, or any other traumatic injury, the skin may tear, allowing the underlying vital structures to dry out. Any bird that has suffered a traumatic injury should be examined carefully by an experienced avian vet.

Bird skin has no sweat glands, and little in the way of other glands. However, it does contain a preen (uropygial) gland, and the wax-producing glands of the ear canal. The preen gland is tulip-shaped and located on the dorsal aspect of the insertion point of the central tail flight feathers (rectrices). The gland varies in size between species, being absent in some (e.g. Hyacinth Macaws and most Amazons). The gland releases an oil, which is spread through the plumage when the bird is preening. The oil provides additional waterproofing, and additional durability of the feathers. The oil is also considered to have some anti-microbial function, and it contains vitamin D3, which plays a vital role in calcium absorption and metabolism.

The ear canal is situated behind and below the hind corner of the eye, and it secretes a waxy material comprising predominantly dead cells.

The skin becomes thicker on the bird's legs and feet, forming scales that protect the feet from rough perches. The scaly feet also help the bird to clean food and dirt from his feathers. It is important to check the base of your parrot's feet on a regular basis. If the normal, rough corrugated appearance has been replaced with smooth, shiny, pink or red skin, this is indicative that the perch surface is inappropriate and should be changed before serious foot infection occurs.

EXTERNAL FEATURES

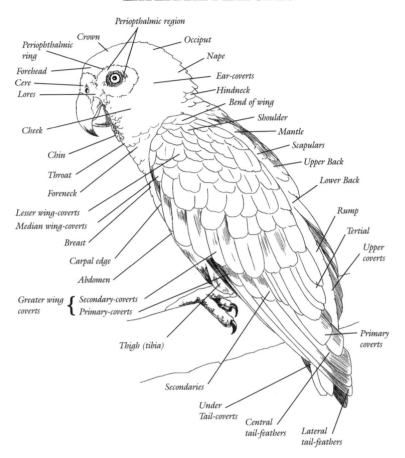

Periopthalmic region
Crown
Periophthalmic ring
Forehead
Cere
Lores
Cheek
Chin
Throat
Foreneck
Lesser wing-coverts
Median wing-coverts
Breast
Carpal edge
Abdomen
Greater wing coverts { Secondary-coverts / Primary-coverts
Thigh (tibia)
Secondaries
Under Tail-coverts
Central tail-feathers
Lateral tail-feathers
Occiput
Nape
Ear-coverts
Hindneck
Bend of wing
Shoulder
Mantle
Scapulars
Upper Back
Lower Back
Rump
Tertial
Upper coverts
Primary coverts

Birds have an area of featherless skin around their face, the amount varying according to species. Some parrots have no more than a small rim of skin around the beak, nostrils and eyes, while others, such as Macaws, have large facial areas of featherless skin. Some birds have a large fleshy mound surrounding the nostrils, which is called the cere. In Budgerigars, this area of skin is sensitive to reproductive hormones, and it may change colour, depending on the sex of the bird and the stage of the reproductive cycle.

The females of many species have a specialised area of skin (the brood patch) below their sternum. At the start of the breeding season, feathers are lost from this area as the blood supply increases, in order to maintain that section of skin at a higher temperature. The brood patch is used in the incubation of eggs.

135

2.2. FEATHERS

Feathers are unique to birds. Feathers do not cover the entire surface of a bird's skin, although the featherless proportion varies according to species. For example, some birds have large featherless areas, such as turkeys and vultures, while other species are almost entirely covered by feathers, such as kiwis, emus, rheas, and ostriches. Overall, feathers make up between 5 and 10 per cent of the body weight of parrots.

Feathers are arranged in tracts, with featherless areas (apteria) lying between the tracts, and there are different types of feathers for different purposes.

2.2.1. FEATHER COMPOSITION

Each feather has a central shaft or a stalk (the quill), which consists of:

- **The calamus**: The tubular, non-pigmented end of a mature feather, which lies below skin level.
- **The rachis**: The part of the shaft above the skin level.
- **Barbs and barbules**: The rachis has two series of filaments (barbs) running at approximately 45 degrees to the rachis. Each barb has two series of even finer filaments (barbules) that are also set at 45 degrees. Barbules are covered in tiny hooks. Barbules of adjacent barbs cross each other at 90 degrees and lock into each other, forming a waterproof barrier termed the vane. When a feather is knocked or damaged, the integrity of the vane is destroyed. However, in most cases, preening forces the barbule hooks to interlock once more, forming a new, apparently solid, sheet. If a bird's feathers become contaminated by any oily substance (beware application of oily creams to a bird), the vane structure will be compromised. As a result, the feathers will look tatty, and they may not be capable of water-proofing.

Structure of a Feather

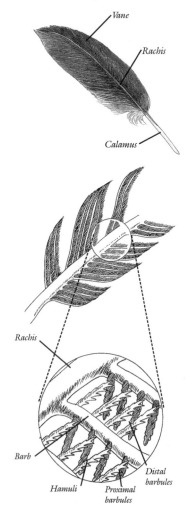

Vane

Rachis

Calamus

Rachis

Barb

Hamuli

Proximal barbules

Distal barbules

2.2.2. CONTOUR FEATHERS

These are the major feathers, giving the bird his colour and shape. Contour feathers are subdivided into flight (tail and wing) and body feathers.

- **Remiges (wing flight) feathers**: There are between 20 and 40 of these feathers on each wing. Remiges feathers are divided into primary and secondary feathers.
  - **Primary feathers** are attached to the metacarpal bones (i.e. below the wrist) on each wing. They are responsible for forward movement in flight. They are numbered 1 to 9-10 from the wrist out to the tip of the wing.
  - **Secondary feathers** are attached from the wrist inwards, towards the body, ending at the elbow. They are attached to the rear surface of the ulna (one of the lower arm bones). The secondary feathers are responsible for providing lift in flight. They are numbered 1 to 12-14 from the wrist to the elbow.
- **Retrices (tail flight) feathers**: Normally, there are 12 of these. Tail flight feathers are divided into left and right, and are numbered from the outside (1) to the centre (6).
- **Covert feathers**: These cover the bases of the remiges and retrices.

2.2.3. INSULATING FEATHERS

Generally, birds are small in size, having a large surface-area-to-volume ratio. As such, they utilise a large percentage of their metabolic energy (derived from their daily food intake), in maintaining body temperature. Interlocking feathers provide an air pocket around the bird's body, which acts as an insulating 'duvet'. When a bird is cold, a small muscle attached to each feather contracts, raising the feather. This increases the depth of the 'duvet', which helps to conserve more body heat. If a bird's feathers become oiled (from pollution or inappropriate oily medications), the barbules lose their ability to interlock. The duvet effect is lost, and, in consequence, the bird loses more body heat than normal. For the same reason, when a vet operates on a bird, he will attempt to do so with the removal of minimal amounts of feathers, to avoid increasing the rate of heat loss and the bird's energy requirements.

- **Semi-plume feathers**: These feathers have a long rachis and an entirely plumaceous vane (shaft). They are located along contour feather tracts, or in feather tracts of their own. They assist with insulation.
- **Down feathers**: These small, fluffy, plumaceous feathers, with a short or absent rachis, provide an undercoat to maintain warmth. These feathers have no barbules, they do not interlock, and they are not waterproof.
- **Powder-down feathers**: These specialised down feathers disintegrate to produce a powder that is spread throughout the plumage as a dry lubricant. The lubricant acts as an aid to preening, as well as being a waterproof agent. African Greys, Cockatoos, Cockatiels, and Macaws have more powder-down feathers than most other psittacines, which is why their beaks tend to be grey and powdery, rather than shiny. Loss or absence of powder down is an important clinical finding, which is typically indicative of Psittacine Beak and Feather Disease (PBFD) (*see page 225*).

2.2.4. FEATHER COLORATION

The colour of a bird's feathers is determined by pigments (melanins, carotenoids, and porphyrins), as well as the structure of the feather.

- **Melanins**: These are pigments produced by special cells, which are laid down early in the chick's development. Melanins colour feathers and help to make them more durable.
- **Carotenoids**: These are pigments synthesised by plants. Birds ingest them when they eat plant matter. Once ingested by the bird, carotenoids act as a colourant, maximising the intensity of the bird's plumage colour. Carotenoids produce yellows and blues, which combine to make green.

   Carotenoid uptake by individual birds is predetermined genetically, so it is dependent on species. However, many cage and aviary birds have duller plumage compared with their wild counterparts. Today, owners of captive birds can purchase food colourants to add to their pet's diet, to maximise the potential genetic intensity of coloration.
- **Porphyrins**: Red and green pigments produced by cells in the bird's body.
- **Structural colour**: The structure of each feather can affect the feather's colour because it acts as a mirror for certain wavelengths of light. Feather structure can result in iridescent sheens, or it may act as a filter, only allowing certain wavelengths to show. The most important structural effect in parrots is Tyndall Scatter – when light hits a feather, it is scattered so that only blue light is reflected. Most blue colours in birds are due to Tyndall Scatter, and many green birds are displaying a combination of the blue effect of Tyndall Scatter and the yellow effect from carotenoid pigments.

Birds perceive different colour spectrums to humans. In particular, birds discern the ultra-red spectrum very clearly. This allows them to distinguish between males and females in what, to humans, appears to be a sexually monomorphic species.

White feathers reflect and refract all wavelengths of light that reach them. They contain no pigments, and the lack of pigments also makes the feathers less durable than similar-coloured feathers.

2.2.5. MOULTING

The feathers of adult birds are replaced at regular intervals, through the process of moulting. Moulting is stimulated by changes in day length, normally occurring after the breeding season. These natural stimulations do not occur in housed pet parrots. Pet parrots tend to have an intermittent, continuous, partial moult, because they are not kept in natural, unfiltered daylight.

   When a bird moults, a new feather emerges from a small mound in the base of the feather follicle known as the dermal papilla. The feather grows downwards, pushing out the old feather. Initially, the new feather is soft, fragile, and blood-filled. It is supported on either side by a tough, mature feather – except when a bird has been badly clipped or has a chewed wing – which ensures that the new feather does not become damaged. If a new feather is plucked or removed, the dermal papillae may become damaged to such an extent that the feather never re-grows, or it grows misshapen. Once feather development has finished, the rachis becomes 'hard-penned' (clear in appearance rather than blue veined), and the blood vessels retract, leaving a mature, durable feather.

Birds hatch with a 'natal down', which they lose after their first moult. From then on, a moulting cycle is established, which lasts from when a particular feather is moulted, to the time when the same feather is moulted again. Most parrots complete a total moult once each year. Exhibition Budgerigars will usually moult, as a flock, over a few weeks in September or October. Other species may moult twice a year (often having different summer and winter plumage), while some of the larger species (e.g. Eagles) complete a moult only once every two to three years. For this reason it is important to preserve a bird's feathers, as they will not be replaced with new ones until the bird next moults.

Growing new feathers is a tremendous drain on the bird's resources – it is considered to increase the metabolic requirement by approximately 30 per cent. Therefore, additional nutrition, especially vitamins and minerals, should be provided during the moulting period. If a bird is subjected to illness, shock, or undue stress during the moult (when feathers are actively growing), fault lines (known as fret bars) may appear on the feathers. These appear at right angles to the length of the barbs. Fret bars are lines of weakness, and, until the feathers are replaced at the next moult, the weakened feathers may become damaged easily.

3. SPECIAL SENSES

3.1. HEARING
Birds do not have externally apparent ears, having, instead, an opening to the ear canal. The small holes are located on either side of the head, behind and below the level of the outer corner of the eye, and are hidden by the bird's feathers. The ear canal leads to an eardrum and middle ear, which is similar to that of mammals. A bird's sense of hearing is very acute.

3.2. SIGHT
Sight is the dominant special sense of birds, which need good eyesight in order to spot predators, food, and mates, across large areas of forest or desert.

In relation to overall body size, the eyes of a parrot are much larger than those of humans, but parrot eyes are similar in structure to human eyes. Parrots have also been shown to have good colour vision. It is believed they see far into the ultraviolet spectrum and the infrared – what looks to be a plain bird to human eyesight may appear extremely bright and colourful to another bird. This is of particular relevance when differentiating between apparently monomorphic (species in which the male and female appear visually identical) species, in which the sexes may look very different to birds.

3.3. SMELL

In parrots, as in most birds, the sense of smell is very poorly developed, and may be absent completely. While mammals have an acute sense of smell, such that a mother will reject a youngster that has been handled by humans, a female bird will be unaware of any human intervention, and should not reject a chick that has been placed, or replaced, in her nest.

3.4. TASTE

Parrots have a much lower number of taste buds than mammals. The taste buds they possess are situated on the roof of the mouth, the floor of the mouth, and in the throat, but there are few on the tongue. However, parrots can taste very well, as anyone who has tried to give medication to birds will know.

3.5. TOUCH

Despite having a solid, horny beak, parrots have a well-developed touch sensation within their mouth, which allows them to cleverly manipulate seeds into the perfect positions for cracking and de-husking.

4. DIGESTIVE SYSTEM

The digestive system consists of all the organs and structures that enable a bird to ingest food, to process and absorb nutrients from it, and to excrete the waste products of food.

4.1. BEAK

The beak and tongue are the most characteristic features of the parrot family. Birds lack teeth and use their horny beaks for prehension and the sharp edge (tomia) for incision of food. Despite a wide range of soft, hard, and even liquid foods, all parrots have a large, curved or hooked upper beak, sitting over a smaller, cup-shaped lower beak. The maintenance of this relationship between top and bottom beak is essential.

The shape and size of beak matches food type and the manner of ingestion, which varies according to species. For example, Lories possess fine, small, delicate beaks for sucking nectar, the large powerful beaks of Macaws are designed for eating large nuts, and the hook-like beak of Kheas are shaped for meat eating.

The beak is formed from a horny outgrowth of skin, originating from the germinal epithelium – similar to a human fingernail – that covers a lightweight, but strong, bony framework. Parrots have the unique feature of the upper beak. While other birds have a degree of elasticity in the upper beak, only psittacines have a fully functional, hinged joint (the 'cranio-facial hinge'), which allows for a much greater degree of movement.

The horny layer of the beak is produced by the skin around the base of the beak. The skin produces this layer continuously, to replace what is worn away during eating and chewing. New beak tissue takes approximately three months to migrate from the skin at the base of the beak to the tip of the beak where it can be worn away. Damage such as bite wounds (common in pairs of Cockatoos), chips, or shallow cracks, will gradually move to the edge of the beak and disappear.

4.1.1. DAMAGE AND DISEASE

Deep cracks may involve the bone underneath, and damage to the skin (germinal epithelium) at the base of the beak can disrupt future horn growth, so veterinary attention should be sought immediately. Modern techniques can allow impressive reconstructions, so, even if part of the beak is lost, it can often be temporarily replaced.

Permanent replacement of a severely damaged beak is very difficult, especially if the bird tries to continue to use his beak to bite hard objects. A permanent prosthesis has to be attached to the underlying bone. Typically, this involves implanting stainless-steel pins into the bone. Each time a prosthesis has to be replaced, new pins have to be inserted, which further reduce the platform to which future prostheses can be attached.

Some diseases affect the growth of the horny layer of the beak. Psittacine Beak and Feather Disease (PBFD), as well as various nutritional problems, can cause the beak to become flaky and crumbly; many overgrown beaks are often symptomatic of an undiscovered liver problem; and, occasionally, tumours of the horn-producing structure (e.g. a keratoma) can lead to rapid abnormal growth.

4.2. TONGUE

Birds' tongues are fleshy and mobile, varying in size, length, consistency, and strength, as appropriate for the lifestyle and food consumption of each species. The tongues of parrots are far more actively involved in ingestion of food than those of other groups of birds.

Ingested food is coated in saliva, which originates from salivary glands under the tongue. These glands can be affected by squamous metaplasia, leading to abscesses in the glands. The condition is caused by vitamin A deficiency, which is a common occurrence in parrots fed on a predominantly sunflower seed- or peanut-based diet.

4.3. CROP

Not all types of bird have a crop. In addition to parrots, it is present in birds such as pigeons, chickens, hawks and finches, but it is absent in owls, waterfowl, gulls and penguins.

When a parrot eats, the consumed food does not go straight to the stomach, as in mammals. Instead, it is stored for several hours within a sac-like structure in the neck area, called the crop. Birds require a constant, but slow, trickle of food to enter the stomach. The crop enables them to eat a large meal in one go, and then let it pass in small amounts down to the stomach. The only disadvantage is that the food is held at body temperature (40 degrees Celsius/104 degrees Fahrenheit) in the absence of any gastric enzymes or acid. If passage of the food into the stomach is delayed for any reason, the food can start to ferment and support abnormal bacterial or yeast cultures.

In baby parrots, the crop is seen very easily, and one of the best indicators of the health of a baby bird is the speed with which the crop empties itself.

4.4. STOMACH

Food passes to the stomach from the crop. In parrots, there are two separate parts to the stomach. The first section is a glandular stomach called the 'proventriculus'. It is a thin-walled organ that secretes the digestive juices ('enzymes') necessary for food digestion.

The second section is the 'ventriculus' or 'gizzard'. Many parrots eat hard seeds and only after these have been ground up can they be digested. The gizzard is a muscular organ with a hard, rough lining that grinds down the seed into a paste. There is considerable debate on whether or not grit is necessary for the gizzard to function properly. Wild birds certainly eat grit in small amounts. It is generally considered that birds should have grit in their ventriculus, but, once grit is present, it will stay there for many months or even years, and it will not need replacing regularly. Captive birds have been known to overeat grit, especially if they are ill, and the gizzard can become blocked ('impacted').

4.5. INTESTINES, LIVER, AND PANCREAS

Most of the remaining digestive system – the intestines, liver and pancreas – are the same in birds as in mammals. Food passes from the gizzard through to the intestines. The pancreas secretes more digestive enzymes that are added to the food as it passes through the intestine. Once fully broken down, the food is absorbed and processed by the liver. The indigestible wastes then travel to the cloaca.

4.6. CLOACA

The cloaca or vent is a complex structure that receives faeces from the intestines, liquid (watery) urine, and white urates from the kidneys. It also receives eggs or sperm from the reproductive tract (*see page 143*). It is composed of three sac-like compartments, which manage to keep all these different products separated until they are expelled from the body. Once voided, the waste products often appear as, or are considered by keepers to be, 'droppings' – owners often describe their birds as suffering from diarrhoea. If a bird's droppings appear to be very liquid, it is important to monitor whether this is due to the faecal element being runny, or if it has arisen because the water part or white urates components are excessive. Only then is it possible to determine whether the bird has an intestinal abnormality or a problem with his kidneys.

5. RESPIRATORY SYSTEM

This is the group of organs involved with breathing, smelling, and talking. The respiratory system includes all the apparatus which is used in inspiring (breathing in) air (nares), warming and humidifying it (nasal

INTERNAL STRUCTURE

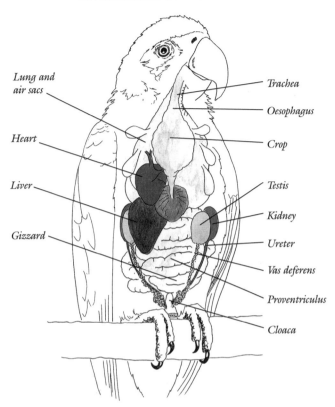

Lung and air sacs

Heart

Liver

Gizzard

Trachea

Oesophagus

Crop

Testis

Kidney

Ureter

Vas deferens

Proventriculus

Cloaca

chamber and sinuses), transferring it down the neck (choana, glottis, and trachea), through the lungs (primary and secondary bronchi) to the air sacs (neopulmonic parabronchi), the air sacs themselves, back to the lungs (paleopulmonic parabronchi), and back out via the cranial air sacs and trachea.

The respiratory system of birds differs significantly from that of humans and mammals.

5.1. SINUSES

While many of us will have suffered headaches from 'blocked sinuses' in the past, we are actually fairly lucky. Human sinuses extend only a little way up the forehead and behind the nose. The sinuses in the heads of birds extend down to the beak, up the forehead, around, behind and beneath the eye, around the ear canal, down the neck, and even down to the jawbones. Each of these diverticuli is a blind-ended passageway, with the entrance and drainage point above the level of any fluid that may be in the sinus.

Sinusitis can be a very serious disease in birds. Any fluid build-up in the sinuses is very difficult to drain out. Moreover, the nares, sinuses, and eyes are all interconnected, so a nose cold, sinusitis, and conjunctivitis will often occur simultaneously. Consequently, treatment needs to encompass all three elements.

5.2. SYRINX

Man and other mammals use their larynx (the 'Adam's apple' at the back of the throat) and their lips to make sounds. In birds, the larynx is further forward – occasionally, it can be seen at the base of the tongue – but it plays no part in vocalisation. Instead, birds use a structure called the syrinx, which lies within the chest cavity at the point where the windpipe (trachea) divides into the left and right primary bronchi. The syrinx consists of a complex combination of muscles, membranes, and folds, which alter in size, shape, and tension to produce the voice. Many birds possess a complex syrinx, allowing them to sing, whistle, and chirp – sometimes, all at the same time! However, the ability of parrots (and birds such as Mynahs and Starlings) to mimic sounds is thought to be a product of the brain function controlling the syrinx, rather than a peculiar feature of the syrinx itself.

The complexity of the syrinx, and its position at the narrowest part of the respiratory system, renders it vulnerable to diseases. In particular, the syrinx is one of the commonest sites where the *Aspergillus spp.* fungus can take a hold, and any bird that appears to suddenly 'lose or change his voice' should be examined by an avian vet as soon as possible, as any delay could be life-threatening. Parasitic infections, fungal infections (e.g. Aspergillosis), viral infections, bacterial infections, or the effects of vitamin A deficiency, can all cause abnormalities at this site.

5.3. LUNGS

When flying, a bird utilises a tremendous amount of energy. This level of energy consumption requires vast amounts of oxygen, and, if a bird had the same lung design as a human, flying would be impossible. In addition, certain species make even further demands on their respiratory system, such as the diving birds that are underwater for a considerable period of time, or birds (e.g. Bar-headed Geese) that have been recorded flying at altitudes of up to 10,000 metres, where the oxygen level is extremely thin.

The respiratory system of birds is estimated to be 10 times more efficient than that of mammals. When humans breathe in, air flows into the lungs and oxygen is absorbed. When we breathe out, however, there is no fresh air reaching the lungs, so half the cycle is wasted. The mammalian system is like driving a car down a one-way street, getting to the far end (the lung) and having to back out again, i.e. half of each cycle is wasted. Birds have developed a system to avoid this. Instead of having lungs that inflate and deflate, sucking in and blowing out air as they do so, birds have a system of 'air sacs' that act as two pairs of bellows. A valve system regulates the flow of air, so that, when a bird breathes in, the air is sucked through the lungs to the caudal (abdominal) air sacs. When the bird breathes out, air passes from the cranial air sacs. This process ensures that fresh air flows across the lungs throughout inspiration and expiration as air passes from the caudal to the cranial air sacs via the lungs. The avian system is more akin to driving around a roundabout. Air passes continuously across the absorptive surface (the paleopulmonic parabronchi), during all phases of the respiratory cycle.

One advantage of having air sacs, from a veterinary point of view, is that it becomes possible to look inside a bird using an endoscope. In a mammal, fat and intestines would obstruct the view of the internal organs, and, in human medicine, keyhole surgery relies on inflating the body cavity with sterile carbon dioxide to create an air space. In a bird, the presence of air sacs means that it is a relatively simple task to make a tiny hole, and, with the endoscope, look directly at the testes or ovary for sex determination, or at the lungs, liver, kidneys, spleen, and many other organs, to look for signs of disease.

5.3.1. LUNG DISORDERS

The way in which birds absorb oxygen renders them more vulnerable to the effects of noxious gases or other substances that may be inhaled. This is why canaries were used to detect gas in coalmines. It is also one reason why parrots are so susceptible to poisoning by fumes from Polytetrafluoroethylene (PTFE or Teflon®). When PTFE becomes hot, it releases fumes that can kill a bird within minutes. Anyone with a parrot should avoid using non-stick cookware, knock-resistant paints, and many other heat-, cold-, and stain-resistant fabrics (e.g. irons, ironing-board covers, baking, or grill sheets, waterproof or outdoor clothing, etc.), all of which may contain this substance.

6. URINARY SYSTEM

Birds excrete urinary wastes in two different forms – liquid urine (the watery part of the droppings) and solid uric acid (the white part of the droppings). The use of solid uric acid allows a bird embryo to develop within a solid eggshell without becoming poisoned by its own wastes. It also provides a means of conserving water for birds living in desert environments. This is why, although the droppings of many larger fruit-eating parrots are wet, those of Budgerigars and Cockatiels are very dry, with very little watery content.

The kidneys comprise three separate divisions on each side, each section found embedded in hollows within the bony pelvis. Several of the major nerves to the legs pass between the kidney and the bone, and sometimes through the kidney itself. Consequently, any disease affecting the kidneys (e.g. infection, inflammation, tumours) may cause paralysis in one or both legs.

7. REPRODUCTIVE SYSTEM

7.1. FEMALE

Most female animals have two ovaries, which are connected to the uterus by two tubes, although the tubes often join before reaching the main part of the uterus. In most birds, the ovary and uterus on the right-hand side are missing. When inactive, the reproductive system comprises a tiny ovary, the size of a pea, and a thin tube that can be further divided into oviduct, uterus (shell gland) and vagina. When the female becomes ready to produce eggs, all these components increase dramatically in size.

7.1.1. EGG PRODUCTION

Follicles on the ovary 'mature' into the yolk portion of the egg. This yolk is released from the ovary and falls into the open end of the tube (the 'infundibulum'). If the yolk cannot enter the tube, or if the developing egg passes backwards from the oviduct, the yolk material is released back into the body cavity. At best, this means that the egg never gets laid, which can render the hen infertile. At worst, the egg white (albumen) can cause an inflammatory reaction known as peritonitis, which can be life-threatening. If the yolk passes successfully into the infundibulum, it passes down the oviduct to the uterus, where much of the albumen is added, and finally the calcified shell. The egg then remains in the vagina until the hen is ready to lay. In larger parrots, the egg's journey from ovary to nest takes between 36 and 56 hours.

FEMALE REPRODUCTIVE ORGANS

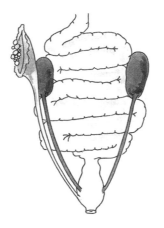

Reproductive system of a non-active female. In a breeding female, the oviduct is approximately 100 times thicker, and the follicles in the ovary have matured into the yolk portion of the egg.

7.1.2. OVERPRODUCTION

In some female birds, the urge to breed is very strong. Birds such as Lovebirds, Cockatiels, and Budgerigars commonly lay multiple clutches of eggs, which puts a tremendous drain on the body's resources and greatly increases the risks of egg peritonitis and egg binding. In other birds, the continual hormonal stimulation of the ovary leads to a weakness of the muscles of the body wall, and the bird develops a hernia. Although behavioural and dietary techniques help these birds, in many cases it is necessary to surgically remove the oviduct and uterus, so that the reproductive system shuts down.

7.2. MALE

As with the female, the male's reproductive tract varies tremendously in size depending on the breeding season and sexual activity of the bird. During the non-breeding season, the testes are a pair of tiny organs situated deep in the roof of the abdomen (i.e. internal rather than being outside the abdomen, as occurs in mammals) near the kidneys. As the breeding season approaches, the testes increase in size by several hundred times. Sperm passes from the testes via the epididymis and the ductus deferens to the cloaca.

7.3. MATING

Among birds, mating is often preceded by an extensive courtship ritual. When mating takes place, the male 'mounts' the female, usually by standing with one foot on a perch and the other over the female's back. The female raises her tail, exposing her cloaca (vent), and the male bird bends his tail

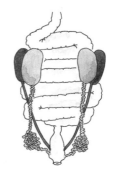

Reproductive system of a male.

around underneath so that their vents meet. In most parrots there is no 'penis' structure. Instead, the vents touch and sperm is transferred. Vasa parrots *(Coracopsis vasa* and *C. nigra)* are an exception – both the male and the female have a prominent enlargement of the cloacal region during the breeding season, which can hang several centimetres below the body of the bird, although the exact function of this structure is not known.

After mating has taken place, the sperm travels into the oviduct. Sperm may be stored for several days inside the female's body, before it passes on to fertilise the egg. There is evidence that, in some cases, a single mating supplies enough sperm to fertilise an entire clutch, which may be laid over a period of many days.

CHAPTER 11

A-Z OF PARROT HEALTH

INTRODUCTION

Parrots are generally healthy creatures, capable of existing for many years in conditions that are far from ideal. Parrots also have a naturally long lifespan, although, sadly, many pet parrots do not have the opportunity to enjoy their longevity. Many parrots are not given optimum conditions, and it is a sad trend that avian vets commonly see parrots that have fallen ill due to poor nutrition, or that have developed severe behavioural problems.

Other common problems seen by today's avian vets are concerned with breeding. Without increased knowledge and skill in the area of parrot breeding, most chicks appear to be hand-reared, given few opportunities for socialisation with their peers, and, consequently, they often develop emotional disorders in later life. Unfortunately, these birds are usually rehomed several times – further adding to the problem – before being rejected as pets completely. This adds to the burden already borne by parrot rescue centres. It is to be hoped that future parrot keepers will develop more effective, practical husbandry techniques, which will help to prevent these easily avoidable disorders.

Avian medicine has made many advances in recent years. Most parrot keepers know of an avian veterinarian, and most general veterinary surgeons are willing to consult with the parrot keeper's choice of an avian veterinarian. This trend has proved extremely useful, with more diseases being correctly diagnosed, and improved treatments occurring as a result. Some parrot diseases (e.g. *Psittacine Beak and Feather Disease*) appear to be on the increase among captive birds, and, unfortunately, there are no cures available to date. However, research is being undertaken in various centres around the world, and, with increased scientific knowledge, there is every possibility of cures or preventative vaccinations in the future.

A

ACHROMATOSIS
A condition affecting the feathers, commonly seen among Cockatiels.
Signs: The flight feathers lack pigmentation, so will appear white.
Causes: Believed to be caused by choline and riboflavin vitamin deficiencies.
Treatment: There is no treatment.

ACYCLOVIR
An antiviral drug, used particularly against *Herpes* viruses, such as *Pacheco's Disease*.

AFLATOXIN
A common fungal toxin that is present on grains and other harvests that have been stored or harvested damp (i.e. with more than 16 per cent moisture content). These toxins primarily affect the liver, causing liver failure, tumour production on occasions, immune suppression, and reduced fertility.

AIR SACCULITIS
Inflammation or infection of the air sacs.
Signs: Fluffed-up appearance, tail bobbing, and weight loss.
Causes: In most cases, the inflammation is caused by infection, the most common pathogens being *Chlamydophila psittaci* and *Aspergillus*. *Chlamydophila* causes a systemic disease (i.e. affecting the whole body), with the greatest effect being on the liver and air sacs. *Aspergillus* spores are present in the environment at all times. Healthy birds inhale spores without developing illness, but exposure and reaction to spores increases if the bird is kept in or fed mouldy food.
Treatment: Diagnosis is usually made on radiology, with the pathogen confirmed through endoscopy and swab or biopsy collection and culture. Treatment depends on the pathogen responsible, but mainly involves systemic therapy (e.g. antifungal or antibiotic treatment) and *Nebulisation*.

AIR SACS

Most species have eight air sacs, comprising three pairs (namely the anterior thoracic, the caudal thoracic, and the abdominal) and two single sacs (the clavicular, and the cervical air sacs).

Air sacs act as a storage and bellows system for the lungs, and assist in keeping the bird's body light enough for flight. Air sacs have a poor blood supply and are prone to infection from parasites (mites or worms), bacteria, and fungal infections. *Chlamydophilia* infection is a common cause of *Air Sacculitis*.

AIR SACS: INTUBATION

The placement of a tube into the caudal or abdominal thoracic air sac, to allow air or *Anaesthesia* to be channelled directly into the respiratory system, bypassing the windpipe. This is particularly useful if the windpipe is blocked by infection (e.g. *Aspergillosis*) or following trauma.

AIR SACS: RUPTURE OF CERVICAL SACS

On occasions, the wall of the cervical air sac may rupture, releasing air under the skin. This is not immediately life-threatening, but veterinary attention should be sought as soon as possible.

Signs: The parrot will develop a swelling on his shoulder or back, having the appearance of a 'hunchback'.

Causes: Trauma, concurrent respiratory infection, or constant exposure to smoke.

Treatment: Diagnosis needs to be made by an experienced avian veterinarian. Treatment is to create a fistula (opening) so that the air can escape, and to maintain this long enough for the internal rupture to heal before the fistula does.

ALBUMEN

Comprises 45 to 70 per cent of serum protein. It functions primarily as a transport protein, moving calcium and other elements about the body.

Albumen acts by osmosis to maintain the blood circulatory volume. It also provides an emergency source of protein.

ALKALINE PHOSPHOTASE

A clinical pathology parameter, which increases if there is damage or disease affecting the duodenum or the kidney, if the bird is about to lay eggs, or in the event of bone disease.

ALLANTOIS

An extension of the embryonic digestive tract.

As the embryo develops, the allantois fuses with the *Chorion*, which is a living-tissue membrane that surrounds the embryo in its shell. When the *Chorion* and the allantois fuse, they create the chorioallantoic membrane, which supports the growing embryo's breathing and helps with calcium mobilisation.

ALLOPURINOL
A drug previously recommended for the treatment of *Gout*, which has now been superseded by uricase.

ALTRICAL
A term for birds that are unable to maintain sufficient feathering by themselves, or newly hatched chicks that are unable to maintain their body temperature because they have yet to develop feathering.

AMAZON HAEMORRHAGIC SYNDROME
A condition that causes internal bleeding.
Signs: Blood in the droppings. It is important to discern whether the blood is in the faeces (i.e. of gut origin), in the water (from the kidneys), or separate (from the oviduct or vent).
Causes: Commonly caused by lead poisoning *(see Toxicity: Heavy Metals)*.
Treatment: Once the diagnosis has been confirmed, the veterinarian will administer twice daily injections of *Chelating Agents*, for at least five days.

AMAZON TRACHEITIS VIRUS
A highly infectious form of the *Herpes* virus that affects Amazons.
Signs: Acute *Tracheitis* (inflammation of the windpipe), causing breathing difficulties.
Causes: Amazon Tracheitis Virus is caused by the *Herpes* virus.
Treatment: Diagnosis is confirmed using endoscopy and cytology, while treatment is based on administering *Acyclovir.*

AMINOLEVULENIC ACID DEHYDROGENASE
A clinical pathology parameter, which gives an early indication of lead poisoning *(see Toxicity: Heavy Metals)*.

AMINO ACIDS
Amino acids are essential protein building blocks required for normal body function. Amino acids are derived from food.
   Deficiency of the amino acid choline causes *Achromatosis* in Cockatiels.

AMNION
A living tissue membrane that forms a fluid-filled sac in which the embryo develops and moves during incubation.

AMPHOTERACIN B
An antifungal therapeutic agent. It is, potentially, damaging to the kidneys, particularly if given to a dehydrated bird. It is normally administered by intravenous (i.e. directly into the vein) injection.

AMYLASE
An enzyme found in the liver, the small intestine, and the pancreas. Moderate elevations may indicate disease in the small intestine, while an increase of fourfold or greater is indicative of pancreatic disease.

AMYLOIDOSIS
Amyloid is a type of protein deposited in the liver. When amyloid is deposited in the liver and/or kidney, it typically causes death. Amyloidosis occurs due to abnormal or long-term immune stimulation, from an infectious agent or other foreign matter.

ANAEMIA
A lack of *Red Blood Cells (Erythrocytes)*.
Signs: Pale mouth and skin, general weakness, and weakness during flight.
Causes: Erythrocytes may decrease due to reduced production (e.g. from marrow damage or nutritional deficiencies), or increased loss (e.g. following an injury or during surgery). Anaemia can also arise when blood cells are broken down more rapidly than usual, as a result of bacterial septicaemia, for example.
Treatment: In severe cases, iron can be administered or *Blood Transfusions* can be given. However, birds form new blood far more quickly than mammals, so, if the cause of the anaemia can be corrected, most birds regenerate their own blood very rapidly.

ANAESTHESIA
Many bird owners are concerned about their birds undergoing anaesthesia. However, in the hands of an experienced avian vet with appropriate facilities, avian anaesthesia is very safe.
It may be achieved by administering *Gaseous Anaesthetic* or by injecting anaesthetic (such as ketamine in combination with medetomidine) into the muscle or vein. It should be remembered that clinical examination is less distressing to an unwell bird if it is performed under anaesthetic.

ANAFRANIL
An antidepressant that may be used in some cases of feather plucking.

ANALGESIA
The relief of pain. Several non-steroidal (e.g. carprofen, flunixin, ketoprofen, and meloxicam) and opioid (e.g. butorphenol) drugs are safe and effective.

ANTHELMINTICS
A term for drugs that act against parasites. Different drugs are effective against different parasites, while certain drugs that are safe in some

species are dangerous in others. Expert veterinary advice should be sought prior to administering wormers.

ANTICOAGULANTS
(See Toxicity: Anticoagulant).

APTERIA
Featherless tracts of skin between swathes of plumage.

ARTHRITIS
There are several causes of arthritis: developmental abnormalities, infection, immune abnormalities, or old age (wear and tear).
Signs: One or more joints that have become swollen and appear to be causing the bird discomfort or pain. In the case of septic arthritis, there are typically a number of joints affected. Joints tend to be hot and very painful.
Causes: Developmental arthritis occurs as a result of incorrect long bone development, leading to angular deformities. As a result, abnormal strain is likely to be placed on proximal joint, leading to arthritis as the bird ages. Also, any injury leading to joint instability is likely to lead to arthritis.

Septic arthritis is caused by one of a number of bacteria (most commonly *Staphylococcus, Escherichia coli, Erysipelothrix, Pasturella*, and *Salmonella*). Infection can arise following the infection of a wound or via haematogenous (i.e. blood-borne) spread.
Treatment: Any developmental abnormality of long bones (e.g. legs or wings) should be presented to an experienced avian veterinarian as soon as possible. Diagnosis is on clinical signs, radiology, cytology, and culture. Extensive therapy may be able to control infection-caused arthritis, but there is normally considerable residual joint damage and pain. Management and surgery can minimise the severity of developmental arthritis, while anti-inflammatory medication can be given over the longer term to alleviate clinical signs.

ARTHROPODS
Mites that cause *Scaly Face* and *Scaly Leg*.

ARTICULAR GOUT
(See Gout: Articular).

ASCARIDS
(See Parasites: Ascarids).

ASCITES
A build-up of fluid in the abdomen (coeliomic cavity) of a bird, which is most commonly caused by severe liver or heart disease. The fluid should

not be drained off, except for a small volume for diagnostic purposes. Medical therapy, to clear the fluid and to stabilise the underlying disease, will be effective in a small number of birds only, and in most cases, the prognosis is grave.

ASPARTATE TRANSFERASE
A clinical pathology parameter. When a blood sample is taken from a bird, this is one parameter that may be tested. Changes related to liver cellular damage, skeletal muscle damage, and heart damage.

ASPERGILLOSIS
An infectious respiratory disease caused by a mould or fungus known as *Aspergillus fumigatus*. The fungus is ubiquitous, but it grows particularly well in damp (more than 16 per cent moisture content) vegetable matter. Aspergillosis is not particularly contagious and will tend to affect birds that are in poor condition; good husbandry will significantly decrease the chances of infection.

Signs: The clinical signs of Aspergillosis vary from acute respiratory distress to slow weight loss (and loss of appetite) without any apparent respiratory signs.

Causes: Parrots will often contract Aspergillosis when subjected to profound 'stress', e.g. on international transportation or quarantine. The disease can occur in birds that have an immune deficiency. On other occasions, infection usually arises when birds are fed on mouldy seed or are supplied with mouldy nesting material. If feeding your birds seed, each new batch should have a sample cracked open and checked for white, brown, green, or grey dust or mould. If present, the seed should be discarded.

Treatment: Diagnosis is made by blood testing, *Radiology* and *Endoscopy*. The prognosis is poor, with the majority of affected birds dying of the disease. The vet can prescribe a range of drugs that may be given in a variety of ways, including *Nebulisation*. If the parrot is very ill, he may also require tube-feeding and other supportive care.

ASTHMA
A term given to a condition that closely resembles asthma in humans. Asthma is most common among Macaws and Amazons, typically when they are housed with African Greys, Cockatoos, or Cockatiels.

Signs: Sudden-onset wheezing and/or difficulty breathing.

Causes: A variety of allergens may trigger the asthma.

Treatment: An extremely thorough diagnostic examination is required for the diagnosis of asthma to be correctly determined. The majority of cases presented to veterinarians have an underlying infection (commonly *Psittacosis*). Once a certain diagnosis has been made, symptomatic treatment may be given by *Nebulisation,* as and when the signs occur.

ATAXIA
(See Nervous Disease).

ATHEROSCLEROSIS
A hardening of the arteries, often correlating to a high blood-cholesterol level.
Signs: Clinical manifestation is usually sudden death, although weight gain and a reluctance to exercise are early warning signs.
Causes: The condition is often seen in older, female breeding birds, or birds fed an excessively fatty diet. Sunflower seeds and peanuts contain approximately 45 per cent fat – seven times more fat than a chocolate bar!
Treatment: Exercise tends to prevent or reduce incidence. Attention should also be paid to the bird's diet.

AVIAN TUBERCULOSIS
(See Tuberculosis).

AVITAMINOSIS
(See Vitamin Deficiencies and Toxicosis).

B

BASOPHILS
White blood cells, which increase in response to tissue necrosis, *Chlamydophila, Respiratory Disease, Anaemia,* or parasite infestation.

BEAK ABNORMALITIES: ABNORMAL GROWTH
When a beak does not grow at the correct rate, so that it eventually becomes malformed.
Signs: The beak will be noticeably malformed, to a greater or lesser extent depending on how early the problem is discovered.
Causes: This is most often associated with *Liver Disease*, usually caused by long-term fat build-up in the liver due to an excessively fatty diet (e.g. sunflower seeds, millet, or peanuts). It can also be caused by *Chlamydophilia* infection, or by a keratoma (a tumour of the beak growth tissue).
Treatment: The underlying cause will need to be treated, and regular beak trimming will be needed.

BEAK ABNORMALITIES: BITE WOUNDS
Just like humans, birds can become frustrated with one another's company, which can lead to physical squabbles resulting in bite wounds.
Signs: The beak will be broken or damaged.

Causes: Bite wounds on the beak are most common among neonates and breeding pairs (especially Cockatoos), which have either not been sufficiently well trained to realise that biting is unacceptable, or else are exhibiting hormone-related behaviour that causes them to become aggressive and to bite. *Treatment:* Damaged areas should be debrided. These crush injuries are typically very painful and pain relief is required in order to ensure normal food intake. The wound should be cleaned and all devitalised material replaced. Once the wound has been cleaned and is free of infection and dead tissue, an acrylic repair material may be placed on the beak to keep the wound clean and intact until regeneration has occurred.

BEAK ABNORMALITIES: INFECTION
A beak may become infected for any number of reasons.
Signs: The beak may alter in colour or texture.
Causes: The common infectious cause of poor beak health is *Psittacine Beak and Feather Disease (PBFD), Aspergillus* infection, or other fungal infections. However, infections following traumatic injuries are not uncommon. The infection may be bacterial, yeast-based or fungal.
Treatment: Samples must be cultured, and effective medication administered systemically (i.e. into the body as a whole), as well as topically (directly on to the lesion). Soft food and pain relief may be needed until full beak recovery has been achieved.

BEAK ABNORMALITIES: MANDIBULAR PROGNATHISM/MAXILLARY BRACHYGNATHISM
The top beak is shorter than the lower beak, curling inside it, rather than closing down over the top of it.
Signs: The top part of the beak will be noticeably shorter than the lower.
Causes: This abnormality is usually present from birth and the cause is unknown.
Treatment: If detected very early, digital manipulation (pulling the beak forward gently for a few minutes during each feeding session) will soon correct the abnormality. If the condition is diagnosed later (but within three months of hatching), a ramp dental acrylic extension is created on the tip of the top beak, so that when the beak closes, the extension forces the top beak forward over the end of the lower beak. Such prostheses will remain on the beak for 10 to 15 days only, but, in a young bird, this is ample time for the beak to correct itself.

BEAK ABNORMALITIES: REPAIR
The aim of beak abnormality correction is to return the beak to as normal a function as possible, for as long as possible.
This may be for a specific period of time only, to allow healing to occur, or,

where healing may be impossible, a prosthesis may be attached. Repair is achieved with one of a number of acrylic materials. Cracks, fissures and other lesions should be cleaned out, infection controlled and then covered with a suitable acrylic material. If the beak is split, wires may be required to pull the edges into adherence, prior to acrylic application over the top. Large deficits may be covered with stainless steel mesh prior to acrylic placement. If the beak is weakened, climbing should be prevented and hard foods restricted until the beak is fully healed.

BEAK ABNORMALITIES: SCISSOR BITE
When the beak does not align properly.
Signs: The top beak will align to one side of the lower beak, rather than over the top of the lower beak.
Causes: This usually develops within a few days of hatching. The causes are unknown, but may be related to feeding methods.
Treatment: Detected early, digital manipulation can be curative within a few days. The beak should be trimmed to minimise the abnormality. If digital pressure alone is insufficient, a ramp is created on the outer edge of the lower beak, so that, as the beak is closed, the top beak is forced down into a normal position. Such prostheses usually fall off within 10 to 15 days, but this is usually ample time for the beak to fully correct.

BEAK ABNORMALITIES: TRAUMA
This is the commonest cause of beak abnormalities, and includes any sort of injury, such as bite wounds, flying into stationary or solid objects, and ceiling fan injuries.

BILE ACID
A green-pigmented enzyme in the blood, which is involved in liver function. When a blood sample is taken, elevations of bile acid indicate impaired liver function.

BILE DUCT CARCINOMA
A terminal, malignant tumour of the bile duct.
Signs: The first indication may be *Choanal Papillomatosis* or *Cloacal Papillomatosis* (i.e. wart-like lesions around the vent and/or the roof of mouth).
Causes: Papilloma are thought to be caused by a virus (possibly *Herpes*), which then spreads to other areas of the body (e.g. small intestine, pancreas and bile duct), causing tumours to develop.
Treatment: Unfortunately, once the tumour has formed, there is no treatment available, although pain relief can be provided. Euthanasia should also be considered. Discuss the matter with your vet.

BIOCHEMISTRY

When blood samples are taken to test for a series of enzymes, minerals and chemicals, which help to determine which organs may be affected by any particular clinical illness. Biochemistry is also referred to as clinical pathology.

BIOPSY

A small sample of tissue, which may be collected for diagnostic testing.

BLEEDING

Blood loss in birds is potentially life-threatening.

Signs: Bleeding from anywhere on the body.

Causes: The most common cause of blood loss in a caged parrot is the rupture of or damage to a *Blood Feather* (also referred to as a pin feather), i.e. a new, soft, growing feather with an active blood supply. Blood loss is also relatively common from bleeding nails, either from accidental damage during nail clipping, or if the bird has caught its nails on something.

Treatment: In any case of significant bleeding, veterinary advice should be sought. In an emergency situation, pressure should be applied to the bleeding point. After several minutes of finger pressure, such bleeding is likely to be controlled unless there is a blood-clotting defect. The application of styptic powder, or flour, is often recommended for bleeding from nails. However, a bar of soap works very effectively as well. The bleeding nail bed should be pushed into the soft, wet surface on the underside of the soap.

BLINDNESS

Blindness occurs when either the eye fails to detect light, or when the brain fails to interpret the messages sent from the eyes.

Signs: The bird will be unable to see properly, which may cause him to walk or fly into objects and to fail to eat and drink.

Causes: The main causes of blindness are trauma (to the eyes or to the brain), heavy metal poisoning (see *Toxicity: Heavy Metals*), and *Cataracts*. One or both eyes may be affected.

Treatment: Diagnosis and treatment will very much depend on the cause of blindness, and should only be carried out by an experienced avian vet.

BLOOD-BORNE INFECTIONS

Blood parasites are normally transmitted by blood-sucking insects. Blood parasites will be seen on a blood film and may be present within the blood cells, or free-floating within the plasma. Some parasites are pathogenic (cause disease), while many others are not.

The presence of blood parasites in UK parrots normally indicates that the bird is a wild-caught parrot, possibly imported illegally.

BLOOD CELLS: RED

Technically known as *Erythrocytes,* avian red blood cells are different to those of mammals in that they each contain a nucleus.

As a consequence, avian blood cells cannot be accurately counted in automated machinery (unlike humans and mammals). However, like mammalian red blood cells, erythrocytes contain haemoglobin and are involved in the transport of oxygen from the lungs to all other areas of the body. These blood cells are made in the bone marrow and are removed by the liver at the end of their functional lives.

BLOOD CELLS: WHITE

Also known as *Leucocytes*, avian white blood cells perform a similar function to those of mammals.

There is far more variation of normal blood values within a species of birds than there is within a similar mammalian species. As such, rather than comparing a bird's blood result with a published supposed 'normal' value, it is far preferable to have a normal baseline value for that individual bird. Keepers should have their birds sampled annually to detect any subclinical (non-visible) abnormalities, but also to generate a normal value for that individual bird.

BLOOD-CLOTTING DISORDERS

Blood-clotting disorders are most commonly associated with vitamin K or calcium deficiencies *(see Vitamin Deficiencies and Toxicosis)*. Clotting problems are most common in birds fed an all-seed diet.
(See also Amazon Haemorrhagic Syndrome).

BLOOD FEATHER

A blood feather is a soft, fragile, new feather, growing to replace a moulted, lost or damaged feather. A blood feather has its own blood supply, hence the name. The shaft of a blood feather appears bluish in colour, compared with the white of a mature (hard-penned) feather.

BLOOD-SUCKING INSECTS

Mosquitoes and ticks are the most common blood-sucking insects, although various midges, blackflies, and gnats are also significant. Any blood-sucking insect can transmit infection and may cause the bird such annoyance that it runs or flies about, crashing into solid objects.
(See also Parasites: Ticks).

BLOOD TRANSFUSIONS

Blood transfusions should be given to any birds with a *Packed Cell Volume* (haematocrit) below 20 per cent.

It is preferable to seek a blood donation from the same species of bird (a homologous transfusion). If no other donor is found, a different species may be used, but the blood cells will last 2 to 3 days only, as opposed to 9 to 10 days for a homologous sample.

BLOOD VOLUME

Between 9 and 13 per cent of a bird's volume is blood. For example, a bird weighing approximately 1 kg (2 lbs) will have a blood volume of 90 to 130 ml. A healthy bird can afford to lose up to 10 per cent of its blood volume, i.e. 9 to 13 ml for a 1 kg bird.

BODY TEMPERATURE

A bird's core body temperature is greater than that of a mammal, ranging from 38 to 42.5 degrees Celsius (100 to 108 degrees Fahrenheit).

Most birds have a large surface area to body ratio. Consequently, birds use a large part of their daily energy in maintaining body temperature. When a bird is unwell, it is important to keep it in warm conditions, between 29.5 and 32.5 degrees Celsius (85 to 90 degrees Fahrenheit), so that valuable energy, needed for the recovery process, is not wasted maintaining body temperature.

BONE: CALCIUM STORAGE

Prior to breeding, female birds lay down additional stores of calcium in their bones, especially the medullary cavity of the femur (thigh). These changes are often evident during *Radiography*. Occasionally, non-breeding females or males may show similar signs, thought to be the result of ovarian activity or oestrogen-secreting tumours.

BONE: DEFORMITIES

This is usually a consequence of metabolic bone diseases due to imbalances of calcium, phosphorus, or vitamin D_3 *('Rickets')*. This may follow a fracture that has healed incorrectly, or it may occur while a bone is still growing and the growth area of the bone has been damaged so that one side grows faster than the other, leading to an apparent bending of the bone.

BONE: DISEASES AND INFECTIONS

(See Osteomyelitis, Rickets, and Valgus).

BONE: FRACTURES

Avian fractures normally occur in the wing or the leg. Some parrots, particularly the African Grey, appear to have a problem in maintaining normal serum calcium levels, which may lead to weak bones that are more susceptible to fractures. For this reason, calcium supplements containing vitamin D_3 are often advised.

There are three main types of fracture:
- **Compound fracture:** where the fracture protrudes through the skin.
- **Greenstick fracture:** where the bone is not totally broken, but bends and returns to near normal.
- **Simple fracture:** where the broken bone does not protrude through skin.

Signs indicating that a limb may be fractured include an inability to bear weight, swelling, pain, and, in the case of a wing fracture, a dropped wing. Old wing fractures, which have healed with poor alignment, may result in a permanent degree of dropped wing. However, unless severe, many birds are still able to fly and do not suffer any obvious handicap (dependent on their natural lifestyle).

If you suspect a fracture, take your bird to your veterinarian immediately. The sooner the damage is stabilised, the less likelihood there is of damage to the surrounding tissue (e.g. nerves, and blood vessels). Wrap the bird in a towel, as this prevents it from making excessive movements, which may further complicate the injury.

Thanks to advanced techniques, experienced surgeons can repair most fractures. Fractures that have been realigned correctly will be largely healed within two to three weeks, and often complete by four (i.e. faster compared with mammals). However, fractures need to be stabilised without hindering the normal function of adjacent joints. If a limb is bandaged for more than 48 hours, there are likely to be long-term effects on joint function. Fractures close to joints, or where the skin is broken, have a less favourable prognosis.

BONE: MALALIGNMENT
When a bone heals out of its natural alignment, following a fracture.

BONE: MARROW
This is present in the centre of all bones that are not filled with air (pneumatic). It is where new blood cells are manufactured.

BROOD PATCH
When female and/or male birds prepare to incubate their eggs, they develop a 'brood patch' (i.e. they lose their feathers over a patch of skin). This happens because the birds are developing an increased blood supply in order to help maintain the temperature of their eggs.

BUDGERIGAR FLEDGLING DISEASE
A widespread disease of Budgerigars that also affects other psittacines (with slightly different clinical signs).
Signs: In young birds, the disease may cause abdominal distension, bleeding under the skin, and a lack of co-ordination. Commonly, young birds die very

suddenly, within the first few weeks of life. In other cases, the virus may follow a more long-term pattern, where the bird survives, but with abnormalities of the wing and tail flight feathers. This non-fatal form of the disease closely resembles *Psittacine Beak and Feather Disease (PBFD)*.

Causes: The disease is caused by a virus called *Polyomavirus*.

Treatment: Unfortunately, there is no treatment available. Birds suffering from this disease should be culled.

BUMBLEFOOT
(See Pododermatitis).

BURNS: CROP

Crop burns are not uncommon in baby birds, but they can easily be avoided by taking appropriate measures.

Signs: Redness or swelling over the area of the crop. As the redness fades, the tissue may become necrotic, which may lead to a hole forming between the inside of the crop and the skin, through which food may leak out.

Causes: Overheating hand-feeding formula, particularly if the formula has been microwaved so that it contains 'hot spots' within it, and has not been mixed adequately prior to feeding.

Treatment: When the redness or swelling first appears, it is difficult to determine which areas of the crop lining and skin are damaged beyond repair, and which areas are healthy, as some apparently healthy tissue may die off over the next few days. After a further four to five days, when all the damaged tissue has died, surgery must be performed, to remove all the devitalised (burned) tissue and to repair the crop wall. Hand-feeding formula should always be tested on the back of the wrist before being given to baby chicks.

BURNS: MISCELLANEOUS

Serious burns may occur if birds are allowed to fly free without sufficient care being taken for their safety. Fires and saucepans of boiling water are among the most common causes of burns among free-flying birds. Treatment involves *Fluid Therapy*, antibiosis, and pain relief, but, if burns are extensive, the bird often dies. All birds suffering from burns should be taken to your veterinarian as soon as possible.

C

CALCIUM BLOOD LEVEL
Calcium is vital for normal muscle and nerve function.

CANCER
(See Neoplasia).

CANDIDIASIS
An infection caused by an overgrowth of yeast, which commonly affects the gastrointestinal tract.
Signs: Delayed gut emptying, reduced appetite, weight loss, and regurgitation.
Causes: Candidiasis infections occur most commonly in newly hatched birds or at weaning. This is because the healthy bacteria in the gut can be affected by giving food at the wrong temperature or consistency. Candida infection may also occur following the use of antibiotics, especially those that are given orally.
Treatment: Diagnosis is achieved by microscopic examination of stained crop or faecal smears. *Nystatin*, given orally for 10 days, is the usual treatment.

CANDLING
A traditional technique used to detect whether eggs are fertile.
Shining a light from a 'candler' (a torch-like instrument) against an eggshell during incubation allows the breeder to see inside an egg, to see if it contains a foetus or if it is empty, and, therefore, infertile. Infertile eggs are likely to 'go off', which may result in bacteria contaminating the remaining fertile eggs. Therefore, if eggs are being artificially incubated, it is important to detect infertile eggs as soon as possible and remove them from the incubator. Candling also allows the breeder to check the health, vitality, development, and position of the embryo.

CARBON MONOXIDE POISONING
(See Toxicity: Carbon monoxide).

CARCINOMA
(See Neoplasia: Carcinoma).

CARDIAC FAILURE
Heart failure is an under-diagnosed avian disease, although more cases are now being recognised and treated.
Signs: Lethargy, weakness, rapid or difficult breathing, depression, and inactivity.
Causes: Heart failure commonly follows a chronic, debilitating disease.
Treatment: Diagnosis may follow a physical examination by a veterinarian. *Radiology*, *Electrocardiogram,* or *Ultrasound* scans may also be used, to confirm the diagnosis. There are a number of medical therapies available, although these have yet to be validated. The chosen treatment may depend on the cause of cardiac failure.

CARDIOMYOPATHY
A serious, life-threatening disease caused by a defect in the heart muscle.
(See also Heart Failure).

CAROTENOID
A pigment found in brightly coloured vegetables, including carrots, sweetcorn, and leafy green vegetables such as spinach. Carotenoids are also a source of vitamins.

When a parrot eats carotenoid-rich vegetables, the pigment and vitamins are absorbed from the food and transferred to the growing feather cells, where the pigments are used to generate feather coloration.

CATARACTS
Opacity of the lens leading to loss of sight.
Signs: The lens of the eye will develop a cloudy appearance, or a white spot or circle will be visible within the pupil.
Causes: Cataracts can develop as a result of trauma, old age, inflammation, nutritional deficiencies, and hereditary disorders. Some parrots may be born with cataracts.
Treatment: Cataracts can be surgically removed, although the bird's ability to focus at close distance will not be as good as before cataracts developed.

CERE
The fleshy area of skin above the top beak, which is dry, smooth and symmetrical in healthy individuals.

The colour of the cere may indicate the sex of a bird or its stage of sexual activity. For example, male Budgerigars have a blue cere, while females have a brown cere. The cere of a Budgerigar is more fleshy than that of other species, and it is frequently affected by *Scaly Face.*

CERVICAL LORDOSIS
A condition affecting young chicks, in which the neck forms at an inappropriate angle (usually folded back against the spine).
Signs: The newly hatched chick will appear malformed, with its head held at an unusual angle.
Causes: Cervical lordosis usually occurs when the chick has taken an abnormal position within the egg, prior to hatching.
Treatment: In some cases, the condition can be corrected by applying a foam splint or support to the chick's neck, to correct the position and orientation of the neck. If successful, the neck will return to the correct position within three to four days.
(See also Toxicity: Pesticides).

CESTODES
(See Parasites: Cestodes).

CHELATING AGENTS
Drugs that bind and enable the excretion of heavy metals from the body.
(See also Toxicity: Heavy Metals).

CHICK: HAND-FEEDING
The following shows the ideal dietary requirements for Cockatiel chicks. Although requirements vary between species, the ratios given here form a good starting point for most other species.

Hand-rearing formula should contain 18 to 22 per cent protein and 1 per cent calcium, with a 2:1 ratio of calcium to phosphorus. Unless you are very experienced at preparing your own homemade feed, it is best to use commercially prepared hand-feeding formula, as the nutritional balance is guaranteed.

The water-to-solids ratio is equally as important as the nutritional content in hand-feeding formula. On the first day of feeding, the mix should be very watery, with only five to ten per cent solids by weight. The solids should generally be increased by two to three per cent each day, until they are at 25 to 30 per cent by day seven.

It is vital that hand-feeding formula is given at the right temperature, which is between 35 and 37.8 degrees Celsius (95 to 100 degrees Fahrenheit). Microwaves should not be used to heat food, because microwaved food can contain 'hot spots' (i.e. parts of the food may be heated to a far higher temperature than the rest), which can cause burns *(see Burns: Crop)*.

CHICK: TEMPERATURE
The normal body temperature of a chick varies between species, but the following may be used as a guideline.
Recent hatchlings: 33.3 to 34.4 degrees Celsius (92 to 94 degrees Fahrenheit)
Older chicks, still without feathers: 32.2 to 33.3 degrees Celsius (90 to 92 degrees Fahrenheit)
Chicks with pin feathers: 29.4 to 33.3 degrees Celsius (85 to 90 degrees Fahrenheit)
Chicks with full feathers: 23.9 to 26.7 degrees Celsius (75 to 80 degrees Fahrenheit)
Chicks at weaning age: Room temperature, i.e. 20 degrees Celsius (68 degrees Fahrenheit).

CHLAMYDOPHILIA
(See Psittacosis).

CHLAMYDOPHILOSIS
(See Psittacosis).

CHOANA
The choana is a slit situated in the roof of the mouth, forming the end of the nasal chamber.

CHOANAL ATRESIA
A widening of the choanal slit, accompanied by the loss of papillae. This is commonly caused by vitamin A deficiency *(see Vitamin Deficiencies and Toxicosis: Vitamin A)*, a common finding among parrots fed a diet high in sunflower seeds for some years.

CHOANAL PAPILLOMATOSIS
Proliferative wart-like lesions located in the *Choana*. Macaws and Amazons are commonly affected.
(See also Papillomata).

CHOCOLATE
(See Toxicity: Chocolate).

CHOLANGIOHEPATITIS
Inflammation of the bile duct and liver.
Signs: The bird will be unwell, often with obvious weight loss and reduced appetite.
Causes: The condition is caused by a reflux of bacteria from the gut back up the bile duct. A virus-induced *Bile Duct Carcinoma* may also be responsible.
Treatment: If the inflammation has been caused by an infection, it will respond well to antibiotics and anti-inflammatories. However, if a tumour is responsible, treatment is not normally recommended.

CHOLESTEROL
A clinical pathology parameter, which can be used to determine the health of a bird's heart and arteries.

Like humans, cholesterol levels tend to be higher in birds fed on a high-fat diet, particularly if the bird takes little or no exercise. Levels are also raised in middle-aged breeding birds following egg laying. Birds with high cholesterol levels may be predisposed to *Atheroschlerosis*. However, a reduced-fat diet and plenty of exercise will reduce or correct this condition.

CHOLESTEROL CRYSTALS
(See Neoplasia: Xanthoma).

CHOLINE
(See Amino Acids).

CHORION
The membrane inside an egg that surrounds the developing embryo.
As the embryonic chick develops, the chorion fuses with the *Allantois* to form the chorioallantoic membrane, which helps with the chick's respiration and calcium metabolism.

CHRONIC ULCERATIVE DERMATITIS (CUD)
A serious skin condition, in which lesions appear on different areas of the body.
Signs: Typically, lesions appear on certain areas of the body, including the propatagial skin web (the soft flap of skin and tissue between the elbow and the leading edge of the wing web), the keel area (on the lower part of the abdomen), and the parson's nose area of the tail (the flap of skin just above the bottom). Left untreated, CUD leads to infection (i.e. septicaemia) of the blood, skin oedemas (where fluid fills the tissues surrounding the lesions), increased redness (due to increased blood supply to the area) and ulceration of the affected areas.
Causes: Skin lesions are normally associated with trauma, often due to repeated crash landings, which firstly break the feathers and then damage the underlying skin tissue. Wounds are often compromised further by infection. Occasionally, CUD may be associated with skin tumours.
Treatment: Diagnosis is made by clinical examination, following which the veterinarian will thoroughly clean the lesions to prevent further infection. Treatment also involves microbiology culture and antibiosis. To prevent further recurrences, attention must be paid to the parrot's environment and its ability to fly, to make sure that further trauma to the skin is prevented.

CIRCOVIRUS
(See Psittacine Beak and Feather Disease).

CLAVICLE
The clavicle is one of the bones that make up the shoulder girdle.
A bird has one clavicle on either side, fused together in the centre of the chest to form the 'wishbone'. The tips of each clavicle meet with the scapula (shoulder blade) on each side of the bird's body, and the coracoids, to form the point of the shoulder (termed the trioseum).

CLOACA
Another name for a bird's vent.

CLOACAL PAPILLOMATOSIS

Usually seen in Amazons and Macaws, this condition is characterised by wart-like lesions located around the cloaca. It is a serious, progressive disease.

(See also Papillomata).

CLOACAL PROLAPSE

This condition occurs most commonly in Cockatoos that demonstrate *Hypersexuality* (i.e. those that exhibit excessive sexual behaviour), although any psittacine species can be affected.

Signs: The *Cloaca* will become red and inflamed. If there is no intervention at this stage, the cloaca may become dilated, which will lead to the bird straining when it tries to excrete, and may eventually cause cloacal prolapse (where the cloaca passes out through the vent , appearing like a small cherry at the opening).

Causes: A bird that exhibits signs of hypersexuality may view its owner (or a favourite toy or mirror) as a mate, becoming frustrated when he or she does not reciprocate. When the potential 'mate' does not respond to the parrot's mating behaviour, the parrot often turns to masturbation, to such an extent that it injures its cloaca.

Treatment: Cloacal prolapses can be repaired using a range of surgical options. However, it is vitally important to treat the cause of the problem or it is bound to recur. The parrot needs to be taught that its owner is in charge. If the bird accepts the owner's dominance, it is unlikely to seek sexual favours, so the problem will be solved. As well as this behavioural modification training, it is also important to change the bird's diet, from a high-energy seed or nut mix (which can stimulate breeding behaviour) to a quality pellet-based complete mix, which will reduce the biological drive to breed.

CLOACOPEXY

A surgical procedure performed to repair a *Cloacal Prolapse*. The *Cloaca* is sewn up inside the body to prevent it from being pushed out again, usually against the eighth rib on either side of the body.

CLOACOPLASTY

A surgical procedure in which the circumference of the *Cloaca* is reduced by 20 to 30 per cent, to reduce the chances of another *Cloacal Prolapse*.

CLOMIPRAMINE

An anti-depressant medication used as a behaviour modifying agent to assist in the control of feather plucking.

Clomipramine is considered to be only marginally effective. Any benefits derived are diminished from 14 days and are negligible by 30 days. It can be useful as an aid to achieving behavioural modification, but it is not a solution in its own right.

CNEMIDOCOPTES
(See Parasites: Cnemidocoptes).

COCCIDIOSIS
(See Parasites: Coccidia Species).

COELIOTOMY
A term to describe surgical access to the coeliom (i.e. the part of the abdomen that contains the liver, intestines, gonads, kidneys and pancreas). In mammals the procedure is known as a laparotomy. If an abdominal problem exists, but the cause is unknown, the procedure may be referred to as an exploratory coeliotomy.

COLCHICINE
A drug used to treat gout, which has now been largely superseded by another drug called uricase.

COLITIS
Inflammation of the lower intestine, often accompanied by infection.
Signs: The condition is characterised by the presence of a jelly-like substance in the faeces, which may also contain blood.
Causes: Bacterial, parasitic, viral or fungal infections are common causes, although food allergies are believed to be another cause.
Treatment: Diagnosis is based on faecal *Cytology*, culture, history, and clinical impression, while treatment will depend on the cause.

COMPLETE BLOOD COUNT (CBC)
A clinical pathology term that refers to the counting and analysis of both red and white blood cells.

COMPUTED TOMOGRAPHY SCAN (CT SCAN)
Better known as a CT scan, this diagnostic aid uses a specialised type of X-ray to build up a three-dimensional image of the inside of the bird's body. It is very useful for assessing areas with great anatomical complexity. The bird is anaesthetised while the scan is carried out.

CONJUNCTIVITIS
Inflammation (usually combined with infection) of the conjunctiva (the lining of the eyelid).
Signs: One or both eyes will appear red and inflamed.

Causes: Bacteria, viruses, or a yeast infection are the main culprits.
Treatment: Your vet will normally prescribe antibiotics and topical treatments. The cause needs to be fully investigated to prevent a recurrence.

CONSTRICTED TOE SYNDROME
(See Toes: Constricted Toe Syndrome).

CORACOID FRACTURES
The coracoid is a bone in the parrot's chest that acts as a strut to keep the shoulders apart. During flight, a strong downward thrust is created every time the bird's wings take a downbeat. The coracoid counteracts this thrust, and so helps the bird to fly.
Signs: If the coracoid is fractured, the bird will be unable to move its wing higher than a 90 degree angle to its body.
Causes: Typically occurs when the bird flies into a solid object, such as a wall, window, or perch.
Treatment: Unless there is major displacement of the coracoid, surgical repair is not required. The bird should be cared for in a restricted area, so that it is unable to flap its wings. Given rest (for approximately three weeks), most birds make a full recovery and return to normal flight.

CORNEA
The superficial, clear, shiny surface of the eye, approximately 0.7mm thick.

CORNEAL LIPIDOSIS
Deposition of fat in the surface layer of the cornea.
Signs: Clinically, this presents very similarly to *Cataracts,* and owners often confuse corneal lipidosis with cataracts.
Causes: The condition is most common in older birds maintained on a high-fat (e.g. seed-based) diet.
Treatment: Your veterinarian will discuss appropriate treatments with you, but it is also important to pay careful attention to the bird's diet.

CORNEAL ULCERATION
Ulceration of the cornea is a painful condition, but one that can be treated in a variety of ways.
Signs: There may be obvious ulceration, and the bird will have inflamed eyes and appear in distress.
Causes: Corneal ulceration most often occurs following trauma, or loss of normal tear production.
Treatment: Various medications and lubricants can be used to assist with healing, which your veterinarian will determine at the time of treatment.

CORTICOSTEROID
This potent anti-inflammatory is rarely used to treat birds because of the side effects. Where the use of corticosteroids is unavoidable, they should not be used for more than a maximum 12-hour duration. Long-acting steroid preparations should never be used.

COUGH
When a bird coughs, it is rarely an indication of a respiratory disease. Typically, a bird that coughs is doing so to mimic its owner.

COXOFEMORAL LUXATION
(See Hip: Dislocation).

CREATININE
A clinical pathology parameter, which may increase in birds suffering active *Kidney Disease.* It is rarely of any diagnostic value.

CREATININE PHOSPHOKINASE
A substance present in skeletal muscle, heart muscle, brain tissue and nerve tissue. Levels become elevated in the event of muscle damage (which includes injections in the muscles) convulsions, vitamin E or selenium deficiency, *Chlamydophila* infection, and lead poisoning.
(See also Toxicity: Heavy Metals and Vitamin Deficiencies and Toxicosis).

CROP: AIR IN
A condition in which air is trapped inside the crop.
Signs: A swollen or distended crop (seen as a swelling on the front of the chest) filled with air.
Causes: Trapped air in the crop is seen most often in chicks that continually beg for food and gulp in air, or chicks fed so slowly they swallow air with food. Trapped air may occur in iodine-deficient Budgerigars.
Treatment: Diagnosis is made by palpation, or by shining a bright light from the side of the crop. Treatment is usually simple, such as extending the neck and very gently massaging the crop to encourage the chick to expel the trapped air. However, care must be taken not to cause reflux of the food back into the mouth, which could then enter the windpipe and kill the chick.

CROP: BURN
(See Burns: Crop).

CROP: DAMAGE
This refers to anything that damages the crop tissue.
Signs: Signs vary depending on the type of damage, but veterinarians most

commonly see crop damage resulting from the use of a metal feeding tube, especially in a chick that is begging and pumping for food. If a puncture occurs in the crop, crop contents tend to leak out between the crop and the overlying skin, giving rise to infection and abscess formation.

Causes: There are many, but using a metal feeding tube is a common cause.

Treatment: In cases where the crop has been punctured, surgery is required to repair the hole and to allow infection to be drained from the area. Antibiotics will be required to prevent reinfection.

CROP: FISTULA
A type of skin ulcer that develops following damage to the crop.
(See also Crop: Damage and Crop: Burn)

CROP: FOREIGN BODIES
A foreign body in the crop is any article or substance that should not be there, or that will cause problems by remaining there.
Signs: A hard swelling in the crop, and/or attempted regurgitation.

Causes: Feeding tubes may be lost inside birds of any age. However, chicks that 'pump' for food most commonly eat oversized or inappropriate items, such as peanuts or grapes. These are too large to pass through to the proventriculus and cannot be digested in the crop.

Treatment: Foreign bodies may be milked up the oesophagus, from the crop to the mouth, and then grasped with forceps, or, in difficult cases, an anaesthetic may be administered and endoscopic retrieval may be required.

CROP: STASIS
Crop stasis is when the crop fails to empty or takes too long to empty.
Signs: The crop will be visibly full and will not appear to empty.

Causes: Crop stasis commonly affects chicks, particularly those fed hand-rearing formula that has been heated to the wrong temperature or mixed to the wrong consistency. It can also occur following trauma, burns, infection, impaction, or overfeeding. Alternatively, crop stasis may arise as a result of some form of blockage further down the gastrointestinal tract.

Treatment: Mild cases can be treated by giving a small volume of warm saline. More complicated cases may require crop emptying (sucking out the contents using a syringe and tube). Your veterinarian may also take microbiology samples to determine the underlying cause, the results of which will affect the medication and treatment required.

CYATHOSTOMA SPECIES
A parasite of the trachea (windpipe) that occasionally affects the sinuses, giving rise to an infection or abscess on the face or under the eye.

CYTOLOGY
A clinical pathology term referring to the collection and microscopic analysis of diagnostic tissue samples (e.g. scrapes, aspirates and swabs). Cytology is used to help form a diagnosis.

D

DAYLIGHT
Birds require ultraviolet light to convert vitamin D_2 into activated vitamin D_3. Activated vitamin D_3 is essential for calcium metabolism.

Birds are considered to absorb sufficient UV light within 45 minutes of natural daylight, which does not seem a great deal of time. Nevertheless, unless a bird is kept out of doors, in an aviary that is well lit by natural, unfiltered sunlight (i.e. without glass), it is likely to be vitamin D_3 deficient, unless UV light is provided in some other manner. Keepers should be aware that glass or plastic filters out UV rays from sunlight.

Many parrots live in equatorial climates and have evolved to cope with conditions within these climates. For example, equatorial parrots tend to live a lifestyle of 12 hours of daylight and 12 hours of night within each 24-hour cycle. Excessive daylight can lead to chronic tiredness and fatigue, and is considered to be a trigger factor in some cases of feather plucking.

DEHYDRATION
(See Fluid Requirements).

DERMATITIS
An inflammatory condition of the skin.
Signs: Skin will appear red and sore, and may, in some cases, be broken. Severe dermatitis may lead the bird to begin self-harming, such as biting or attacking its own skin.
Causes: Dermatitis sometimes occurs as a secondary reaction to environmental irritants or allergens, such as dust, cigarette smoke, insect bites, chemical disinfectants, or a build-up of ammonia. Alternatively, it may occur following trauma or infection (whether bacterial, parasitic, viral or fungal). Occasionally, nutritional deficiency may cause a dry skin condition, which can become inflamed and develop into dermatitis.
Treatment: Diagnosis is made on the basis of clinical examination, swabs, *Cytology, Biopsy,* or as a response to exclusion or therapy. Treatment will involve the avoidance of any trigger factors, systemic or topical anti-inflammatory therapies, plus any relevant antibiotic. Skin conditions are complicated to diagnose and to treat, and require expert avian veterinary care.
(See also Skin).

DIABETES MELLITUS

A condition in which the body fails to produce adequate amounts of the hormone insulin, or fails to respond to the presence of insulin.

Signs: The most obvious clinical signs of diabetes are an increased water intake and increased water content of the droppings.

Causes: Diabetes mellitus is most common among Budgerigars and Cockatiels, although obesity is, in many cases, the primary factor among all species.

Treatment: Diagnosis cannot be made on clinical signs alone, and must be confirmed through blood tests, or, more accurately, by testing for the presence of fructosamine (an enzyme that indicates the stability of glucose metabolism within the body). Treatment depends on the underlying causes and complications of the condition. Obese birds will need to lose weight, and the fibre content of their diet should be increased. Insulin replacement therapy is not particularly successful in treating birds. This is because, while glucose metabolism is controlled entirely by insulin in mammals, in birds the greater control is achieved by *Glucagon*. This means that the supplementation of insulin does not achieve a return to normal as is seen in mammals. Insulin therapy can be attempted in birds, but in many cases no response is noted. Unless an improvement is achieved, the long-term consequences of diabetes result in *Liver Disease* or fibrosis, due to the build-up of fats.

DIARRHOEA

Clinically speaking, diarrhoea is a very serious condition that can be life-threatening. However, the term is normally used to refer to the excess production of faeces that contain too much fluid.

Signs: Bird droppings contain three different types of waste products. There is a dark, (usually green or brown) solid part, which is the *Faeces* (i.e. from the gut). There is also a white part (uric acid) and a watery part, both of which come from the kidneys. In true diarrhoea, there is too much fluid in the faecal part of the droppings, to the point where faecal matter is not excreted as a well-formed stool.

Causes: Common causes include infectious disease, an infestation of parasites, dietary changes, foods with a high water content, a foreign body in the intestines, *Liver Disease, Kidney Disease* or pancreatic disease, poisons, or heavy metal poisoning.

Treatment: Diagnosis is based on medical history, clinical signs and physical examination, *Haematology, Biochemistry, Radiography,* and faecal examination for parasites and bacteria. Treatment usually involves *Fluid Therapy* and nutritional support, as well as relevant antibiosis or other therapeutic agents.

DIET
(See Nutrition).

DIMERCAPTOSUCCININC ACID (DMSA)
A therapy used to treat heavy metal poisoning. It is used widely in the US, but it is not available in the UK at the current time.
(See also Toxicity: Heavy Metals).

DOXYCYCLINE
The drug of choice for treating *Psittacosis (Chlamydophila psittaci).*

DROPPINGS
Monitoring droppings is a great way to keep a check on your bird's health. They should be checked on a daily basis, and any changes from normality should be investigated further.
(See also Diarrhoea).

DRUG TOXICITY
(See Toxicity: Drugs).

DRY GANGRENE
(See Gangrene: Dry).

DUSTER FEATHER
A lethal genetic disorder found in Budgerigars.

Affected birds are abnormally large with long, filamentous feathers. Such birds do not live for more than a few months, normally. However, many are highly prized exhibition specimens during their short lives.

DYSPNOEA
A clinical term that means difficulty in breathing.
(See also Respiratory Disease).

DYSTOCIA
(See Egg: Binding).

E

EAR CANAL
A bird's ear canals are situated behind and below the outer corner of the eye on each side of the head. Feathers cover the opening to the ear canal. The ear canals of Old World psittacines (e.g. African Greys and Cockatoos) open at hatch, while those of New World parrots (e.g. Amazons and Macaws) open between 14 and 25 days after hatching.

EAR CANAL PROBLEMS

Although well documented, it is generally quite rare for a bird to suffer from a problem with its ear canals.

Documented cases include problems with the ear canal opening up at hatch or shortly after. Occasionally, the ear opening does not open at the expected time, a condition known as persistent ear membrane. This occurs mainly in Macaws (particularly the Military Macaw). In these cases, the ear canal will need to be surgically opened.

Another problem to affect New World psittacine species is that of infection building up in the unopened ear canal. It takes 14 to 35 days for the canal to open, which can lead to infectious bacteria travelling into the ear canal from the throat. This leads to a build-up of pus in the unopened ear canal. In these cases, the membrane needs to be opened surgically, and the infection cultured and treated.

ECG
(See Electrocardiogram).

EGG: BINDING

When a female parrot carrying eggs is unable to lay them.

Signs: Unfortunately, many parrot owners find their parrot dead before realising that she is suffering from egg binding. However, common signs are those of a distressed bird: fluffed-out feathers, panting with the beak half open, and straining. Some parrots will attempt to move when disturbed, and their legs may appear weak or even paralysed. Sometimes, there may be a visible lump in the vent area, which is the trapped egg. In some cases, the egg may protrude from the vent as the bird strains to pass it, but it will disappear when the muscle contraction relaxes.

Causes: One of the most common causes of egg binding is the wrong temperature. The ideal temperature for egg laying is 32.5 degrees Celsius (90 degrees Fahrenheit). A temporary blood calcium deficiency, or lack of a nest box, can also be a contributory factor.

Treatment: Often, elevating the temperature is enough to resolve the problem, as this helps to relax the muscles sufficiently for the egg to pass. Prior to placing the hen in such heat, oral fluid therapy (electrolytes) should be administered at a rate of 15 mls per kg of body weight (approximately 0.5 UK fluid ounces per 2 lbs). When giving electrolytes, it is sensible to add a single oral dose of a suitable calcium and vitamin D_3 supplement as well. If you are breeding African Grey parrots, a maintenance calcium supplement should be given, not only for egg laying, but also for the developing chicks. Following treatment, it is essential to give the hen peace and quiet, which will allow her to relax and get on with the business. If no egg has been produced after a few hours, the parrot will need to be seen by the veterinarian as a matter of urgency, as the parrot's life could be in danger. Indeed, unless you are an experienced breeder who is used to egg binding problems and treatment, the veterinarian should be called in all cases.

EGG: CHILLING

Eggs are very sensitive to the effects of chilling once incubation has begun, especially in the first 10 days. In the last third of incubation, it is far less critical because, by this stage, the eggs have become exothermic (i.e. they generate their own heat).

EGG: DISINFECTION

Eggs may be disinfected prior to incubation if they have been collected from a nest and are to be artificially incubated. A number of proprietary egg dips and washes are available for disinfecting eggs. Formaldehyde may also be used to disinfect both incubators and eggs.

The success rate of eggs hatching following artificial incubation is greatly improved if eggs are 'set' under the hen (i.e. spend the first 8 to 10 days of incubation under the hen). Disinfecting eggs is not as safe once incubation has commenced. In particular, if eggs are immersed in any liquid that is cooler than the egg, the egg will cool. This results in the egg contents shrinking and drawing in any surrounding liquid or air through the shell, which can lead to infection or intoxication of the embryo.

EGG: FERTILITY

In parrot keeping, the term 'fertility' refers to the measurement of how many eggs, out of all those that have been laid, are fertile. The term is not used to describe the breeding pair's fertility in general terms. A pair will be deemed fertile or not depending on whether they have the will and ability to produce fertile eggs.

EGG: INCUBATION TEMPERATURES

Small eggs should be incubated at a temperature of 37.5 degrees Celsius (99.5 degrees Fahrenheit), while large eggs should be 0.25 to 0.5 degrees lower.

EGG: INFECTION

If eggs are known to be infected during the incubation period, it may be possible to treat them with antibiotics. This is done by injecting antibiotics into the air sac inside the egg. However, this is not a commonly used technique.

Infection may enter an egg in several ways:
• Direct from the hen's ovary prior to the egg being laid.
• Once an egg has been laid, it cools, and, in so doing, it draws in air from

around it. If the surrounding environment is contaminated, the egg may become infected by bacteria within three minutes of being laid.
• During incubation in a nest (which will not be sterile) or in an incubator, contamination may pass from an infertile and/or infected egg to viable eggs.

Therefore, it is recommended that eggs be candled regularly, so infertile or dead eggs may be removed before they pose a risk to healthy, fertilised eggs.

EGG: NECROPSY
If an egg fails to hatch for any reason, it should be examined by an experienced avian veterinarian or pathologist. Detecting the cause of failure may save other eggs that year, or improve the chances with other eggs in subsequent years.

EGG: STORAGE
Eggs may, on occasion, be stored, so that a whole group of eggs can be 'set' (i.e. placed under the hen) at the same time to synchronise hatching and rearing dates. However, egg storage tends to reduce hatchability by approximately 10 to 14 per cent for every week the eggs are stored. Consequently, long-term storage is not recommended.

Stored eggs should be kept at a temperature of 13 degrees Celsius (55 degrees Fahrenheit), and with 75 to 85 per cent humidity. Once a day, the eggs should be warmed to 27 degrees Celsius (80 degrees Fahrenheit) for 5 minutes. Once the eggs have been warmed, they should also be turned.

EGG: TRAUMA
Eggs are very fragile, but no more so than during the first 10 days of *Incubation*. During this time, they are very sensitive to knocks, jarring or other trauma, which may easily lead to death of the embryo, so if eggs are incubated artificially, great care must be taken when handling them.

EGG: TURNING
It is crucial that eggs are turned regularly, especially in the first third of *Incubation*, otherwise the membranes may stick, leading to embryonic death.

EGG: WEIGHT
Eggs naturally lose weight during *Incubation*. While natural incubation will control the rate of weight loss, in an artificial incubator the rate of loss will be affected by temperature, environmental humidity, altitude, and the thickness and porosity of the shell.

If incubating eggs artificially, the eggs should be weighed at the start and regularly thereafter. Eggs should lose between 12 and 13 per cent of their fresh weight by the time of internal pip *(see Hatching)*, and between 15 and 16 per cent by hatch. Weight loss can be reduced by adding water to the incubator (to increase humidity), or increased by adding desiccating crystals if the weight loss is insufficient.

ELECTROCARDIOGRAM (ECG)
A recording of the heart's electrical impulses and changes, as well as the rate of the contraction cycle. It is used to help diagnose *Heart Disease*.

EMBRYONIC ASSISTED HATCH
When the keeper or breeder assists the chick to hatch.

Embryonic assisted hatch can be very dangerous. An assisted hatch should not be attempted until at least 48 hours after internal pip *(see Hatching)*. Chicks with a retracted yolk sac and no blood vessels in the membranes can be safely removed from the shell. Chicks that have themselves rotated at least a quarter of the shell circumference of the external pip can usually be safely removed.

EMBRYONIC DEATH
When the embryo dies inside its shell. Any fertile egg that fails to produce a live chick at the end of incubation is a case of embryonic death.
Signs: The egg will fail to hatch and the chick will be found dead.
Causes: There are numerous causes, including incorrect temperature, incorrect humidity, poor hygiene leading to infection, trauma, parental age or nutrition, parental lethal genes, toxic insult (e.g. pesticides, petroleum products, carbon monoxide, tobacco, antibiotics), and embryonic malpositions.
Treatment: There is no treatment once death has occurred, but breeders can minimise embryonic death by taking sensible precautions when breeding and incubating. All embryonic deaths should be investigated *(see Egg: Necropsy)*.

EMPHYSEMA (SUBCUTANEOUS)
(See Subcutaneous Ephysema).

ENDOSCOPY
The use of a fine-diameter telescope which may be inserted into body cavities or orifices in order to perform visual diagnostic examinations, biopsy collections, or for surgical sexing. This is an invaluable diagnostic tool. There is little risk involved in the procedure when in the hands of an experienced clinician.

ENTERITIS
An infection of the intestines.
Signs: The bird will appear depressed and unwell, and may have *Diarrhoea*.

Causes: The infection can be caused by bacteria, parasites, a virus, an overgrowth of internal fungi, or food that is too old or has been contaminated.
Treatment: Diagnosis is based on history, and an examination of faecal material. Treatment is symptomatic and would normally include nutritional support, antibiosis and possibly probiotics.

EPILEPSY
Seizures or fits that can range from mild to severe.
Signs: In mild cases, there may be no apparent signs, but, at its most extreme, the bird will appear to have severe muscle spasms and may even die. Usually, however, the clinical signs are repeated seizures that do not become more severe in nature.
Causes: There are many causes of abnormal physical behaviour that must be eliminated before a diagnosis of epilepsy can be accepted. Primary epilepsy (characterised by repeated seizures) is caused by a non-progressive, non-pathological brain disease. Primary epilepsy may also arise secondary to brain trauma (where there is residual brain damage). Heavy metal poisoning or calcium deficiency commonly cause epilepsy (e.g. fits).
Treatment: The main treatment is the use of anticonvulsant therapy, once other causes have been eliminated.

EPISTAXIS
(See Blood: Clotting).

ERGOT
A fungal toxin commonly found in stored seed, which causes dry gangrene of the extremities *(see Gangrene: Dry).*

ERYTHROCYTES
(See Blood Cells: Red).

ESCHERICHIA COLI
More commonly referred to as *E. coli*, this bacterium is a normal inhabitant of the intestines of many animals, and does not always cause disease.

There are different forms (serotypes), which have varying pathogenicity (ability to cause disease). Where the presence of *E. coli* leads to disease, it causes *Enteritis, Septicaemia,* and *Yolk Sac Infection.*

EXCESSIVE LAYING
It is not unknown for hens that have not been mated to lay eggs, sometimes repeatedly. This should be discouraged.
Signs: A hen beginning to lay eggs even though she has not been mated.

Causes: Often, the hen has overbonded with the keeper, viewing him or her as a mate, but even a toy or mirror can become the object of the bird's desire.
Treatment: Any nest should be removed, although the eggs should be left. The amount of daylight to which the bird is exposed should be reduced to 8 hours, which will fool the bird into believing that the breeding season has passed. The person, bird or toy that the bird has focused on should be prevented from having contact with the affected bird until successful behavioural modification training has taken place. *Leuprolide Acetate* (a drug which acts on the brain to stop egg laying) may be administered every fortnight on three separate occasions. The parrot's diet should be adjusted to reduce the energy content, as this is often the trigger behind egg production.

EYE DISCHARGE
Any infection of, trauma to, foreign body in, failure of tear drainage in, or inflammation around the eye will lead to an abnormal discharge. This should be urgently investigated by a specialist veterinarian.

EYE REMOVAL
Eye removal is possible, and, on occasions, necessary for birds.
During surgery, great care must be taken not to pull on and damage the optic nerve (which joins the back of the eye to the brain), as this can result in damage to the optic nerve of the other eye, which may, therefore, lead to complete blindness.

EYE SWELLING
Any swelling around the eyes should be investigated immediately.
Signs: There will be visible swelling around the eyes, which may be accompanied by inflammation and discharge.
Causes: Swelling around the eyes is typically associated with abscess formation. This is most common among birds suffering from vitamin deficiencies *(see Vitamin Deficiencies and Toxicosis)*.
Treatment: The abscess will need to be drained or removed, followed by an appropriate course of antibiosis and vitamin supplementation.

EYELIDS: MALFORMED
When the eyelids have not formed in the manner characteristic of the species generally.
Signs: Depending on the extent of the malformation, they eyelid will be visibly malformed.
Causes: Lack of eyelids, or an abnormally small eye opening between the lids (microphthalmia), is sometimes seen in Cockatiels, which suggests that it is linked to genetics.
Treatment: Most birds adapt well to seeing through a smaller eyelid opening.

F

FAECES
(See Droppings).

FEATHERS: BLEEDING
A common cause of bleeding among pet parrots.
Signs: The feather will be bleeding.
Causes: Blood (newly growing) feathers are soft, blood-filled, and prone to damage.
Treatment: The affected feather is normally removed. One disadvantage of this is that plucking can damage the dermal papillae, preventing or damaging future feather regrowth, leading to a distorted or non-existent feather.

FEATHERS: BROKEN
If a blood (newly growing) feather breaks, it will bleed copiously. If a hard-penned (mature) feather breaks, it will naturally be replaced during the next moult. If it is important that the bird is fully flighted, a secondhand feather can be glued in *(see Imping)*.

FEATHERS: CYSTS
A common finding among canaries, although very rare among psittacine species as a whole.
Signs: A cyst or cysts will be visible as a swelling where a feather should be.
Causes: It is suggested that feather cysts are virus-induced, although genetic susceptibility also plays a role. Feather cysts commonly develop subsequent to some type of infection.
Treatment: Cysts will recur unless removed totally during surgery.

FEATHERS: DISCOLORATION
When feathers lose their pigment or change colour from the colour that is normal for that bird in terms of age, sex, and species.
Signs: Affected feathers will differ in colour from what would normally be expected.
Causes: Diets deficient in *Carotenoids*, xanthophyll, copper, essential *Amino Acids* and vitamin B_2 (riboflavin) may result in birds with abnormal feather coloration. Excess beta carotene in African Greys can cause additional red feathers, while *Liver Disease* or zinc toxicity may also cause discoloration *(see Toxicity: Heavy Metals)*. *Psittacine Beak and Feather Disease* is another common cause, especially among African Greys.
Treatment: Treatment varies according to the underlying causes, but, if the cause is possible to treat, normal feather coloration may return in time.

FEATHERS: OIL CONTAMINATION

Oil contamination covers a variety of complaints with varying causes.

Signs: Depending on the cause, some birds may change colour (e.g. the Rose-breasted Cockatoo may become more pink in colour). Otherwise, the feathers may take on an oily or dirty appearance.

Causes: Oily feathers may be seen when a bird is fed a greasy diet that causes an increase in preen gland secretion (e.g. Rose-breasted Cockatoos). A greasy appearance may also occur if the bird has been handled with greasy hands, had oil-based creams or ointments applied, or if there is any malfunction with the preen gland, in particular because of vitamin A deficiency *(see Vitamin Deficiencies and Toxicosis: Vitamin A)* or general *Malnutrition.*

Treatment: A change of diet and a change of grooming products will often rectify the situation, but veterinary attention must be sought to rule out the possibility of preen gland problems and to advise on a suitable diet. Plumage may not return to normal until after the subsequent moult.

FEATHERS: PLUCKING

When a bird grooms itself to excess, resulting in bald patches or a total absence of feathers.

Signs: The bird will spend an excessive amount of time grooming, may be seen to pluck out feathers, and will develop bald patches.

Causes: Typically, there are multiple causes behind feather plucking. Although psychological problems are usually the root cause of feather plucking, most experts try to rule out husbandry and medical causes before assuming that the problem is psychological.

Husbandry causes: Poor environment (e.g. too dry, too smoky, too much direct sunlight), insufficient opportunity to bathe, inadequate *Nutrition,* as the result of poorly executed wing clipping, subsequent to trauma or any other cause of pain.

Medical causes: Allergies, parasites, metabolic or systemic disorders (e.g. thyroid deficiency, *Liver Disease, Air Sac Infection, Septicaemia),* previous trauma to feathers, lead or zinc toxicosis *(see Toxicity: Heavy Metals),* Chlamydophila infection, feather follicle infections, skin infections, *Psittacine Beak and Feather Disease (PBFD), Polyomavirus, Polyfolliculitis, Neoplasia.*

Psychological causes: Attention seeking, boredom, overcrowding, lack of environmental stimulation, *Stress,* as a development of excessive preening, as a result of nest-building behaviour, *Sexual Frustration,* lack of behavioural training, overdominance, separation anxiety, *Obsessive Compulsive Disorders.*

Treatment: Feather plucking is a serious condition, and help should be sought from an experienced avian veterinary surgeon as well as an avian behaviour specialist. If the veterinarian is able to rule out an underlying medical problem, and changes in husbandry have not produced an improvement, behavioural modification training is likely to be required.

FEATHERS: TRAUMATIC LOSS

When an entire feather is lost as a result of trauma.

Signs: The feather will be missing.

Causes: There are many reasons why a feather may be lost (e.g. if the bird flies into an object, damaging its wing).

Treatment: Most feathers will grow back, either immediately or during the next moult. However, if damage is sustained by the dermal papillae (from which the feather grows), the feather may never grow back. There is nothing that can be done to speed up or increase the chances of regrowth.

FEET CONDITIONS

(See Toes, Gout: Articular, Herpes, and Pododermatitis).

FEMUR FRACTURES

Any bird with a suspected fracture should be taken to a veterinarian immediately. The bird will be unable to stand and will be in considerable pain.

(See also Bone: Fractures).

FIBRINOGEN

A clinical pathology parameter that increases rapidly in the event of any inflammatory or infectious condition. It usually returns to normal following resolution of the problem.

FIBROSARCOMA

(See Neoplasia: Fibrosarcoma).

FIRE

Any bird involved in a fire should be presented to a veterinarian immediately.

Many birds manage amazingly well (air sacs may help in this respect). *Fluid Therapy*, non-steroidal anti-inflammatory therapy, antibiotics, and supplementary feeding (if necessary) should be provided.

FLUID REQUIREMENTS

As they originate from varying climates, different psittacines have different fluid requirements. However, as a general rule, parrots are considered to require 50 mls of fluid intake (including the fluid contained in food) per kilogram of body weight each day.

Sick birds may manage for a day or two without eating, but it is vital that they have an adequate intake of water. More birds are saved by suitable fluid and nutritional support than any other medical or surgical treatment.

FLUID THERAPY

This is essential for any traumatised or sick avian patient.

Fluids may be given orally, using a gavage tube *(see Gavage Feeding)*, or fluids can be administered intravenously (directly into the vein). Alternatively, fluids may be given intraosseously (direct into a non-pneumatised bone), or subcutaneously (under the skin), which can be made more effective by the addition of hyaluronidase.

FLUOROSCOPY

A form of 'real time' radiographic imagery that allows changes and movements within a bird's body to be recorded as they happen.

The technique has become very useful for the screening of psittacines for *Proventricular Dilation Disease,* by assessing not only proventricular size but also whether the gut motility is normal.

FOLLICULITIS

Inflammation of the feather follicles.

Signs: The feather follicle will appear sore, swollen, reddened or inflamed. The feather will become itchy, and the bird may begin feather plucking.

Causes: Folliculitis usually occurs as a result of infection.

Treatment: Swabs must be collected to test for infection and antibiotic sensitivity. Antibiotics are generally required for an extended period (e.g. three to six weeks).

FOREIGN BODIES

(See Crop: Foreign Bodies and Proventricular Dilation Disease).

FRACTURES

(See Bone: Fractures).

FRENCH MOULT

(See Polyomavirus).

FROST BITE

(See Gangrene: Dry).

FRUCTOSAMINE

A clinical pathology parameter used to measure the long-term stability of glucose metabolism. If levels are elevated, it is an accurate indication that the bird is suffering from *Diabetes Mellitus*.

G

GANGRENE: DRY

A rare condition in which the tissue, usually of the extremities (e.g. wing tip or toes), develops a dry necrosis.

Signs: The tissue will be red and sore initially, eventually becoming black and dry as the necrosis becomes more severe. Eventually (within three to four weeks), the blackened tissue drops off.

Causes: A number of conditions can cause these signs, although the necrosis is caused by restricted blood supply to the affected area. Often there is a clogging of the blood vessels in the extremity, such that tissue is starved of blood and dies completely. Fungal toxins (e.g. *Ergot* or *Aflatoxin),* immune reactions, or trauma are all thought to play a part.

Treatment: After a period of time (usually between 5 and 8 weeks), the dry, blackened areas drop off to expose healed healthy tissue. However, the lost extremity will not be replaced.

GAPEWORMS

(See Syngamus Trachea).

GASEOUS ANAESTHETIC

Gaseous anaesthetic is used when a bird needs to be rendered immobile for examination or surgery by a veterinarian. It is more widely used than a 'local' (i.e.topical) anaesthetic.

Gaseous anaesthetic consists of *Isoflorane* or *Seyoflorane*, both being significantly safer than *Halothane*.

GASTROINTESTINAL TRACT

A term used to describe the entire digestive system, from beak to *Cloaca*.

GAVAGE FEEDING

A method of supplementary feeding using a metal or plastic tube.

The bird should be held under the left elbow, with its chest facing towards the ceiling and its head towards the handler's wrist (the head should be held between the thumb and fingers of the left hand). With the bird's head and neck extended, the tube is introduced from the left side of the beak and passed gently over the tongue down the throat (oesophagus) to the crop. This is a fast, safe and effective method to maintain a bird's nutritional levels while he is too unwell to eat voluntarily.

GIARDIA

(See Parasites: Giardia Species).

GLOBULIN

Immune system proteins generated in response to infection or other antigen stimulation.

There are three types: alpha, beta and gamma fractions. Alpha fractions are generated in response to parasites, beta fractions in response to kidney or liver problems, and gamma fractions in response to immune system problems.

GLUCAGON

(See Diabetes Mellitus).

GOITRE

Enlargement of the thyroid gland, producing a large swelling on the throat.

Signs: A swelling on the throat, which may increase in size. The swollen thyroid gland presses on the trachea (windpipe) or *Syrinx,* causing a clicking noise when the bird breathes in.

Causes: Goitres are produced as a result of iodine deficiency, and are most common among Budgerigars fed a seed-based diet with no iodine supplementation.

Treatment: The bird should be given iodine supplements, usually achieved by adding *Lugol's Iodine* to the water.

GOUT: ARTICULAR

A common cause of lameness among small parakeets and psittacines.

Signs: Small, white swellings will be present around the joints, particularly the intertarsal and the metatarsophalangeal joints (i.e. around the foot and ankle).

Causes: The causes are not fully understood, but are thought to be related to excessive dietary protein levels, and the inability of the kidney to remove uric acid waste from the blood. Such kidney malfunction is usually caused by infection, immune damage, renal mineralisation due to vitamin D toxicity *(see Vitamin Deficiencies and Toxicosis: Vitamin D)*, or cancer *(see Neoplasia)*. When excessive levels of uric acid remain in the body, uric acid crystals are deposited in the joints or on the viscera, which is why the white swellings are formed.

Treatment: Diagnosis can be confirmed using *Cytology.* Certain medications can be used in an attempt to reduce blood uric acid levels, but the condition is very painful and many cases are euthanased on welfare grounds.

GOUT: VISCERAL

An extreme form of gout occurring as a result of renal failure and usually found during post mortem.

Signs: In most cases, visceral gout is discovered after a bird has presented with acute renal failure *(see Kidney Disease)*. Post mortem, a cloudiness and white grainy covering is found over the fibrous sac around the heart (pericardial sac) and the coeliomic membrane (which covers the guts), while uric acid crystals are found at large levels in the kidneys. Typically, the bird becomes sick and dies in less than 12 hours.

Causes: Kidney failure is the cause of the signs, but the cause of the kidney failure may vary. Infection, immune damage, vitamin D toxicity and cancer may be responsible, as may a diet too rich in protein.

Treatment: Unfortunately, most cases present too late for treatment.

GRAM STAIN
A diagnostic, microscopy stain used to check bacteria levels.

Bacteria are divided into two main groups depending on whether they are gram positive (stain blue with gram stain) or gram negative (stain pink with gram stain). Veterinarians commonly collect swabs from the *Choana* (slit in the roof of the mouth connecting the mouth with the nasal chambers), or the *Faeces*. The swabs are stained with gram stain to check if the range of bacteria present is normal.

GRANULOMA
Firm masses of fibrous tissue.

Signs: There will be a firm, fibrous lump present on the bird's body.

Causes: Granulomas are typically caused by infection, and the fibrous tissue is produced by the body to surround the infection. Tuberculosis is the most common cause of a granuloma, although other types of bacteria and fungi can have the same effect.

Treatment: Your veterinarian will try to treat the underlying infection, although the lesions can be difficult to control because the infectious organisms are often walled off inside the granuloma.

H

HAEMATOLOGY
The study of blood cells, in order to determine the health or disease status of a patient.

HAEMATOMA
A technical term for a large blood blister.

Signs: A large, blood-filled blister, which may slowly increase in size.

Causes: Haematomas are quite common following a traumatic injury.

Treatment: It is best if the haematoma is not punctured in any way, so that infection does not enter. In time, the haematoma will regress. However, a haematoma of any size should be examined by a veterinarian, to ensure that there is no underlying tissue damage.

HAEMATOZOA
(See Parasites: Blood).

HAEMOCHROMATOSIS
(See Iron Storage Disease).

HAEMOLYSIS
Rupture or destruction of blood cells in the blood vessels.
When red blood cells rupture, haemoglobin is released into the fluid surrounding the cells. This 'free' haemeoglobin within the circulation interferes with the normal function of blood.
Signs: The bird will appear very weak or may collapse.
Causes: Haemolysis can arise as a result of certain infections, blood parasite infestations, poisoning, or immune reactions.
Treatment: Fluid Therapy and *Blood Transfusions* are normally administered, although the underlying cause will need to be identified and treated also.

HAEMOLYSIS OF BLOOD SAMPLES
Occasionally, after a blood sample has been collected, some of the blood cells in the sample may disintegrate, leading to *Haemolysis* of the sample. This may cause false results in some of the tests carried out on the blood sample.

HAEMOPARASITES
(See Parasites: Blood).

HAEMOPROTEUS
(See Parasites: Blood).

HAEMORRHAGE
(See Bleeding).

HALOPERIDOL
A behavioural modification drug used to assist in the treatment of psychological or behavioural disorders, such as feather plucking.

HALOTHANE
A gaseous anaesthetic, generally avoided in the treatment of birds because of contraindications, such as heart dysfunction.

HATCHING
Hatching commences when the chick inserts its beak into the air cell (which should be in the large end of the egg). This stage is termed the

internal pip. Once the chick has reached this stage, it should be transferred from the incubator to the hatcher and should hatch within approximately 48 hours.

As an approximation, Budgerigar eggs hatch within 18 days, Cockatiels within 21 days, Moluccan Cockatoos within 29 days, Eclectus Parrots within 28 days, African Greys within 30 days, and Macaws within 25 to 27 days. These approximations are taken from the beginning of incubation to the point of hatching, rather than from laying to hatching.

HEART DISEASE
A condition affecting the ability of the heart to function effectively. It has been greatly underdiagnosed in the past.
Signs: Lethargy, loss of flight ability, and, on occasions, a fluid-filled, swollen abdomen *(Ascites)*.
Causes: Heart disease is caused by a variety of factors, although, like mammals, diet quality and exercise levels are thought to play a role. Birds fed a high-fat diet (e.g. too many sunflower seeds) are particularly at risk.
Treatment: Diagnosis is assisted by *Radiology, Ultrasound* and *ECG*. Some mammalian medications have been used, but efficacy is not as yet quantified.

HEART FAILURE
(See Cardiac Failure).

HEAVY METAL POISONING
(See Toxicity: Heavy Metals).

HELMINTHS
Another name for a 'worm' or gut parasite.

HEPATIC ENCEPHALOPATHY
When the liver's ability to function is so impaired that levels of metabolic waste in the blood increase and begin to affect the brain and nervous system.
Signs: Depression, behavioural disorders, loss of co-ordination, and seizures.
Causes: This occurs most commonly as a result of *Liver Disease* (particularly *Liver Cirrhosis,* fatty build-up or *Iron Storage Disease*).
Treatment: The suspected diagnosis of Hepatic Encephalopathy will be confirmed through blood tests and liver biopsy, but treatment is not straightforward. *Lactulose* can be administered by mouth, which is considered to reduce blood ammonia levels and hence reduce the burden of the liver. A low-protein, high-carbohydrate, high-quality diet, with vitamin supplementation, may also help.

HEPATIC LIPIDOSIS
(See Liver: Fatty).

HEPATITIS
Any disease causing an inflammatory reaction in the liver.
Signs: Depending on the extent of the condition, the signs are the same as those described under *Liver Disease.*
Causes: Common causes are *Chlamydophila* infection, viral infection (e.g. *Pacheco's Disease* caused by *Herpes)*, or a bacterial infection, such as *Yersinae pseudotuberculosis.* Toxic agents can also be responsible (e.g. *Aspergillus* producing an *Aflatoxin).*

HEPATOMEGALLY
A technical term for an enlarged liver.

HERBICIDES
(See Toxicity: Herbicides).

HERNIA
Avian hernias are not the same as mammalian hernias. They are a splitting of the overstretched muscle bands, which results in a muscular lesion.
Signs: They appear as a ventral swelling or distension of the abdomen. On occasions, they appear on the ventral abdomen just in front of the *Cloaca.*
Causes: Abdominal hernias are most common in overweight birds, in particular Cockatoos.
There is also an association between hernias and long-term, excessive oestrogen levels (associated with *Hypersexuality).*
Treatment: The current consensus is that overweight birds must be put on a low-fat diet to lose weight. In the past, surgery has been used to correct hernias, but it is now found that as long as the birds lose the appropriate weight, the hernia becomes unimportant. Hernias should not be operated on unless the distension becomes traumatised and infected.

HERPES
A family of highly infectious viruses. Although the viruses do not live long in the external environment, any infected individual is likely to be a life-long carrier (often while appearing in perfect health), and, therefore, poses a risk to other birds.

HETEROPHILS
This is a type of white blood cell, which increases when there is an active infection.

HIP: DISLOCATED
When the ball and socket of the hip joint are forced out of correct alignment.
Signs: The bird will be unable to bear weight on the affected leg, and the leg may hang limply underneath the bird.
Causes: The avian hip is significantly supported by ligaments, and can only dislocate if severe trauma has occurred to these ligaments. Dislocations occur most commonly when the bird traps its leg, or if the leg ring becomes caught, and the bird tries to fly away while caught.
Treatment: The joint will need to be stabilised using surgery, and repair of the joint may be necessary.

HUMAN CHORIONIC GONADOTROPIN (HCG)
A treatment commonly advocated for the treatment of *Excessive Laying* of eggs (common among Cockatiels). HCG has now been superseded by the use of *Leuprolide Acetate*.

HYPERCALCAEMIA
High calcium levels in the blood.
Signs: Analysis of the blood will reveal elevated calcium levels. No external signs will be evident.
Causes: Calcium levels become elevated during egg laying. In most cases, this is a natural side effect. However, excessive supplementation of the diet, particularly of vitamin D, can also result in excessive levels of calcium *(see Vitamin Deficiencies and Toxicosis: Vitamin D)*.
Treatment: If the calcium levels are elevated because of egg laying, they should return to normal once laying has ceased. If the excess calcium has been caused by poor diet, attention will need to be given to the diet, to make sure the event does not occur again. The veterinarian who diagnoses the problem will advise you on the appropriate therapy.

HYPEROESTROGENISM
(See Cloacal Prolapse, Hernia, and Sexual Frustration).

HYPERSEXUALITY
(See Sexual Frustration).

HYPERVITAMINOSIS A
(See Vitamin Deficiencies and Toxicosis: Vitamin A).

HYPERVITAMINOSIS D
(See Vitamin Deficiencies and Toxicosis: Vitamin D).

HYPOCALCAEMIA
Low levels of calcium in the blood.
Signs: Weakness and a lack of co-ordination. Falling from the perch is a common sign, while in severe cases, the bird may have fits.
Causes: Hypocalcaemia often occurs if the parrot is receiving inadequate levels of *Daylight* or vitamin D$_3$. It may also occur following *Excessive Laying* of eggs. *Kidney Disease*, parathyroid disease, or gut absorption deficits, can also be responsible for this condition. Hypocalcaemia can occur without any apparent reason in African Grey Parrots.
Treatment: Diagnosis is based on blood tests. Treatment involves oral and/or intravenous (i.e. directly into the vein) supplementation with calcium, but the underlying cause needs to be addressed. *Egg Binding* is a common sequel to Hypocalcaemia. Young, growing birds may develop *Rickets*.

HYPOGLYCAEMIA
Low blood glucose levels.
Signs: Depression, weakness, and possibly seizures.
Causes: Hypoglycaemia is often associated with *Anorexia, Malnutrition, Septicaemia*, or *Liver Disease*.
Treatment: Initially, an injection of dextrose will be given to return blood glucose levels to normal. However, the cause will need to be determined so that the situation does not arise again. The benefits of glucose injections are short-lived, and the bird will require *Gavage Feeding* until the underlying problem is resolved.

HYPOTHERMIA
Reduced body temperature. This is a significant risk while a bird is anaesthetised, and is a factor of which the surgeon will be aware.

HYPOTHYROIDISM
A lack of thyroid hormone within the body.
Signs: Obesity, non-itchy feather loss, feather picking, discoloured feathers, long-term, low-grade skin infections, and impaired moult.
Causes: Thyroid is the hormone responsible for setting the internal metabolic rate, and a number of factors can affect the amount of hormone produced by the thyroid gland, such as diet, management, and exercise.
Treatment: Diagnosis needs to be confirmed through laboratory testing. Thyroid hormone can be administered by mouth, but care must be taken not to overdose.

HYSTERECTOMY
(See Salpingohysterectomy).

I

IDENTICHIP
(See Microchip Transponders).

ILEUS
A loss of gut tone or muscle activity, usually giving rise to dilatation of the gut.
Signs: Weakness and loss of appetite, and reduced faecal production.
Causes: Heavy metals, *Proventricular Dilation Disease,* intestinal foreign bodies, gut parasites, tumours, *Granulomas,* and twists in the guts all play a role.
Treatment: Diagnosis is confirmed using *Radiology* and *Endoscopy,* but the initial cause will need to be determined and treatment is symptomatic.

IMPING
A traditional falconer's technique for gluing a secondhand feather on to the stump of a previously broken flight feather.

The technique involves cutting a suitable feather to length, and trimming the stump of the broken feather. A small piece of bamboo or similar is then glued into the shaft of the replacement feather. Once the bamboo has set solid, the replacement feather is glued into the open shaft projecting from the wing. Imping is useful for repairing severely clipped or damaged flight feathers.

IMPRINTING
When a bird is hand-reared, it can mature believing that it is human or that its human keeper is another parrot.

Until the bird reaches sexual maturity, imprinting does not usually create any problems. However, as the bird becomes sexually mature, it may begin to exhibit problematic behaviour, including *Hypersexuality,* and overdominance. This sexual behaviour is normally focused on the owner.

INCUBATION: ARTIFICIAL
Artificial incubation plays an important role in breeding captive-bred parrots. However, it requires great skill, as hygiene must be closely regulated, the eggs must not be jarred or knocked, and control needs to be exercised over temperature and humidity.

The recommended relative humidity is 48 per cent. There should be a 13 per cent weight loss by pip (when the chick starts to break into the internal air sac of the egg), and a 15 to 16 per cent weight loss by hatch. Turning of the eggs, especially during the first 10 days, is essential, and should normally be done at least 5 to 8 times a day.

INCUBATION: NATURAL

Natural incubation refers to the eggs being incubated by the breeding pair that produced the eggs, or, where that is not possible, by foster parents of a similar size and genus, if not species.

There are several advantages to natural incubation:

- Separate facilities are not required for natural incubation, and, should a power cut occur, the eggs will not be affected if they are being incubated naturally.
- Natural incubation may improve the parents' ability to rear their own young, and stimulate them to lay more eggs in subsequent years.

However, there can be some disadvantages to natural incubation, mainly:

- Young, inexperienced or disturbed parents may drop, break or otherwise damage their eggs.
- The risk of egg contamination from other eggs, parents, and nest material is greater than that of eggs kept in a well-managed, artificial incubation facility.
- There may be an increased risk from predators.
- The parents may abandon the nest.
- Embryo development cannot be readily monitored.
- The parents will not lay a further clutch immediately.

INFERTILITY: FEMALE

When a female is unable to produce fertile eggs, despite being mated repeatedly with a known fertile male.

Signs: Despite repeated matings with a fertile male, the female will fail to produce fertile eggs or any eggs at all.

Causes: As with male infertility, the causes are complex. However, common causes include *Peritonitis*, generalised debility or disease, *Excessive Laying*, abnormal egg quality, inflammation, infection or disease of the oviduct, sexual immaturity, and physical or psychological incompatibility with the male.

Treatment: Depending on the underlying causes, there may or may not be a cure. Your veterinarian will need to assess the bird to identify the problem and to advise on any possible treatment.

INFERTILITY: MALE

When a male is unable to fertilise a female.

Signs: Despite repeated attempts at mating, the female fails to produce fertile eggs or any eggs at all, and the female is known to be otherwise fertile.

Causes: The causes behind male infertility are complex, but are thought to include *Orchitis* (testicular inflammation), generalised disease or debility, a physical inability to mount the hen, cloacal inflammation, a low sperm count, sexual immaturity, and physical or psychological incompatibility with the female.

Treatment: Depending on the underlying causes, there may or may not be a cure. Your veterinarian will need to assess the bird to identify the problem and to advise on any possible treatment.

INFILTRATIVE SPLANCHNIC NEUROPATHY
(See Proventricular Dilation Disease).

INFRAORBITAL SINUSITIS
Inflammation or infection of the infraorbital sinus, which is situated between the nares (the opening of the nostrils) and the eyes.
Signs: A bird suffering from infraorbital sinusitis will have swelling or distension around the eyes and head.
Causes: The swellings usually develop as a result of an infection, with a build-up of fluid or pus.
Treatment: Microbiology testing is important, and will be followed by sinus flushing and drainage. Flushing normally takes place on a daily basis for 10 days or more.

INGLUVIOTOMY
A surgical procudure that opens the crop. It is frequently used to remove foreign bodies from the crop *(see Crop: Foreign Bodies).*

INHALATION TOXICITY
(See Toxicity: Polytetrafluorethylene and Fire).

INSECT BITE ALLERGIES
Some birds, particularly Amazons and Macaws, can be highly sensitive to the bites of certain insects.
Signs: The site of the bite will become reddened and swollen, typically on the face (where reduced feather density makes it easier for insects to bite).
Causes: Biting insects.
Treatment: The affected area is normally treated with a soothing topical application. Antihistamines, anti-inflammatories, and pain-relieving medication may be administered also.

INSECTICIDE
(See Toxicity: Insecticides).

INSULIN
(See Diabetes Mellitus).

INTRAMEDULLARY
A term used to describe a type of fracture repair, in which a stainless steel

pin is passed up the middle of a bone in order to achieve stabilisation.
(See also Bone: Fractures).

INTRAOCULAR DISEASE
A disease affecting the internal parts of the eye.
Signs: The bird may appear in pain and be rubbing at the eye. There may also
be abnormal swelling or discharge from the eye. However, more commonly,
there may be few or no clinical signs.
Causes: Infection, parasitic infestation, penetrating wounds, trauma to the
head, or tumour formation.
Treatment: An avian veterinarian should check the internal working parts of a
bird's eye once each year.

INTUBATION
**During an operation under anaesthetic, a plastic or rubber tube is placed
down the windpipe, through which the *Anaesthesia* is administered.**

This prevents contamination of the operating environment with anaesthetic
gases, and also helps to maintain respiration artificially should the bird stop
breathing unexpectedly. Another reason why intubation is used is that, should
a bird regurgitate food or fluid from the crop, the tube prevents the food from
entering the windpipe, from where it could travel into the lungs and cause a
potentially fatal pneumonia.

IRIS
**The coloured circle around the pupil of the eye. The colour of the iris
alters in some species in relation to age and sex. For example:**
African Grey: Juveniles have dark brown or grey eyes, while adults have
yellowish-grey or silverfish-white eyes.
Blue and Gold Macaw: Juveniles have brown-grey eyes that lighten in colour
in the first three years of life. Adult eyes become more yellow with age.
Cockatoos: Many Cockatoos have black eyes as juveniles, which change to
reddish pink in adult females, and brown in adult males. An exception is the
Moluccan Cockatoo, which has black eyes if male, or dark brown if female.
Amazons: Juveniles have brown eyes that become more red as the bird ages.

IRON STORAGE DISEASE
**A liver disease most often reported among Toucans and Mynah birds, but
occasionally seen in psittacines.**
Signs: Any bird suffering from this disease will be extremely and obviously
unwell. The liver will be significantly enlarged.
Causes: The full mechanism of the disease is complex and is not fully
understood. However, the disease results in an excessive build-up of iron in the
body's tissues (in particular the liver), which leads to illness.

Treatment: Diagnosis may be suspected on *Radiology* or *Endoscopy,* but requires a liver *Biopsy* and microscopic interpretation to be sure. Treatment involves blood-letting, with the removal of one per cent of the bird's body weight weekly for up to one year. Dietary modification is essential in order to reduce iron uptake. Iron-sparing drugs (e.g. desferoxamine) may also be useful.

ISOFLORANE
A volatile gas used for *Anaesthesia* that, used correctly, is relatively safe. It is significantly safer than *Halothane.*

ITRACONAZOLE
Normally the drug of choice used to treat *Aspergillosis.* African Greys can develop side effects to this drug, and are usually given lower doses as a consequence. An alternative therapy for African Greys is terbinafine.

IVERMECTIN
A drug used to treat parasitic infestations.

J

JERUSALEM CHERRY
(See Toxicity: Plants).

JUGULAR VEIN
The main vein found either side of the neck, which draws blood from the head back to the heart.

K

KEEL
The keel or 'carina' is the central bone running down the front of the chest. The prominence of the keel can be used to assess the overall condition of the bird.

KIDNEY DISEASE
An illness in which the kidneys fail to function normally, also referred to as renal disease. Kidney disease may develop slowly, with clinical signs apparent for a long time (i.e. chronic renal failure), or it may occur very suddenly and severely, often leading to the rapid demise of the bird (i.e. acute renal failure).

Signs: Affected birds will drink more and produce a large volume of watery droppings. In severe or chronic cases, the sciatic nerve may be affected, which will lead to leg weakness or paralysis.

Causes: The underlying causes include infection, parasitic infestation, tumour formation, *Diabetes Mellitus,* and vitamin D toxicity *(see Vitamin Deficiencies and Toxicosis: Vitamin D)* leading to mineralisation of the kidneys.

Treatment: The veterinarian will need to determine the underlying cause of the disease. Blood tests, *Radiography,* and, if necessary, a *Biopsy,* may be used to discover the cause. Treatment normally concentrates on alleviating the signs, and preventing further deteriation.

KIDNEY NEOPLASIA

A tumour or tumours present in the kidney.

Signs: The condition is fairly common, especially among Budgerigars. As the sciatic nerve becomes affected by the size of the tumour, the legs may become weak or even paralysed.

Causes: The causes of tumours are not fully understood, but, in birds, many are caused by viral infection.

Treatment: Some tumours can be treated medically or surgically, if a diagnosis is made early enough. However, this is rarely the case with internal tumours.

KIDNEY NEPHRITIS

Inflammation or infection of the kidneys.

Signs: Signs may not be obvious, but increased water consumption and the production of watery droppings may occur. In extreme cases, the bird may become very lethargic, lose weight, and die very suddenly.

Causes: Bacterial infection is the most common cause.

Treatment: The cause of the inflammation will need to be determined, which is usually done using *Radiography.* Blood testing reveals results only once the condition has caused extensive damage. A more accurate diagnosis can be made using *Endoscopy* with *Biopsy* collection and microscopic examination of samples. Treatment involves aggressive *Fluid Therapy,* antibiotics, and anti-inflammatory medication.

KYPHOSIS

A malformed, arched back.

Signs: The back will be abnormally arched, to a greater or lesser extent, depending on the severity of the condition. The condition normally arises in neonatal life, although it may not become noticeable until later in life, if ever.

Causes: Kyphosis can be caused by genetic susceptibility, incubation problems, or calcium deficiency.

Treatment: No treatment is likely to be effective.

L

LACTATE DEHYDROGENASE
A clinical pathology parameter, elevated in the event of disease affecting the skeletal muscle, heart muscle, liver or kidney tissue.

LACTULOSE
A polysaccharide (sugar) solution given by mouth, especially for liver cases. It helps to balance the gut bacterial colonies and reduces the workload placed on the liver.

LAMENESS
Lameness may arise following trauma or as the result of an underlying medical problem. Any noticeably lame bird should be presented to a veterinarian.

LAPAROTOMY
(See Coeliotomy).

LEAD POISONING
(See Toxicity: Heavy Metals).

LEG SPLAY
A condition affecting chicks, also known as 'spraddle leg'.
Signs: A young chick will have a noticeable deviation of the leg from the stifle or hip joint.
Causes: The condition is normally seen in chicks that have been reared on a smooth surface.
Treatment: The chick's legs must be forced under its body and maintained in that position. This may be achieved by placing the chick in a round-bottomed bowl or by applying paper or tape hobbles between the legs. An alternative method is to cut two holes in a piece of foam and place the legs in the holes. As long as the chick is still growing, the condition should rectify itself as the chick grows.

LEGUMES
Legumes are vegetables that grow in a pod.
There are two types of legumes. Some have a high fat content (e.g. soya beans and peanuts), and should be fed in limited amounts only. The other type is very nutritious, and includes peas and beans.

LENS
Birds use the lens of their eyes to a greater extent than mammals. As a result, birds have greater visual acuity (an ability to focus better at different distances and to achieve greater detail in vision). A bird's lenses are 'soft', which means they can change shape in order to focus on an object.

LENS LUXATION
When the lens dislocates from its normal position, either forwards (anterior lens luxation) or backwards (posterior lens luxation).
Signs: The eye will be inflamed, and may have some discharge. Typically, the bird will be in obvious pain and may show signs of *Blindness*.
Causes: Trauma, tumour formation, or hereditary susceptibility.
Treatment: In cases discovered early enough, the lens may be surgically moved. However, if more than 24 hours have passed since the luxation, sight in the affected eye is likely to be lost, in which case it is preferable to remove the eye.

LEUCOCYTES
(See Blood Cells: White).

LEUCOCYTOSIS
A term used to describe an increase in white blood cells.

LEUCOPENIA
A term used to describe a decrease in white blood cells (often linked to a viral infection).

LEUPROLIDE ACETATE
A hormone-controlling injection that turns off the gonads (i.e. ovary and testicle). It is used in very small doses in birds as an agent to prevent or stop egg laying, and to control *Hypersexuality*.

LIPAEMIA
An increase of fat in the bird's blood.
Signs: There are very often no presenting signs, but the condition is common among obese birds.
Causes: Obesity and a high-fat diet are normally responsible. It should be appreciated that the fat content of sunflower seeds or peanuts is seven times that of the average chocolate bar. Such diets are not suitable for parrots. However, Lipaemia can occur as a natural side effect before egg laying.
Treatment: Overweight birds should be put on a low-fat diet.

LIPOMA
(See Neoplasia: Lipomas).

LIPOSARCOMA
(See Neoplasia: Liposarcoma).

LIVER CIRRHOSIS
Chronic fibrous scarring of the liver, to the extent that it becomes too diseased to function effectively.

Part of the role of the liver is to remove metabolites (waste products) produced by the body's normal metabolism (where nutrition derived from food is converted into living matter). When the liver ceases to function properly, metabolite levels become raised, and may result in *Hepatic Encephalopathy.*

LIVER DISEASE
There are numerous types of liver disease, each with their own causes, although signs are similar across the board.
Causes: A diet containing too much fat, infectious organisms, metabolic diseases, tumours or poisons.
Signs: An excessive rate of beak growth, *Anorexia,* weight loss, lethargy, weakness, *Diarrhoea, Polyuria* and *Polydipsia,* poor feathering, abdominal swelling, black or bloody faeces, haemorrhaging into the beak or claws, and liver enlargement.
Treatment: A *Biopsy* may be taken to determine the cause and extent of the damage, although it will not necessarily reveal the specific cause. An *Endoscopy* and a *Coeliotomy* may also be carried out, along with clinical history and examination, blood testing, *Radiology,* and microscopic examination of samples. The veterinarian's choice of treatment will depend on the underlying cause.

LIVER FATTY (HEPATIC LIPIDOSIS)
A bird with a fatty liver will have a seriously enlarged liver *(see Liver Disease).*
Signs: See Liver Disease.
Causes: A high-fat diet is often responsible.
Treatment: Affected birds should be handled very gently, as rough handling could cause the liver to rupture. Nutritional support is essential for these cases, and will involve *Gavage Feeding* with a high-carbohydrate, low-fat formulated diet, with supplementary vitamins and plenty of fluids. Blood-clotting, glucose and vitamin storage and release, and the ability to combat infection are all compromised in birds with a fatty liver.

LIVER FUNCTION
The liver has many functions, including the storage and release of glucose,

production of immunoglobulins to fight infection, production of blood-clotting factors, breakdown of old blood cells, storage of vitamins, and the excretion of metabolite waste products.

LOCAL ANAESTHETIC
An anaesthetic technique that removes feeling from a desired area, rather than rendering the bird unconscious.

Local anaesthetic is rarely used on birds because there is a high incidence of death and because most birds find the procedure very stressful. In nearly all situations, gaseous general anaesthetic is preferable.

LUGOL'S IODINE
An iodine supplement used to treat iodine deficiency.

LUNGWORM
(See Parasites: Syngamus Trachea).

LYMPHOCYTES
A type of white blood cell.

LYMPHOCYTOSIS
Elevated levels of *Lymphocytes*.

LYMPHOSARCOMA
(See Neoplasia: Lymphosarcoma).

LYSINE
(See Amino Acids).

M

MACAW WASTING SYNDROME
(See Proventricular Dilation Disease).

MAGNETIC RESONANCE IMAGING
More commonly known as MRI scanning, this is one of the most significant advances in medical imaging. The resulting image has far better soft-tissue contrast than conventional *Radiology*, CT or *Ultrasound* scanning, and it is an invaluable diagnostic tool.

MALNUTRITION
(See Nutrition).

MANDIBULAR PROGNATHISM/MAXILLARY BRACHYGNATHISM
(See Beak abnormalities: Mandibular prognathism/maxillary brachygnathism).

MASTURBATION
(See Sexual Frustration).

MATE TRAUMA
This is common among breeding birds, particularly Cockatoos, and usually presents as bite wounds to the beak.
(See also Beak: Trauma).

MEDROXYPROGESTERONE
A type of progesterone injection that was once used to control multiple egg laying. However, this hormone therapy has been found to have dangerous side effects, and *Leuprolide* is now used instead.

MEGABACTERIA
A very common disease of the digestive system, particularly among Budgerigars.
Signs: Vomiting and Regurgitation, and passing soft droppings, which may contain undigested seed. Weight loss is a common sequel.
Causes: Megabacteria are present in the proventriculus and ventriculus of many birds, causing no problems as long as they remain in low numbers. However, in situations where gastric acid production is reduced, megabacterial populations increase, and begin to cause digestive upsets.
Treatment: Antifungal therapy (e.g. amphoteracin) must be given by mouth every day for 14 days. In very severe cases, it may be necessary to euthanase the bird.

MENINGITIS/MENINGOENCEPHALITIS
Inflammation of the brain or the membranes surrounding the brain.
Signs: The bird will appear sick and depressed, with loss of co-ordination and possible development of fits.
Causes: Infectious organisms (e.g. bacteria, viruses, parasites and fungi), a build-up of fluid, and a restricted blood supply can all lead to meningitis.
Treatment: Blood tests, and cerebral fluid analysis and culture are used to confirm diagnosis, while treatment is based on alleviating the signs (e.g. using a sedative such as valium) and treating the causes (e.g. administering antibiotics).

METABOLIC DISORDERS
Major metabolic disorders may affect the liver, kidney, pancreas, reproductive or endocrine systems.

The clinical signs will vary greatly, depending on the system affected, but the owner will be left in no doubt that their bird is seriously unwell. Affected birds should be taken to an experienced veterinarian as soon as possible, so that the cause can be determined and the appropriate treatment provided. Such diseases are serious, and hold a grave prognosis.

METACARPAL FRACTURES

Fractures to the wing tip usually occur as a result of flying injuries.
Signs: The wing may be held unusually, or, in more serious cases, the tip may be set at a very strange angle to the rest of the wing. Feathers may be missing, and there may be bleeding and broken skin.
Causes: Wing tip fractures are normally caused when a bird flies into a stationary object.
Treatment: Any bird suffering from a suspected fracture should be taken to a veterinarian immediately, so that the fracture can be stabilised.

MICROBIOLOGY CULTURE

The controlled laboratory growing of bacteria for the purpose of identification and testing for drug sensitivity (i.e. to determine which drug will be most effective).

MICROCHIP TRANSPONDERS

Also known as passive identification transponders (PITs) or *Identichips,* these are tiny implants inserted into the bottom left-hand side of a bird's chest. Each implant contains a unique code, which enables each individual bird to be identified.

It is highly recommended that pet birds are chipped, so that if they are stolen or lost and their identification ring is removed, the real owner can be located. In addition, identification is invaluable to maintain health and breeding records.

MILKWEED
(See Toxicity: Plants).

MITES
(See Parasites: Cnemidocoptes).

MONOCYTES
A type of white blood cell.

MONOCYTOSIS
A term used to describe an increase in *Monocytes.*

MULTIPLE EGG LAYING
(See Excessive Laying).

MYCOBACTERIOSIS
(See Tuberculosis).

MYCOPLASMA INFECTION
An organism responsible for respiratory infection.
Signs: Sneezing, nasal discharge, *Sinusitis, Air Sacculitis,* and *Conjunctivitis.*
Causes: The organism is passed from bird to bird, often with no clinical signs manifested. The onset of clinical disease is often triggered by stress.
Treatment: Unfortunately, fatalities can reach up to 20 per cent. Diagnosis is difficult, as mycoplasma is very difficult to culture, but suspected cases are normally treated with drugs, including enroflaxacin, tylosin and tiamutin. Although some poultry mycoplasma vaccines are available, they have not been tried or tested on psittacines. Daily nasal flushing for several days may be necessary.

MYCOTIC GRANULOMA
A type of *Granuloma* that forms around a fungal infection (typically Aspergillus).

MYCOTOXINS
Toxins produced by fungal growths. These may occur on damp or decaying vegetable material (including seeds), or within the bird's respiratory system.
Signs: These vary, but can include gangrenous lesions, reduced egg production, reduced growth rates, liver necrosis, liver tumours and death.
Causes: Mycotoxins grow on poor-quality vegetation. The two main types to affect psittacines are ergot and aflatoxin. Ergot grows in poorly stored seed, while aflatoxin is a common cereal contaminant, especially when the cereal or seed is grown, harvested or stored in damp conditions.
Treatment: Mycotoxins suppress the immune system, so there may be secondary complications to treat. Antibiotics may be prescribed to prevent infection, and *Fluid Therapy,* nutritional supplementation, and additional vitamins may be required. In addition to treatment, keepers will need to ensure that, in future, only food of the highest quality is fed to their pets.

MYENTERIC GANGLIONEURITIS
(See Proventricular Dilation Disease).

N

NARES
Symmetrical, paired entrances to the nasal chamber located in the *Cere*. Air travels through the nares into the nasal chamber, where it is warmed and humidified before passing into the sinuses or via the *Choana* into the trachea.

NARES: DISCHARGE
A discharge from the nares, similar to the human 'runny nose'.
Signs: Discharge from the nares.
Causes: Discharge from the nares is a common consequence of an upper respiratory infection, which may also affect the sinuses and eyes.
Treatment: The underlying cause of the discharge will need to be found so that it can be treated. The discharge should then clear up on its own. Nasal flushing may be necessary in some cases.

NARES: RHINOLITH
A concretion in the nares, most commonly seen in African Greys.
Signs: A hard, round concretion present in the nares.
Causes: Rhinoliths are typically caused by a low-grade nasal infection, and are often secondary to vitamin A deficiency *(see Vitamin Deficiencies and Toxicosis: Vitamin A)*.
Treatment: The infection will need to be treated, and, if vitamin A deficiency is believed to be responsible, attention will need to be given to the bird's diet. Weekly vitamin A injections will need to be administered for three weeks, by which time the improved diet should be proving effective.

NEBULISATION
A technique 'borrowed' from human medicine, which is typically used to treat respiratory problems, such as *Asthma*.

A drug in liquid form is placed inside a small chamber. Oxygen or air is pumped through this chamber, forcing the liquid drug to reform as a fine mist consisting of various-sized particles. The smaller the particle, the better, as smaller particles can be inhaled deeper into the respiratory system. The bird is placed into an enclosed space (possibly just a towel over the cage) and the medication is pumped inside. Birds are usually medicated for 20 to 30 minutes, 3 to 4 times a day.

One great benefit of nebulisation is that drugs used are not absorbed elsewhere into the system, so very potent drugs, which are potentially toxic to other organs, may be safely administered by nebulisation. Moreover, nebulisation is a very stress-free, 'hands-off' method of administering medication.

NECROPSY
(See Post Mortem).

NEMATODES
(See Parasites: Nematodes).

NEONATE
A newly hatched chick.

NEOPLASIA
Another name for a tumour. There are two types of neoplasia, benign and malignant.

Malignant tumours can metastisise (spread) in the blood or lymphstream, which means they can spread. Benign tumours do not spread, although they can continue to increase in size, which may cause further problems.

Tumours are complicated to treat, particularly in birds, because of the significant number of avian viruses that can trigger tumours. There are very many different types of tumours, each originating from different tissue types, spreading or not spreading with variable prognosis.

NEOPLASIA: CARCINOMAS
A carcinoma is a technical name for a particular type of tumour.
Signs: If the carcinoma is present in an internal organ, it is unlikely that the bird will present with signs until the tumour has progressed beyond the point at which it can be treated. If the carcinoma is present on the surface of the body (e.g. a *Squamous Cell Carcinoma* of the skin), the tumour should be visible as a lump or area of skin with abnormal tissue.
Causes: The causes of cancer are not entirely understood, although certain viruses are known to play a part.
Treatment: If the carcinoma is internal, the prognosis is not good. However, for skin tumours and preen gland adenoma carcinomas, it may be possible to save the bird's life if the tumour is spotted in time and the bird is taken to an experienced avian veterinarian immediately. No abnormal lumps or bumps on a bird should ever be ignored.

NEOPLASIA: CHEMOTHERAPY
There is a range of chemotherapy agents available for the treatment of avian neoplasia, some of which have achieved remarkable results without causing the bird any discomfort.

To date, the drugs used as chemotherapy agents include prednisolone, doxorubicin, cisplatin, carboplatin, and chlorambucil. These may also be used in combination.

NEOPLASIA: FIBROSARCOMAS
Malignant tumours of fibrous tissue, common among Budgerigars and Cockatiels.
Signs: Fibrosarcomas are normally found on the legs and wings, and will take the form of lumps of fibrous tissue.
Causes: The causes are not fully understood, but many believe these tumours are virus-induced.
Treatment: Fibrosarcomas, although malignant, do not have a strong tendency to spread. As a result, surgical removal of the affected area can be curative.

NEOPLASIA: LIPOMAS
Benign tumours found in fat cells, particularly common in Budgerigars, Cockatiels, Amazons, and certain Cockatoos.
Signs: The tumours are commonly situated on the abdomen, hip, breast and neck, and may be felt as fatty lumps underneath the skin.
Causes: As with most forms of neoplasia, the causes are not entirely understood. However, lipomas are more common among birds fed a high-fat (e.g. seed-based) diet.
Treatment: Lipomas can be effectively controlled, in many cases, by a strictly controlled diet.

NEOPLASIA: LIPOSARCOMAS
Malignant tumours found in fat cells, particularly common in Budgerigars and Cockatiels.
Signs: Liposarcomas are normally found on the face, neck and preen gland, and will be present as fatty lumps.
Causes: As with all cancers, the causes are not fully understood, although a high-fat diet may play a part.
Treatment: Often, it is difficult to distinguish between a lipoma and a liposarcoma, except by the use of microscopic examination, which would require a *Biopsy*. Removal of the tumour is often the first course of action, followed by biopsy. Further treatment will depend on the results from the biopsy.

NEOPLASIA: LYMPHOSARCOMAS
Malignant tumours in the lymphoid cells.
Signs: Weakness and weight loss.
Causes: The causes are not fully understood, but many believe these tumours are virus-induced.
Treatment: The tumours may be present in the bone marrow alone, or throughout the body, and the extent of the cancer will determine the treatment chosen. Chemotherapy will be effective in some cases.

NEOPLASIA: SQUAMOUS CELL CARCINOMAS

Malignant tumours of the skin, common in Budgerigars and Cockatiels.
Signs: The skin tumours appear on the face, legs, and preen gland.
Causes: The clinical signs are caused by abnormal cell changes, although the factors that trigger these changes are not fully understood.
Treatment: Tumours can be treated very successfully by surgical removal, followed by topical or systemic chemotherapy.

NEOPLASIA: SURGERY

If a tumour can be removed, removal is usually the first choice of treatment. If tumours are located in positions where surgery is not appropriate, or if tumours recur, chemotherapy may also be considered.
(See also Neoplasia: Chemotherapy).

NEOPLASIA: XANTHOMAS

Abnormal areas of skin tissue, often found on the extremities.
Signs: Yellow-coloured, waxy plaques or areas of raised skin.
Causes: Xanthomas are not true tumours. They tend to occur in areas where there has been some trauma previously, often over the site of another pathology (e.g. a lipoma). They tend to be more common among Budgerigars, Cockatiels, and some Cockatoos and Macaws.
Treatment: If possible, xanthomas should be surgically removed. However, xanthomas often have a rich blood supply and removal may be dangerous, especially in small birds.

NEPHRITIS

(See Kidney Nephritis).

NERVOUS DISEASE: GENERAL

Any disease of the nervous system, which affects the bird's balance and motor control.
Signs: The affected bird may hold its head to one side, develop a habit of turning around in circles, hold its head upside down (opisthotonous), make jerky, unco-ordinated movements, lose balance on occasion, and may also suffer from seizures.
Causes: Commonly caused by vitamin deficiencies, although toxins (especially heavy metals or pesticides), fungal, bacterial or viral infections and head trauma can also be responsible.
Treatment: Radiography and blood testing will confirm the diagnosis and help give the veterinarian suggestions for treatment. If caused by dietary deficiencies, the diet will need to be changed. Seizures should be controlled where possible, and the bird placed in a warm, quiet, dark environment. Anti-inflammatories may be administered, as will sedatives and *Anaesthesia*, if deemed necessary.

NERVOUS DISEASE: NEOPLASIA
Space-occupying lesions of the nervous system are rarely reported as a cause of nervous disease. When they do occur, treatment is not usually possible.

NEW BIRD CHECK
Any new bird should come from a reputable source, and, preferably, should be health-screened prior to leaving the source. When arriving at the new home, the bird should be placed in quarantine for at least 21 days (preferably 35), regardless of whether the bird is from a neighbouring town or another country. The bird should then undergo more health screening when in quarantine (i.e. a 'new bird check'), to ensure it is well and that it does not pose a risk to other birds on the site.

The content of the health screen should be decided by your avian veterinarian, taking into account the disease risks of your species and area. A basic screen for most psittacines would include a physical examination, a standard haematology and biochemistry profile, together with a *Chlamydophila* test. Polymerase Chain Reaction Tests for *Psittacine Beak And Feather Disease* and *Polyomavirus* are also sensible. As yet, there is no specific laboratory test for *Proventricular Dilation Syndrome*. A lateral body X-ray remains the best screening method for this disease. If suspected, a *Crop Biopsy* is indicated.

NEW CAGE SYNDROME
(See Toxicity: Heavy Metals).

NEWCASTLE DISEASE
An extremely serious viral disease that occurs in a wide variety of birds, including parrots.

Newcastle Disease is so serious it is classed as a notifiable disease, which means that the relevant government department must be notified of all cases. This is because the disease is so infectious that affected poultry are culled to help prevent infection spreading. Birds confined to small areas will quickly pass on the infection to one another with disastrous consequences.

As with many viral infections, there appear to be waves of infection, which can often be predicted with some accuracy. Newcastle Disease tends to appear every 10-12 years. Interestingly, Slender-billed Conures have suffered greatly from this disease. Slender-billed Conures are very social birds. Large flocks roost in close proximity to one another at night, passing on the infection at such a rate that huge flocks can die as a result.

Signs: The clinical signs are very varied, ranging from sudden death to a much slower onset of signs, which include respiratory distress, digestive problems, and signs typical of *Nervous Disease*. In parrots, the incubation period is normally 3 to 16 days after exposure to the virus, but there is a documented case of an

Amazon Parrot continuing to shed the virus for a year after exposure without showing any clinical signs.

Causes: The disease is caused by the *Paramyxovirus* virus and can be transmitted via respiratory and oral routes, as well as from *Faeces.* It is highly infectious.

Treatment: Although some birds appear to have a greater resistance than others, the mortality rate is nearly 100 per cent. Affected birds, or those assumed to be affected, are normally euthanased. Parrot keepers should always remember that prevention is better than cure, and should never buy birds from an unreliable source. In the event of a local outbreak, parrots may be vaccinated to prevent infection.

NEW WIRE DISEASE
(See Toxicity: Heavy Metals).

NICOTINE
(See Toxicity: Plants).

NICTITANS
This is commonly referred to as the third eyelid.

In birds, the nictitans functions to spread the tear film across the eye, wipe away any debris, and protect the cornea from sudden trauma, especially when in flight. The nictitans should never be removed in mammals, although removal in birds, especially small ones, seems less disadvantageous.

NIGHTSHADE
(See Toxicity: Plants).

NORTHERN POULTRY MITE
(See Parasites: Ornitysluss Sylvarium).

NUTRITION
Surveys have shown that 75 per cent of sick parrots are suffering from a nutritional deficiency that contributed to their illness.

NYSTATIN
A standard treatment for yeast infestations in the mouth or gut.
(See also Candidiasis).

O

OAK
(See Toxicity: Plants).

OBESITY

A clinical term used to describe any animal (including humans) that is significantly overweight.

Signs: Obesity is easy to diagnose because the bird will be obviously overweight. However, in cases of very gradual weight gain, the owner may not 'notice' that their bird is overweight until the bird has been obese for some time. You can check your parrot's weight by feeling for the keel bone, in the centre of the bird's chest. If it cannot be felt, the bird is overweight. Obesity is a serious killer, and, left unchecked, can lead to *Heart Disease, Hernias, Atherosclerosis, Liver Disease,* and fat embolisms.

Causes: There are a number of medical causes (e.g. hormone problems), but poor diet is the usual factor, particularly among birds fed a high-fat, seed-based diet. Cockatoos are particularly susceptible.

Treatment: The first step is to put the bird on a healthier diet and to rule out any underlying medical problem. Provided that poor diet is the main reason, a change of diet should eventually see the bird reach a far healthier condition.

OBSESSIVE COMPULSIVE DISORDER (OCD)

Any activity carried out by a bird to which it devotes an inappropriate amount of time, or which can be self-harming.

Signs: This depends on the form the OCD takes, but the most common example is feather plucking.

Causes: Lack of attention, boredom, and excessive dominance are common causes, although there are many potential triggers.

Treatment: In the case of feather plucking, medical therapy is often required to break the disorder (clomipramine, prozac, or haloperidol), but it is also important to make substantial changes to the bird's environment, so that he has a constant source of activity and interest. Causes of severe itchiness should be eliminated before assuming a diagnosis of OCD.

OESOPHAGUS DILATION
(See Proventricular Dilation Disease).

ORNITHOSIS
(See Psittacosis).

OSTEOMYELITIS

An infection of the bone.

Signs: Lameness.

Causes: Osteomyelitis tends to occur following trauma, surgery, or as a consequence of infection (e.g. *Tuberculosis*).

Treatment: A long-term course of antibiotics (e.g. around four to six weeks) will be necessary.

OVIDUCT: INFLAMMATION
Technically known as *Salpingitis*, an inflamed oviduct hinders eggs passing naturally.
Signs: If eggs are able to pass through, they may take longer to be passed, or arrive with rough, irregular, or contoured shells.
Causes: Bacterial or viral infection, tumours, or scar tissue in the oviduct.
Treatment: Antibiotics and anti-inflammatories will be administered by the veterinarian.

OVIDUCT: PROLAPSE
Fortunately rare, prolapse of the oviduct refers to a condition in which the oviduct is forced out of the cloaca (vent).
Signs: Unfortunately, the condition is fatal very rapidly, so presenting signs may not be noticed until it is too late. One warning sign to look out for is a hen that appears to be straining, without success, to pass an egg. If she strains too much, a prolapse may occur.
Causes: Typical causes include *Peritonitis*, *Egg Binding* and *Salpingitis*.
Treatment: Veterinary attention should be sought immediately if prolapse is suspected. This condition causes a vast shock-effect on the bird. Emergency veterinary care will involve treatment for shock, then replacing the oviduct. The vet is likely to perform a *Coeliotomy* in order to correct the problem. However, the timing is critical – if the procedure is done too early, the shock will be too much, but if it is performed too late, blood poisoning may set in.

OVIDUCT: REMOVAL
Removal of the oviduct, the technical term for which is *Salpingohysterectomy*.
 Oviduct removal is generally performed in cases of multiple egg laying (which are non-responsive to dietary and husbandry changes). The surgery is delicate and requires considerable expertise and specialist equipment in order to be safely performed. In the case of birds, the ovary is not removed, as it is attached too closely to the dorsal wall of the abdomen, close to a major artery from the heart. However, in psittacine species, the ovary is not stimulated to release follicles once the *Oviduct* has been removed.

P

PACHECO'S DISEASE
A very dangerous, highly infectious form of the *Herpes* virus, which affects the liver.

Signs: Clinical signs vary from depression, *Anorexia, Diarrhoea,* regurgitation, yellow-green urates staining the urine, or sudden-onset nervous signs.
Causes: The affected bird will have been infected with this strain of the *Herpes* virus.
Treatment: Clinical signs, *Haematology, Biochemistry, Radiology* and *Endoscopy* may be used to confirm diagnosis, although absolute confirmation can only be made post mortem, through a microscopic examination of a liver biopsy. The disease is typically fatal, so great care must be taken to ensure that all in-contact birds are treated with the antiviral agent *Acyclovir.* Birds that survive are likely to be lifelong carriers of the disease and will present a risk to other birds in the future.

PACKED CELL VOLUME (PCV)

A measure of the solid (cellular) portion of the blood, otherwise known as haematocrit.

Normal values in psittacines vary between 45 and 55 per cent. Lower levels indicate *Anaemia,* while higher levels indicate *Dehydration.*

PANCREAS

The pancreas produces enzymes (amylase, lipase and trypsin) that help to digest food in the small intestine.

PANCREATIC PROBLEMS

Any problem that interferes with the normal function of the pancreas.
Signs: Clinical signs vary from pale, foul-smelling, fatty faeces, increased thirst and fluid production in the droppings, and vomiting. Diagnosis is by blood testing, *Endoscopy, Biopsy* and microscopic examination.
Causes: Diabetes and *Neoplasia,* especially following *Cloacal Papillomatosis,* can affect the function of the pancreas.
Treatment: Treatment will depend on which part of the pancreas is compromised.

PAPILLOMA OF FEET/LEGS IN COCKATOOS

A form of the *Herpes* virus, which causes dry, proliferative lesions on the feet and legs of Moluccan, Lesser Sulphur-crested, and Umbrella Cockatoos, but is rare in Black Cockatoos.
Signs: Abnormal tissue on the feet and legs.
Causes: Papilloma of the feet and legs is caused by a particular strain of the *Herpes* virus.
Treatment: Diagnosis is confirmed by microscopic examination of a *Biopsy.* Treatment includes treating the papillomas with a topical form of *Acyclovir,* together with systemic administration of *Acyclovir.*

PAPILLOMATA

Lesions present in the *Cloaca* or *Choana,* which are most commonly found among Amazons and Macaws.

Signs: There may be a small amount of blood present in the faeces and the affected bird may appear to be straining. Left untreated, papillomatas can be linked to tumours in the pancreas, small intestine, or bile duct, and so can, eventually, lead to death.

Causes: Papilloma form as a result of a *Herpes* virus infection.

Treatment: Vaccinations can help breeding collections of birds, but your veterinarian will need to advise about the suitability of this. Capsicum (chilli peppers) at two per cent in the diet is claimed to be effective at controlling further development of the lesions, although, if the supplement is removed, the lesions can recur.

PARAMYXOVIRUS

A group of highly infectious, virulent viruses, which vary in pathogenicity. The most dangerous form of these viruses is known as *Newcastle Disease.*

PARASITES: ASCARIDS

Also known as *Nematodes* (roundworms), heavy infestations of these *Ascarids* can block the gut and lead to death.

Conures and Australian Parakeets are particularly susceptible to infestation by this type of parasite, but all species can be affected, particularly if the bird has access to the ground or is kept in an outdoor aviary.

Signs: Often, there may be no signs. However, symptoms to watch for include unexplained weight loss, loss of condition, and blood present in the droppings.

Causes: Young birds normally become infected through eating regurgitated food from their parents, which will contain the worms. Ascarid eggs can remain alive for some time on the floor of an aviary, waiting until they find a new host before beginning the cycle once again. Caged birds housed indoors are rarely affected, but a bird needs to be allowed outdoors only once in order to pick up the parasites.

Treatment: The veterinarian will diagnose an infestation following examination of *Faeces* under a microscope. There are several commercial preparations available to kill the worms, but they are bitter-tasting, and, therefore, they are not easy to administer. The best way to administer them is to feed them directly into the crop, using a feeding tube, or by dripping the preparation into the beak. Your veterinarian will advise you further on the type of medication to choose, the correct dosage, and the best way to administer it. Worming medication is extremely effective, but a course of probiotics (healthy gut bacteria) may be needed following use, in order to re-establish harmony in the intestines.

PARASITES: BLOOD

Blood parasites are rare among pet birds, being found more commonly among wild birds. However, as some parrots are illegally captured from their natural habitat, cases have been documented.

Blood parasites are not normally life-threatening, but they should also be treated by an experienced avian veterinarian. The best way to avoid problems is to ensure that you acquire your birds from a reliable source.

PARASITES: CAPILLARIA SPECIES

Nematode roundworms.

Signs: Regurgitation of food, *Anorexia, Diarrhoea,* and weight loss.
Causes: Infestations are normally acquired from another bird, usually from infected droppings on an aviary floor. Less often, birds can pick up the parasites by eating earthworms.
Treatment: This parasite can be immune to some worming treatments, so you will need to consult your veterinarian for advice about treatment and to check that treatment has been effective.

PARASITES: CESTODES

Tapeworms rarely seen in pet birds.

PARASITES: CNEMIDOCOPTES

A microscopic mite that causes *Scaly Face* in Budgerigars. The same mite causes *Scaly Leg* in Canaries, but rarely affects other species unless there are unusual circumstances.

Signs: Scaly Face in Budgerigars and *Scaly Leg* in Canaries.
Causes: The parasite is normally transferred from one bird to another.
Treatment: Diagnosis is confirmed following the collection of a skin scrape and microscopic examination. Treatment involves a weekly application of an *Ivermectin Anthelmintic* on any part of the bird's skin for three weeks. All in-contact birds should be treated.

PARASITES: COCCIDIA SPECIES

A common protozoal parasite of many avian species but not thought to be of any significance in psittacines.

PARASITES: DERMANYSSUS SPECIES

Also known as the red poultry mite, these mites are unusual because they live away from their host for most of the time, feeding only at night.

Signs: Usually, this parasite affects aviary birds only. It causes severe irritation of the skin with resultant *Self-Mutilation, Anaemia* and weakness. Using a torch, the mites can be seen at night as small, brown-to-red or black dots, scuttling between the feathers at skin level.

Causes: The parasites may be caught from the aviary floor or by direct contact with an infested bird.

Treatment: Affected birds will need to be sprayed with an appropriate parasitic preparation, recommended by your veterinarian. The bird's environment should also be treated.

PARASITES: GIARDIA SPECIES

A protozoal parasite that lives in the top of the small intestine.

Signs: A significant infestation may cause *Diarrhoea, Anorexia,* and juvenile mortality. However, less severe infestations may not reveal any obvious signs. Some cases of feather plucking and severe *Pruritis* (itching) have been caused by this parasite.

Causes: The life cycle of *Giardia* is direct with infective cysts being shed in the *Faeces.* The cyst survives for an extended period in water and faeces, and susceptible birds pick up the parasite by coming into contact with contaminated water and faeces.

Treatment: Fenbendazole or metronidazole applications, together with rigorous environmental cleaning and disinfection normally solve the problem.

PARASITES: NEMATODES

Roundworm parasites, including *Capillaria*, *Syngamus*, and *Ascarids*. Most of this group can be treated with benzimidazole and *Ivermectin*, both of which are *Anthelmintics*.

PARASITES: ORNITHONYSSUS SYLVARIUM

A mite, similar to *Dermanyssus*. However, unlike *Dermanyssus*, *Ornithonyssus* does not survive off the host. Only the affected bird will need to be treated.

PARASITES: PROTOZOAL

A collective description for single-cell parasites (e.g. *Giardia, Trichomonas,* and *Coccidia).*

PARASITES: SYNGAMUS TRACHEA

A *Nematode* roundworm that lives in the lungs and trachea (windpipe), also known as *Lungworm*. They are rare among pet birds, usually being found in young aviary-kept birds, and, even then, cases are rare.

Signs: Affected birds will have raspy breathing and their voices may change.

Causes: The parasites are passed on through *Faeces* and matter coughed up by an infested bird.

Treatment: Standard wormers, thorough cleaning, and preventing access to the ground are normally effective.

PARASITES: SARCOCYSTIS
An often-fatal disease of young fledgling birds transmitted by biting insects, which affects youngsters as they are leaving the nest.
Signs: Clinical signs are rare, the first indication being sudden death.
Causes: Biting insects are responsible for transmitting the parasite that causes this disease.
Treatment: If the condition is spotted early enough, sulphonamide antibiotics can be given, and repellents can be used to deter biting insects.

PARASITES: TICKS
A blood-sucking parasite that attaches to the skin of birds, which commonly affects birds kept in aviaries. With the exception of mosquitoes, ticks transfer more infections than any other insect vector. Some of these infections are very serious and often fatal.

As so many infections are transmitted by ticks, it is impossible to describe the clinical signs, as these will depend on the type of infection contracted. However, all infections can easily be avoided through proper tick control. Ticks attach to their hosts when the host passes vegetation that a tick lives on. Therefore, you can minimise risk by removing aviary plants during the tick's breeding season (the late summer months). Your veterinarian will be able to provide further advice about prevention.

PARASITES: TREMATODES
An extremely rare parasite hardly ever seen among pet birds. It requires the ingestion of an intermediate host, and is normally seen in wild-caught birds only.

PARASITES: TRICHOMONAS
A protozoal parasite usually seen among smaller psittacines.
Signs: Slow crop emptying, reduced appetite, and *Vomiting and Regurgitation*.
Causes: Chicks are infected when fed by infected parents.
Treatment: Microscopic examination of fresh swabs will confirm the diagnosis, and treatment (e.g. carnidazole or metronidazole) can be administered orally.

PARROT FEVER
(See Psittacosis).

PERIORBITAL SWELLING
(See Eye Swelling).

PERITONITIS
Inflammation, often with concurrent infection, of the peritoneal cavity (pelvic area).

Signs: These include loss of appetite, lethargy, and respiratory distress.
Causes: Peritonitis occurs most commonly when a follicle released from the ovary falls into the abdomen (coeliomic cavity) rather than down the oviduct.
Treatment: Intensive *Fluid Therapy,* antibiosis, and, on occasions, flushing of the coeliomic cavity. It is common for a hen to suffer adhesions between the oviduct and the guts following peritonitis, and, if this occurs, the bird may have problems with egg laying in the future.

PESTICIDES
(See Toxicity: Pesticides).

PHILODENDRON
(See Toxicity: Plants).

PHOBIAS
Change is a form of stimulation, and all birds should be accustomed to change. However, for some birds, change is very stressful, and can result in phobias of anything new or different. This is most common among birds that are 'institutionalised' (i.e. have become accustomed to solitary confinement).
Signs: The bird will show signs of great distrust and fear when exposed to anything new, which could be anything from a new toy to a change of room.
Causes: There are various causes, but most phobias stem from a previous bad experience, or insufficient socialisation.
Treatment: The first step in overcoming phobias is to generate more confidence in the bird, which may require the help of an avian behaviour specialist. Once this has been achieved, the bird should be exposed, very gradually, to changing situations, firstly in his own room, and then in different rooms, but always at a distance, initially. Once the bird accepts this without distress, the item can be brought closer to the bird, until he can accept unfamiliar objects being positioned next to him. Try to make a game out of it, and encourage the bird to play near or with the previously phobic item.

PHOSPHORUS
Phosphorus is a chemical element that is essential for many bodily functions.
Blood phosphorus levels can be used as a diagnostic tool, as levels decrease or increase in response to certain illnesses, in particular, *Kidney Disease* or parathyroid disease.

PLANT TOXICOSIS
(See Toxicity: Plants).

PLASMA BIOCHEMISTRIES
Also known as clinical pathology tests, these are blood tests taken to indicate damage or malfunction in specific organs.

PLASMODIUM
A blood parasite affecting *Red Blood Cells*, the liver, spleen, hearts or lungs.

PNEUMONIA
A serious infection of the respiratory system.
Signs: Difficulty breathing, a blue discolouration of the mouth membranes, weight loss, and tail bobbing.
Causes: Pneumonia may be caused by a number of different causes, including bacterial organisms (e.g. *Tuberculosis)*, fungal infections, viruses, *Parasites* (*Syngamus, Sarcocystitis, Cyathostoma*), toxins (e.g. Teflon) or inspired allergies.
Treatment: Diagnosis is based on blood tests, *Radiography,* tracheal swabs and culture, *Endoscopy,* and *Biopsy.* Treatment will depend on the cause, but is often a type of antibiotic administed orally, by injection, or through *Nebulisation.*

PODODERMATITIS
An inflammatory condition of the foot, usually, but not always, referring to the underside of the feet.
Signs: Inflammation of the foot, particularly on the underside.
Causes: Pododermatitis is usually caused by inadequate perching arrangements or previous trauma or infection. It is normally a husbandry-related disease. If a bird spends too long standing on a smooth hard perch, bearing all its weight on one part of the foot, the skin of the underside becomes smooth, shiny and reddened. Continued pressure results in inflammation, followed by infection.
Treatment: Veterinary attention must be sought as soon as possible. A normal, healthy parrot will respond quickly to antibiotics. However, care must be taken to ensure that, in future, adequate perching arrangements are provided.

POINSETTIA
(See Toxicity: Poinsettia).

POLYDIPSIA
Increased thirst, often linked to *Kidney Disease.*

POLYOMAVIRUS
Also known as *Budgerigar Fledgling Disease,* this virus commonly affects young budgies, often causing death within the first weeks of life.
Signs: Many cases die, but early warning signs include abdominal distension, bleeding under the skin, and a lack of co-ordination. Birds affected by the

longer-term variety of the disease may develop abnormalities of the wing and tail flight feathers. Older, larger psittacines may show signs of depression, *Anorexia, Vomiting and Regurgitation, Diarrhoea, Dehydration,* and bleeding under the skin 12 to 48 hours before death.

Causes: Polyomavirus is contracted through contact with other infected birds.
Treatment: A vaccine is available in the US but not in the UK or Europe.

POLYTETRAFLUOROETHYLENE (PTFE).

Commonly known as Teflon®, this is a common cause of poisoning in parrots.

PTFE is found in non-stick cookware, and some self-clean ovens, irons and ironing board covers. Knock-resistant paint, heat lamps and all-weather clothing may also contain PTFE. When PTFE is overheated, it produces toxic fumes, and can cause death extremely rapidly (often within minutes).

POLYURIA

An increase in the fluid proportion passed in the droppings.

POST MORTEM

A clinical examination carried out on a dead subject, used to determine the cause of death.

A post mortem procedure is divided into two parts. The first procedure is termed the gross post mortem, which examines the external tissues of the bird, as well as the internal organs. The second procedure, known as histopathology, involves the taking of samples, fixing them in formalin, slicing the fixed samples, and then examining them under a microscope.

The costs of a full post mortem can be high, but as well as determining the cause of death (although this may not be established in all cases), such procedures can discover whether changes in husbandry, nutrition or preventive medicine may help avoid future deaths.

POSTERIOR SEGMENT

The area of the eye behind the pupil comprising the vitreous fluid, retina, choroids and optic nerve.

POX VIRUS

A virus that can take several different forms, affecting different species, although Blue-fronted Amazons are most commonly affected.

Signs: The most common form of the virus is known as the dry, subcutaneous (under the skin) form. It presents as nodular or crusting lesions on non-feathered areas of the skin, especially around the eyes, beak, nares and feet. On occasions, birds will suffer the caseous (diphtheritic) form, which affects the mouth, and, on occasions, the oesophagus.

Causes: The virus has to enter the system via a breach in the skin, which might be a wound or an insect bite.

Treatment: As with any virus, there is no treatment. However, the disease is self-limiting and birds generally make full recovery within three to six weeks.

PRALIDOXIME
A treatment for organophosphorus poisoning. It is only effective if administered within 24 to 48 hours of poison ingestion.

PROLAPSE
When an internal organ is pushed out of the body.

PROPATAGIUM
The elasticated skin web running from the shoulder to the wrist, forming the leading edge of the wing. This tissue is essential as an aerofoil for normal flight. It is easily damaged by trauma or tight bandages placed around it.

PROPULSID
An orally administered drug used to stimulate muscular gut activity.

PROPYLENE GLYCOL
A heavy liquid chemical added to many drugs in their injectable form.

Once injected, propylene glycol can cause some irritation. Likewise, if used to dilute any drugs and given by mouth, some species (especially Toucans) have been recorded to suffer from propylene glycol toxicity.

PROTOZOA
(See Parasites: Protozoa).

PROVENTRICULAR DILATION DISEASE (PDS)
A virus that attacks the nerve supply to the guts. First diagnosed in 1977, it is known by several other names, including Proventricular Dilation Syndrome, Proventricular Hypertrophy, Macaw Wasting Syndrome, Psittacine Wasting Syndrome, Psittacine Proventricular Dilation Disease, Myenteric Ganglioneuritis, Infiltrative Splanchnic Neuropathy, and Encephalomyelitis.

Cockatoos, African Greys and Macaws are most commonly affected, but any psittacine species is at risk. Cases have been reported in more than 50 species of psittacine, while suggestive lesions have also been reported in Toucans, Honey Creepers, Canaries, Weaver Finches, Roseate Spoonbills, and two free-living Canada Geese. Birds of all ages are vulnerable. Individual birds can be affected, but epidemics are equally possible.

Incubation periods vary from 11 days to 2 years or more. The disease is not considered to be highly infectious, and the causative virus is not considered to be stable outside of the host for more than a maximum of 3 days. However, because of the severity of the illness, it is a disease to which all parrot keepers should be alerted.

Signs: The intestinal signs include crop impaction, regurgitation, slow crop emptying, abdominal distension, and progressive weight loss (often in spite of a good appetite), while the signs of encephalitis include limb weakness, limb or head tremors, *Ataxia,* seizures, and loss of balance or difficulty in perching. Usually, the gut signs become apparent first, but there are cases where signs of *Nervous Disease* have manifested first. In nearly all cases, it will be obvious that the bird is unwell, to a greater or lesser degree, although some birds can remain asymptomatic for up to three months after exposure to the virus. Some remain asymptomatic for far longer, although some dilation may be visible under *Radiography* or *Endoscopy.* Keepers should also check their pet's droppings, as undigested seed is a classic sign.

Causes: The virus damages some or all of the autonomic ganglia (splanchnic nerves), which supply parts of the guts (the proventriculus, ventriculus, and duodenum). The guts become dilated, preventing the passage of food through that part of the gut. In addition, encephalitis may affect the brain and spinal cord.

Treatment: Unfortunately, there is no blood screen available to test for PDS, so the condition can be difficult to diagnose with absolute certainty. However, birds believed to have contracted the virus do not have a good prognosis. There are reports of birds showing signs suggestive of PDS appearing to recover from the disease; however there are no documented cases of birds confirmed as suffering from PDS surviving. Failure to respond to treatment is typical of birds affected by PDS, although secondary complications arising from the virus (e.g. *Air Sac Infections)* can be treated with good results. Asymptomatic birds usually survive, although they are unlikely to regain full gut normality. In such cases, parrots should be provided with small, regular meals of soft, high-energy, easily digestible, high-fibre gruel or pelleted foods. Housed in a stress-free environment, and with close veterinary control of any secondary infections that may arise, these birds can survive for months or even years. However, the affected bird poses a serious infection risk to other birds and should be kept in strict isolation.

PROVENTRICULAR DILATION DISEASE: PREVENTION AND QUARANTINE

PDS can occur in any aviary, despite excellent hygiene, effective quarantine precautions and the absence of new additions to the flock. However, by taking sensible precautions, you can minimise the risk to the psittacines in your care.

There have been suggestions that infection may be spread by feral birds visiting aviary birds. Therefore, if at all possible, aviary birds should be housed as a closed collection.

New additions to the aviary should be quarantined for at least three weeks, however reliable the source they have come from. Imported birds must be quarantined for at least five weeks. Towards the end of the quarantine period, the birds should undergo a screening process, to check for *Psittacine Beak and Feather Disease, Poloma,* and *Chlamydophila,* as well as routine blood and biochemistry tests. In view of the risk of PDS, keepers are further advised to have any new birds tested with lateral *Radiography* (if necessary, with barium contrast medium), so that any signs of a dilated proventriculus or delayed gut emptying may be detected.

Birds that have been exposed to the virus should be kept in quarantine for at least one year following exposure, although this may not be long enough to allow detection of all latent cases. PDS can remain dormant for up to two years. As a consequence, the owner of any aviary collection that has suffered with PDS will be prevented from breeding or selling any birds for at least two years, and, in addition, is likely to lose between 15 and 30 per cent of the collection. In an aviary situation, after the loss of a number of birds in a short period, an interval of one to two years may pass with no signs of the disease; however, the virus may resurface unexpectedly after this time. However, it is not recommended that in-contact birds are euthanased as a precaution, as they may never develop the disease.

PROVENTRICULAR DILATION DISEASE: TESTING
There is no specific blood test for PDS, so veterinary diagnosis is based on clinical, signs, *Radiography* (using a barium meal) and *Fluoroscopy.*

Diagnostic confirmation may be achieved by *Biopsy.* Biopsies harvested from the proventriculus or ventriculus normally yield a definitive diagnosis. However, in birds sufffering from PDS, the proventricular wall is so stretched that a real risk of post-surgical rupture exists. Consequently, a crop biopsy or partial-thickness ventricular biopsy is preferred.

PROZAC ®
Also known as fluoxetine, this is a human antidepressant sometimes used to assist in the treatment of avian behavioural problems.

PRURITIS
The technical term for itchy skin.

PSITTACINE BEAK AND FEATHER DISEASE (PBFD)
A viral disease that typically damages the beak and feathers of affected birds. It is sometimes referred to as Cockatoo Rot, because the disease

was first noted among Cockatoos. Some species appear more susceptible than others, with neotropical parrots being the least susceptible.

Signs: The symptoms of PBFD fall into two main areas, depression of the immune system, and beak, feather and skin abnormality. Birds suffering from a depressed immune system will pick up a series of normally minor infections, which can quickly become serious and even cause death. External signs usually include substantial feather loss, including areas where it would be impossible for the parrot to pluck out feathers by itself. Sometimes, the feathers never regrow. When feathers do regrow, they are often twisted, with small haemorrhages within the pin feathers. These feathers tend to be very brittle, breaking easily. Other birds do not lose their feathers, although the coloration may change (e.g. Vasa Parrots turn white). The beak initially takes on a glossy appearance, eventually losing its strength, causing parts of the beak to break. The beak and the nails will overgrow; this is particularly noticeable in a beak where one mandible has broken, therefore preventing normal wear. Parrots with this condition often appear depressed, and may appear in some pain from the feather, nail and beak abnormalities.

Causes: PBFD is caused by a virus named *Diminuvirus* (a member of the *Circovirus* family). PBFD is contagious and it occurs in wild birds as well as among pets. It is not thought that a carrier state exists.

Treatment: A blood test will confirm diagnosis, but at present there is no cure, although there is some promising research being undertaken that may result in effective vaccination. Treatment is limited to controlling pain and secondary infection. Birds suffering from a suppressed immune system may be given drugs to boost their immunity. Parrots that have lost feathers will need to be kept warm, so that they do not suffer from *Hypothermia*. The disease is progressive, although at different rates depending on the individual bird. Young birds tend to progress more rapidly. Adult birds, given good care (which must include psychological care as well as physical), often have a life expectancy of a few years. However, the owner must keep a constant eye on the affected bird's quality of life. Once the bird's quality of life is questionable, or if it is in significant pain, euthanasia should be considered.

PSITTACINE BEAK AND FEATHER DISEASE: PREVENTION AND QUARANTINE

PBFD is a highly contagious disease, and, therefore, one that all parrot owners must be vigilant against at all times.

The virus is easily transmitted among birds, and it is thought that feather dust plays a major role in the transmission of this disease. Where possible, birds should be prevented from having contact with any bird not absolutely known to be clear of the disease. This means that outdoor aviaries should be kept closed, where possible, and access to the aviary floor prevented.

PSITTACOSIS

A zoonotic (i.e. can be passed to humans) disease, also known as *Ornithosis, Chlamydosis, and Chlamydophilosis,* that can affect a wide variety of psittacine and non-psittacine birds, as well as cats, dogs and cattle.

Signs: A major problem in controlling the disease is that some birds will be asymptomatic (i.e. they carry the disease, shedding the organism and infecting other birds, but do not show any signs themselves). The clinical signs normally include respiratory and digestive problems. Some parrot species have a tendency to demonstrate particular signs (e.g. Budgerigars and Pionus Parrots exhibit respiratory distress, while Amazon Parrots lose weight and develop lime-green faces).

Causes: Psittacosis is caused by an organism called *Chlamydophilia psittaci*, of which there are several different strains, each causing a different severity of the illness. Evidence suggests that affected birds may already have a supressed immune system that places them at a greater risk of contracting the disease.

Treatment: Many different signs can be indicative of a *Chlamydophilia* infection and for this reason, vets will commonly test to confirm this condition. Today, antibody test kits for Psittacosis are available, although retests will need to be taken at regular intervals as the disease can remain in incubation for 45 days. The standard treatment for Psittacosis is antibiotics for 45 days. Prognosis is variable and much depends on the strain of psittacosis acquired. It is vital that further tests are carried out at three- and six-month intervals after treatment. It is also important to follow your veterinarian's instructions about caring for your other birds and your own health, as Psittacosis is highly contagious and zoonotic.

PSITTACOSIS: HUMAN INFECTION

Psittacosis can infect humans. It is a serious – potentially fatal – disease that should be treated immediately.

Signs: Initially, the disease will present as 'flu-like' symptoms. The sufferer will develop a high temperature, along with a dry cough, lethargy, headaches and nausea. Untreated, Psittacosis can lead to pneumonia, which, left untreated, can cause death.

Causes: The disease is contracted after exposure to infected birds.

Treatment: You should inform your doctor of your involvement with parrots, so that he or she is aware that Psittacosis is a possibility. Antibiotic treatment, if administered early enough, is very fast and effective, and most affected humans will make a full recovery. However, be aware that having suffered the disease once does not make you immune to another infection at a later date.

PSITTACINE WASTING SYNDROME
(See Proventricular Dilation Disease).

PUBERTY
The point at which a young bird begins to mature sexually.

Budgerigars, Lovebirds and Cockatiels reach puberty at approximately 6 to 12 months, Conures, Parakeets and other small psittacines at 1 to 2 years, and larger psittacines at any time between 3 and 6 years.

Q

(No entries).

R

RADIOGRAPHY
The taking of X-rays.

X-rays use ionising radiation rays, which are directed on to the bird. The bird's skeleton and internal organs deviate or block some of the rays. The rays that are not blocked fall on to a sheet of photographic film, held within a cassette, on the underside of the bird. Once developed, the film reveals an image of the bird's internal structure, commonly known as an X-ray.

Birds are normally anaesthetised for this procedure, as health and safety regulations prevent humans from holding a bird still while radiography is being carried out. However, there is no appreciable danger to the bird, and, indeed, radiography can save a bird's life by helping to make the correct diagnosis, so enabling the appropriate treatment.

RADIOSURGICAL INSTRUMENTS
Extremely valuable instruments used in avian surgery, that allow body tissues to be cut while controlling bleeding.

During surgery, it is vital that bleeding is controlled, as even a small amount of blood loss can prove fatal.

RED BLOOD CELLS
(See Blood: Red Blood Cells).

RENAL FAILURE
(See Kidney Disease).

RESPIRATORY DISEASE
Respiratory diseases are fairly common among psittacines. They are always serious and veterinary attention should be sought immediately.

Respiratory infections tend to affect either the upper respiratory tract (i.e. the nares, nasal cavity, sinuses, and trachea) or the lower respiratory tract (i.e. the lungs and air sacs).

Signs: Common signs include difficulty in breathing, coughing, wheezing, sneezing, discharge from the nasal cavities, and tail bobbing (where the tail bobs up and down as the bird breathes). Loss of, or a change in, the voice is another significant sign.

Causes: Respiratory disease can be caused by infection, parasitic infestation, foreign bodies, tumours, and, often the underlying cause in many cases, vitamin deficiencies. Vitamin A deficiency is a common cause, and any bird on a sunflower seed or peanut-based diet is certainly susceptible to respiratory infection.

Treatment: Speed is of the essence, so the bird should be taken to a veterinarian as soon as signs present themselves. Your veterinarian will depend on an appropriate course of treatment as soon as the cause behind the problems has been determined.

RETAINED EGG
(See Egg Binding).

RHINITIS
Inflammation or infection of the nasal chambers.

Signs: Swollen, reddened *Nares,* discharge, or the formation of deposits in the nares.

Causes: Rhinitis is normally caused by respiratory infection.

Treatment: The cause of the infection should be determined and treated with the appropriate antibiotics.

RICKETS
A metabolic condition of young birds leading to malformed, bent or distorted long bones.

Signs: Affected birds will have a tendency towards 'greenstick' fractures (i.e. bending fractures), which typically occur in the ends of the bones. The condition normally becomes apparent in young birds *(see Bone: Fractures).*

Causes: For correct bone growth, birds require certain ratios of calcium, phosphorus and vitamin D_3. Rickets occur when there is insufficient calcification of the bones in young, growing birds. It is common among birds fed a diet high in pulses and meat and low in calcium, or birds kept without sufficient exposure to unfiltered sunlight. Rickets is most common in chicks produced by hens that have bred repeatedly, as each successive egg contains lower levels of calcium.

Treatment: It is important to change the bird's diet, which your veterinarian will advise you about. The bird will also need to be exposed to sufficient levels of ultraviolet light, either using a special lamp or by allowing them access to 45 minutes of natural sunlight every day. If the bones are ricketic, the bird's quality of life should be considered. Bent bones may require surgical correction.

ROUNDWORM
(See Parasites: Nematodes).

S

SALIVARY GLANDS
Saliva-producing glands situated under the tongue.

SALMONELLOSIS
A bacterial infection that affects embryos as well as adult birds.
Signs: Unfortunately, affected embryos will die during incubation, or within two weeks of hatching. Adult birds may develop *Enteritis, Septicaemia,* and may die.
Causes: The *Salmonella* bacteria may be picked up in food. When the bacteria is passed to the embryos, it normally happens because of an ovarian infection. It can also occur in a cooling egg. As the egg cools after laying, air is drawn into the egg through the pores in the shell. If the shell is contaminated, this infection will be drawn into and infect the egg.
Treatment: Diagnosis in either case is determined by blood tests or faecal swabs, while treatment will be decided on the basis of bacterial cultures and sensitivity testing.

SALPINGITIS
(See Oviduct: Inflammation).

SALPINGOHYSTERECTOMY
(See Oviduct: Removal).

SARCOCYSTIS
A common protozoal parasitic infestation in the US. It infects parrots through contact with the opossum and cockroaches.
Signs: The disease affects young fledglings at the age when they first leave the nest. Usually, the bird is found dead. White grains may be found in the breast muscle post mortem, and the lung may also be inflamed.
Causes: Parasitic infestation.
Treatment: It is important to implement effective insect control in the aviary. Other youngsters that may be at risk should be treated with antibiotics.

SCALY FACE
A condition caused by *Cnemidocoptes* parasites that causes scaly patches on the affected bird's cere.
Signs: There will be scaly patches around the area of the bird's cere.
Causes: The condition is caused by a microscopic mite *(Cnemidocoptes)*.
Infestation often occurs in immune-compromised individuals.
Treatment: An *Ivermectin* preparation will treat the condition, but all in-contact birds will also need to be treated. All in-contact birds should be treated once a week for three to four weeks.

SCALY LEG
A condition caused by parasites that causes scaly patches on the legs of affected birds. It may occur in all species, but it is particularly common among Canaries. Domestic poultry may also be affected.
Signs: There will be scaly patches on the bird's legs.
Causes: The condition is caused by a microscopic mite *(Cnemidocoptes)*.
Infestation often occurs in immune-compromised individuals.
Treatment: An *Ivermectin* preparation will treat the condition, but all in-contact birds will also need to be treated. All in-contact birds should be treated once a week for three to four weeks.

SCOLIOSIS
Severe curvature of the spine. Many affected birds lead normal lives.

SECONDARIES
The inner main flight feathers on the wings, which are responsible for 'lift' in flight.

SEIZURES
(See Epilepsy).

SELF-MUTILATION
This problem is essentially an extension of excessive preening, except that it can also be seen in birds who show signs of attention seeking.

SEPTICAEMIA
A bacterial infection of the blood system.
Signs: The bird will become sick very suddenly.
Causes: A blood-borne bacterial infection. The bacteria may enter the bloodstream from a wound, an insect bite, or from the gut.
Treatment: Veterinary attention should be sought immediately, as septicaemia can be fatal very rapidly. Antibiotics will kill the bacteria.

SEROLOGY
A clinical pathology test used to determine the level of protection a bird has against a given disease.

The test is commonly performed to test whether the bird has recently suffered from an infection, and to monitor progress following treatment for an infection.

SEVOFLORANE
A gas used in *Gaseous Anaesthetic,* which is generally used in preference over *Halothane.*

SEX DETERMINATION
The method of determining the sex of an individual parrot.

At first glance, many psittacines appear to be identical (monomorphic). However, there are often subtle differences. For example, African Grey Parrots tend to be darker if male and more grey if female. Male Orange-winged Amazons have much broader heads than females. Male Pionus Parrots have larger eyes than females. In some species, the differences are more obvious. For example, male Eclectus Parrots are green, while females are red and purple. Cockatiels tend to develop different-coloured plumages once they have reached sexual maturity. Many female Cockatoos, once mature, have brown irises, while the male's is black; while in Budgerigars, the male has a blue cere while the female's is usually brown.

In cases where sex cannot be determined on appearance alone, it is possible to use DNA samples or *Endoscopy* to discover the sex of a particular bird. DNA sampling requires the extraction of genetic material, usually from a blood sample, or, occasionally, from a feather. The technique does not cause too much distress to the bird and is normally very accurate. Results can be obtained within 7 to 10 days in most cases.

Endoscopic sex determination is extremely accurate in the hands of a well-equipped, experienced avian veterinarian. An endoscope is passed into the bird's air sac, allowing the operator to see the internal sex organs and so determine the sex of the bird. A disadvantage to this technique is that it is invasive and requires the bird to be put under a general anaesthetic, although this also has the advantage of allowing the surgeon to perform a thorough health check on the bird while checking the sex organs.

Split stainless steel rings are often applied to birds after surgical sexing, typically bearing the initials of the veterinarian in question, plus a unique number. There should be a certificate to accompany the bird. In the event of the certificate being lost, the result may be traceable through the veterinarian's initials. However, it should be remembered that these rings are, on occasion, placed on birds by dealers, even though the bird may not have had its sex determined.

SEXUAL FRUSTRATION

This is responsible, in part, for many of the behavioural problems seen in Cockatoos and African Greys.

Signs: Parent-reared birds mature at five to six years of age, but hand-reared birds can become sexually active from the age of six months onwards. Sexual activity can be manifested in a variety of ways, although aggression or mating displays towards other birds and towards the keeper or the keeper's family are the most common. Some birds will regurgitate food to their keeper, a toy or a mirror, while others may present their cloacal region in a mating display.

Causes: Having two birds in separate cages, but within each other's view, can lead to sexual frustration and may trigger plucking. Other birds may focus their sexual urges on human family members, usually as a result of overbonding. Very often, the signals are not understood, the bird becomes frustrated, and more disturbing behaviour can occur as a result (e.g. jealousy of the keeper's partner, or extreme sexual displays).

Treatment: One option is to inject the bird with *Leuprolide Acetate* (leupron) once every two weeks, over a period of six weeks. This stimulates the pituitary gland, resulting in a decrease in the sex hormones produced. While this treatment is carried out, the human object of the bird's desires must not have any contact with the parrot. The amount of daylight to which the bird is exposed should also be reduced to six to eight hours each day, so that the parrot is fooled into believing that winter is approaching, which is a bad time to breed. Although these treatments will defuse the situation temporarily, a long-term solution is required, the best option being to re-establish the owner's dominance over the bird.

SHOCK

Technically, shock refers to a collapse of the circulatory system due to a loss of the circulating volume of blood.

Signs: Shock normally occurs after trauma, although illness may also cause an onset. Any traumatised or unwell bird should be considered as suffering from shock and taken to a veterinarian before signs develop.

Causes: Shock develops when fluid leaks from the circulation into extra-circulatory cavities in the body. This normally happens following illness, trauma, or surgery.

Treatment: Shock is normally treated with *Fluid Therapy*, and the provision of a dark, warm space in which to recover.

SINUSES

Extensive blind-ending diverticulae (tubes) that begin between the *Nares* and eyes. They pass around, behind and between the eyes, passing around the ear canal and neck, as well as into the top beak. The main function of the sinuses is to reduce the weight of the head to assist in flight.

SINUSITIS

Inflammation or infection of the sinuses. Amazon Parrots seem particularly prone.

Signs: There is normally a discharge from one or both nostrils, which is clear and watery. There may also be swelling between the nares and eyes. Sometimes, the swelling can affect a large part of the face, giving a noticeably distorted appearance.

Causes: Sinusitis may be caused by allergies, environmental irritants (e.g. cigarette smoke or paint fumes), symptomatic of an underlying *Respiratory Disease,* a trapped foreign body, a vitamin deficiency, or an unrelated infection caused by bacteria, a virus, or fungi. Rarely, the condition may be caused by tumours or parasites.

Treatment: Usually, antibiosis clears the condition, although regular flushing of the sinuses will also be required. The veterinarian will often take samples, in order to determine the underlying cause. If the cause is an irritant or allergic response, the parrot must be removed from the irritant. An ionizer and improved ventilation may assist this. Chronic vitamin A deficiency is unfortunately more common that it should be, and is often seen in African Greys *(see Vitamin Deficiencies and Toxicosis: Vitamin A)*. If this is thought to be the cause, there is a need to ensure that the parrot eats foods which are rich in vitamin A (e.g. dark greens, sweetcorn and carrot). Alternatively, vitamin A can be provided as a dietary supplement (as long as the bird ingests the supplements – many refuse).

SKIN

Avian skin does not contain any glands, except in the ear canal and the preen gland. The condition of the skin is a useful indication of the overall health of a bird.

The skin gives a good indication of a chick's degree of hydration, becoming wrinkled when the bird is dehydrated. If the chick is cold, the skin will be white and cool. In adult birds, where the skin cannot normally be assessed because of the covering of feathers, examination of the skin on the bird's feet can be useful. Many birds suffer from vitamin A deficiencies, and, as a result, the skin on their feet is dry, flaky, or, in extreme cases, inflamed, broken and crusty.

SNEEZING

A rarity among birds, sneezing is normally a sign of an upper respiratory infection, although it may be nothing more than a parrot copying an owner who sneezes.

SPAYING

(See Oviduct: Removal).

SPINAL ABNORMALITIES
(See Cervical Lordosis and Kyphosis).

SPLAY LEG
(See Leg Splay).

SPLEEN
An internal organ responsible for developing the immune system in chicks, and fighting infection in adult birds.

SPLENOMEGALY
A technical term referring to enlargement of the spleen.
Signs: There are no clinical signs while the bird is alive. Signs become apparent only on an X-ray taken post mortem.
Causes: Splenic enlargement (splenomegaly) occurs when there is active infection throughout the body. It is commonly caused by *Chlamydophila*.
Treatment: The veterinarian will use *Radiography* to determine the extent of the enlargment. The spleen should never exceed 1.5 times the diameter of the thigh bone. If the cause of the infection can be determined, appropriate antibiotics can be given.

SPRADDLE LEG
(See Leg Splay).

SQUAMOUS CELL CARCINOMA
(See Neoplasia: Squamous Cell Carcinomas).

STAPHYLOCOCCUS SPECIES
A common bacterium found naturally on the skin of birds, which can cause infection if it enters the underlying tissue.

STERNOSTOMA SPECIES
Air sac mites that commonly affect Canaries and other soft-billed species.

STERNUM
The bony breastplate that protects the internal organs. It has a midline ventral projection (the keel or carina), to which the major flight muscles of the breast are attached.

STEREOTYPIC BEHAVIOUR
Birds require environmental change. They should be accustomed to a variable life, and, as long as they are used to it, they will enjoy it and find it stimulating.

Signs: Stereotypic behaviour is any behaviour that is harmful or inappropriate, with feather plucking being the most common manifestation. It tends to be a repeated pattern of behaviour.

Causes: Birds unaccustomed to change are unable to tolerate it. Recent change, or a disorganised, constantly changing household, may lead to feather plucking. Additions or losses of any members of the household (including other pets) may also trigger plucking.

Treatment: If the bird becomes scared when moving the cage to a new room, when coming out of the cage, or when new toys are added to the cage, it is an indication that the bird has become institutionalised (i.e. acclimatised to solitary confinement), with all the abnormal behaviour patterns that accompany it. In this case, the first steps should be to give the bird far more attention and to begin socialisation training.

STEROIDS
Potent drugs used to treat a wide variety of conditions.

Steroids are used sparingly as they tend to have side effects. Some species are more susceptible than others. Steroids should be used as a one-off treatment, and only short-acting varieties (i.e. 12-hour preparations) should be used.

STIFLE
The joint of a bird's leg, equivalent to the human knee.

STIFLE LUXATION
When the stifle joint moves out of its correct alignment.

Signs: The bird will be unable to bear weight on the affected leg, and the leg may be held at an inappropriate angle.

Causes: Stifle luxations can occur following major trauma to the ligaments supporting the joint.

Treatment: The joint will need to be stabilised by a veterinary surgeon, using pins and wires. Given time and support, stabilising fibrous tissue should build up around the joint, leading to near-normal function.

STOMATITIS
Inflammation of the mouth.

Signs: The bird's mouth will be inflamed.

Causes: Stomatitis can occur after eating hot or caustic compounds that can easily damage the lining of the mouth. Vitamin A deficiency can increase the incidence, especially if there is an underlying infection or tumour *(see Vitamin Deficiencies and Toxicosis: Vitamin A)*.

STOOL
(See Droppings).

STRESS

Stress comes in many varied forms and can affect birds to differing degrees.

Signs: A bird's normal reaction to fear or threat is to flee, but, if the bird is unable to escape, it may produce a 'fear response', which may include plucking or self-mutilation. Stress is a common factor involved in much *Stereotypic Behaviour.*

Causes: Some causes may be obvious (e.g. if the bird's cage is situated close to a window and predators are able to stare at the bird through the window). However, some causes can take some time to be discovered. For example, *Sesame Street* is excellent entertainment for parrots, but *Wildlife on One* may be distressing – the sight of a swooping, predatory bird, even when on a television, is naturally stressful, even if the parrot has never seen such a bird before.

Treatment: If the cause of the stress or fear can be discovered, it should be eliminated. Making the bird more confident (e.g. through behavioural modification training), and allowing it more opportunity to fly, can help greatly. *Haloperidol, Clomipramine* and *Prozac* may be used in the initial stages of retraining. Such drugs help to calm the bird, reducing anxiety and allowing the bird to adapt to improved husbandry techniques.

SUBCUTANEOUS EMPHYSEMA

Trapped air under the skin.

Signs: An air-filled distension of the neck or back.

Causes: The condition occurs when there is a rupture of the air sac (usually cervical), such that air escapes from the air sac and takes up a position under the skin.

Treatment: This serious condition requires treatment from an experienced avian veterinarian, who will create a hole for the air to escape through while the internal rupture heals.

Signs: Often, it is the lower neck that is affected most severely, and the bird typically looks like a hunchback.

Causes: It occurs due to the rupture of an air sac, usually the cervical *(see Air Sac: Rupture of Cervical Sacs)*, from which air leaks into the subcuticular space.

Treatment: The condition is addressed by draining the emphysema and allowing the internal rupture to heal.

SURGICAL SEXING

(See Sex Determination).

SYNGAMUS TRACHEA

A type of *Nematode* parasitic worm, commonly affecting the trachea, otherwise known as *Gapeworm* or *Lungworm*.

SYRINX
The avian voice box.
   The syrinx is situated at the point where the trachea divides into the primary bronchi (which lead to the lungs). If the syrinx is affected by *Lesions* or *Aspergillosis,* a change of voice, or, indeed, a complete loss of voice, is a common result.

T

TAPEWORMS
(See Parasites: Cestodes).

TARSOMETATARSUS
The bone of the lower leg.

TESTICULAR INFECTION
Infection of one or both testes, usually (though not always) occurring when the bird is in breeding condition).
Signs: Testicular infection can be difficult to spot in live birds, although the bird is likely to appear depressed and sick.
Causes: Typically caused by bacterial infection.
Treatment: Antibiotics and pain relief should be administered. However, infection commonly occurs as the bird comes into breeding condition – a time when the keeper is reluctant to disturb the bird. Typically, this condition is confirmed post mortem only.

THERMAL BURNS
(See Burns: Crop and Burns: Miscellaneous).

THROMBOCYTES
A constituent of blood used for clotting, equivalent to platelets in mammals.

THRUSH
(See Candidiasis).

TIBIOTARSUS
The middle leg bone, running from the knee to the hock.

TICK-BORNE INFECTIONS
(See Parasites: Ticks).

TOES: CONSTRICTED TOE SYNDROME
A condition that affects the skin and soft tissues of the toes, usually seen in African Grey, Eclectus and Macaw chicks.
Signs: A fibrous, circular constriction will form around one or more toes. The toe beyond the constriction may become swollen and full of fluid.
Causes: This normally arises in chicks reared in a too-dry environment.
Treatment: The constriction should be removed surgically, although care must be taken to correct the temperature and humidity of the rearing environment from then on.

TOES: DEFORMITIES
Any deviation from the normal development of the toe or toes, usually seen in young chicks.
Signs: The toes develop differently to what is normally expected for the species.
Causes: Incorrect incubation and vitamin deficiencies are common causes.
Treatment: A change in diet is often beneficial. If the toe deformity is discovered very early (i.e. within hours of hatching), it is possible to manipulate the toe into the proper position by taping it to the adjacent toe. The affected toe should then develop normally. If more than one toe is deformed, the chick will need to wear a 'snow shoe', which will encourage the toes to develop in the normal fashion.

TOES: DRY
(See Gangrene: Dry).

TOES: FRACTURES
Any partial or full breakage of the bones in the toe *(see Bone: Fractures).*
Signs: The bird may favour the other foot, have difficulty perching or balancing. There may be a simultaneous bite wound on the foot. Toe fractures are normally very painful, and there is likely to be damage to the surrounding tissues, so the bird is likely to be depressed with obvious damage to its foot.
Causes: Most toe fractures occur as a result of a bite wound from a cage mate.
Treatment: The fracture will need to be stabilised, and the entire foot bandaged. Normally, a 'ball bandage' is applied, which consists of a ball of cotton wool (cotton) placed in the ball of the foot. The toes are then taped around the ball. The bird is likely to try to remove the bandage, so care must be taken to check it regularly.

TONGUE
Parrots have very mobile and prehensile tongues, which they use to manipulate their food and other objects. Injuries to the tongue are rare but usually heal very quickly.

TOTAL PROTEIN

A clinical pathology test used to test for levels of protein in the blood. Levels decrease in long-term *Liver Disease* or *Kidney Disease, Malnutrition, Malabsorption, Blood Loss, or Neoplasia*. Levels may increase if the bird is suffering from *Dehydration* or *Amyloidosis*.

TOXICITY: ALMONDS

While green, almonds are highly toxic. Dry almonds are unlikely to pose a risk.

Signs: Sudden death.

Causes: While almonds are green they have a high cyanide content, which is toxic if eaten in excessive volumes.

Treatment: There is no treatment as the bird dies very quickly, before help can be sought.

TOXICITY: ANTICOAGULANTS

Anticoagulants include rodenticides (i.e. rat or mouse bait). Any vermin-controlling poison should be kept well away from parrots.

Signs: Clinical signs include weakness, depression, loss of appetite, breathing difficulties, and blood spots under the skin or in the mouth. Typically, the bird is found dead before the problem is suspected.

Causes: Anticoagulants contain poisons, to which birds are susceptible. It leads to abnormal haemorrhages.

Treatment: Treatment should involve vitamin K daily, for between 10 and 28 days depending on the type of poison swallowed. *Fluid Therapy* and *Blood Transfusions* may be required also.

TOXICITY: CARBON MONOXIDE

Just like humans, parrots are susceptible to the effects of this poisonous gas, which can prove fatal even in relatively small concentrations.

Signs: Affected birds normally die very suddenly, although lethargy is an early warning sign.

Causes: Faulty car exhausts and badly maintained gas appliances (e.g. central heating boilers) are normally at fault, particularly if the poisonous fumes are released in a confined area.

Treatment: If carbon monoxide poisoning is suspected, the bird should be moved into fresh air immediately.

TOXICITY: CHOCOLATE

Chocolate should never be fed to parrots, even as a very occasional treat.

Signs: Chocolate consumption leads to high blood pressure, raised body temperature, signs of *Nervous Disease,* an excessively fast heart rate, and *Diarrhoea.*

Causes: Chocolate contains theobromine, which is toxic to birds.
Treatment: Excessive amounts of chocolate can lead to death, but, in less serious cases, *Fluid Therapy* and diazepam drugs (to control the nervous signs) can help.

TOXICITY: COPPER

Some species of birds can tolerate copper better than others, but it is best to take precautions and prevent your bird from coming into contact with the metal.

Signs: General weakness, *Blood Loss, Liver Disease* and *Kidney Disease.*
Causes: Copper is found in some fungicides, old pennies, antifouling paints used on boats, and copper wire.
Treatment: A blood test will confirm the toxin, and treatment is normally *Chelation Therapy.*

TOXICITY: DRUGS

All medications have the potential to create side effects, which will, on occasion, be detrimental.

It is most important that, when medications are prescribed, the bird's weight is recorded, so that an accurate dose is administered. It is important that medications prescribed for a given condition in one species are never used for a different condition or in a different species. Incorrect or deteriorated drugs can easily prove fatal.

Signs: It is normally the kidneys, liver and intestines that are affected, although drug toxicity can also cause signs of *Nervous Disease.*
Causes: Normally, side effects arise as a result of a previously undiscovered *Allergy,* or as a result of too high a dosage being administered.
Treatment: As soon as side effects are observed, take your bird to your veterinarian.

TOXICITY: HEAVY METALS

In the case of parrots, this is normally zinc or lead.

Fortunately, lead poisoning is decreasing, as lead is not found in such high proportions in modern homes. However, zinc poisoning may be on the increase, as zinc is commonly used to form cages and aviary wire.

Signs: Heavy metal poisoning usually leads to signs typical of *Nervous Disease,* including unco-ordinated movements and loss of balance, sometimes accompanied by paralysis. Droppings should be checked for traces of blood or *Diarrhoea.* Unfortunately, the clinical signs are not clear-cut and can vary enormously (some birds may develop sudden-onset blindness, for example).
Causes: Your bird is particularly at risk if allowed free access throughout the house, as it can then come into contact with a number of substances that, if ingested, cause heavy metal poisoning. Today, aviary or cage wire is the usual

cause of zinc poisoning. If the wire has been dip-galvanised, there will be little droplets of galvanised material attached to the wire. Many birds pull off these droplets, which contain high levels of zinc, and eat them.

Treatment: Blood tests and *Radiography* will confirm heavy metal poisoning and determine the levels of the toxicity. *Chelating Agents,* such as sodium calcium edetate, D penecillamine, or dimercaptosuccininc acid, is the normal treatment. However, in some cases, it is necessary to remove metal particles from the intestines if they will not clear by natural processes. It should be remembered that, unless the cause of the poisoning is discovered, the bird is likely to suffer from heavy metal toxicity again. For this reason, it is important to identify and remove the source. Your veterinarian may suggest further retests, to confirm that the source has been correctly identified. In cases of zinc poisoning, problems can be avoided by choosing quality, electroplated wire, and scrubbing it with acetic acid (strong vinegar) or having it powder-coated.

TOXICITY: HERBICIDES

Embryos in their shells are most sensitive to the effect of herbicides.

Signs: Embryos may die. If chicks are born live, they may have slow growth rates and abnormal liver enzymes. Adult birds are likely to be infertile. *Altrical* chicks are more susceptible than precocial (i.e. born self-sufficient) chicks.

Causes: Herbicides most commonly affect eggs laid by aquatic birds. The eggs absorb the contaminants from the water.

Treatment: Typically, treatment is not indicated (most embryos die). There are antidotes for some groups of herbicides, although this is only relevant if the exact cause of poisoning is known.

TOXICITY: INSECTICIDES
(See Toxicity: Pesticides).

TOXICITY: LEAD
(See Toxicity: Heavy Metals).

TOXICITY: NEW WIRE DISEASE
(See Toxicity: Heavy Metals).

TOXICITY: ORGANOPHOSPHATES/CARBAMATES

Birds are 10 to 20 times more susceptible to poisoning from organophosphates and carbamates than mammals.

Signs: If the poisoning is sudden, the bird will show signs of *Nervous Disease,* tremors, convulsions, *Diarrhoea, Vomiting,* respiratory distress, slowed heart rate, weakness, collapse, and eventual death. Alternatively, it may present as delayed-onset poisoning, in which case the signs include loss of balance, weakness, failure to perch normally, and paralysis.

Causes: Disease occurs as a result of ingestion or inhalation of these poisons.
Treatment: If the poisoning is discovered early enough, drugs can control the signs fairly well. Normally, atropine, diphenhydramine, or pralidoxime chloride are administered.

TOXICITY: PESTICIDES
Pesticides comprise a wide range of products, including organophosphates (see above), organochlorines, carbamates, rotenone, arsenicals, and nitrates.
Signs: These compounds can cause embryo deformities, including twists and deviations of the spine (in particular of the neck), and they can also cause beak abnormalities and abnormal feathering.
Causes: Toxins may be ingested or inhaled.
Treatment: Medical antidotes are available for some poisons, although this is only useful if the actual poison in known.

TOXICITY: PLANTS
Poisoning by plants is rare. Occasionally, birds will chew plants, which can cause oral irritation but no further damage is caused as insufficient material is swallowed.
Signs: The most usual signs are *Diarrhoea* and *Vomiting and Regurgitation.*
Cause: The following plants are potentially dangerous to birds, and should be removed from their vicinity: arcacea family (diffenbachia, calla lily, philodendron), avocado, castor bean, coffee bean, lily of the valley, oak, oleander, poinsettia, nightshade, jerusalem or christmas cherry, potatoes (green), milkweed, tobacco (nicotine), and yew. The absence of a plant on this list does not imply that it is safe.
Treatment: The bird should be taken to a veterinarian immediately. Inducing vomiting, flushing the crop, *Fluid Therapy* and sedatives, combined with nursing and support care, are usually the relevant treatments.

TOXICITY: POLYTETRAFLUOROETHYLENE.
(See Polytetrafluoroethylene).

TOXICITY: STRYCHNINE
An extremely potent poison that usually gives no signs prior to death. Most birds are found dead and the cause discovered during post mortem.

TOXICITY: TEA AND COFFEE
Parrots should never be given tea or coffee.
Signs: High blood pressure, raised body temperature, signs of *Nervous Disease,* increased heart rate, and *Diarrhoea.*
Causes: Tea and coffee contain caffeine and theophylline, which, while safe for

humans, are toxic to birds.
Treatment: The veterinarian will adminster *Fluid Therapy,* along with diazepam (e.g. valium) to control the nervous system signs.

TOXICITY: TEFLON
(See Polytetrafluoroethylene).

TOXICITY: ZINC
(See Toxicity: Heavy Metals).

TRACHEAL BYPASS
A surgical procedure that allows the bird to breathe without using the windpipe.

A tracheal bypass is normally carried out when the windpipe is obstructed. An 'air sac breathing tube' is inserted directly into the bird's abdominal air sac, through which the bird can breathe. The tube can also be used to administer *Anaesthesia.* The tube is removed once the obstruction has been removed and any damage repaired.

TRACHEAL OBSTRUCTION
Any obstruction in the windpipe.
Signs: The bird will show signs of breathing difficulty.
Causes: Obstructions are usually caused by trauma, which may have pressed part of the windpipe in on itself, inhalation of a foreign body, or by *Aspergillosis.*
Treatment: The obstruction will need to be removed by a veterinarian.

TRACHEITIS
Inflammation or infection of the windpipe.
Signs: Wheezing, difficulty breathing.
Causes: Common causes include infection (viral, bacterial, or mycoplasma), parasitic infestation (e.g. *Syngamus*), foreign body inspiration, trauma, or nutritional deficiency.
Treatment: A tracheal lavage or wash may be performed on an anaesthetised bird, to take samples to determine the cause of the problem. Appropriate antibiotics, antifungals and anti-inflammatories should be administered. Surgical intervention may be warranted in some cases.

TRACHEOTOMY
A surgical procedure that opens the windpipe, usually performed to remove a lesion or foreign body.

TRANSFUSION
(See Blood: Transfusions).

TREMATODES
(See Parasites: Trematodes).

TUBERCULOSIS
A type of bacteria that cause long-term, chronic *Granulomas,* typically leading to the bird's death.

There are several strains of these bacteria, but most birds are affected by *Mycobaterium avium*. Occasionally, *M. genavense* may be contracted, and, even less often, birds may acquire the human form, *M. tuberculosis*.

Signs: Chronic wasting and weight loss. Internally, the bird will have multiple *Granulomas* affecting many organs, notably the gastrointestinal tract and liver, although any organ can be involved, including bones, lung and skin.

Causes: Infection is normally transmitted via contact with wild birds, soil, or from the owner. The organism can remain dormant for months, so it is not always easy to diagnose when the disease was acquired. For this reason, it is important to treat all birds that have been in contact with the diseased bird for the last year.

Diagnosis: Blood tests, *Endoscopy* and *Biopsy* will confirm the disease. Treatment for the disease involves twice-daily crop-tubing of the infected bird for at least two months, although euthanasia is more often advised because of the risk to humans.

U

ULTRASOUND
A diagnostic technique used to create images of internal organs.

Ultrasound does not require the bird to be anaesthetised and is harmless. It cannot work through air so cannot be used to create images of the air sacs. However, it is useful for diagnosing problems with the liver, gonads and heart.

ULTRAVIOLET
(See Daylight).

URATES
White, pasty deposits of uric acid which contain metabolic waste.

Urates can be a useful diagnostic tool, as discoloration is normally an indication of some abnormality. A green discoloration is relatively non-specific, indicating an increased blood breakdown, *Liver Disease* or simply that the bird has had very little food to eat. Pink-coloured urates turning to red are highly indicative of lead poisoning in Amazons. Cream or yellow-coloured urates, especially in the absence of faeces, is indicative of anorexia. Yellow or orange discoloration also occurs if the bird has received an injection of B vitamins.

UREA

A clinical pathology parameter. Increased levels indicate *Dehydration,* but have no bearing on kidney function *per se*.

UROLITH

Urine contains tiny crystals, which, in most cases, do not cause a problem. However, sometimes these crystals combine to form a urolith (the human equivalent is a bladder stone).

Signs: The bird will appear to be straining when attempting to excrete waste products from the body. A small amount of fresh blood may be apparent in the bird's faeces.

Causes: Uroliths are formed when uric acid crystals build up within the cloaca, often in birds that have been incubating eggs for prolonged periods.

Treatment: Diagnosis is made under anaesthetic, when the veterinarian will perform a physical examination of the cloaca. If uroliths are found to be present, they can be broken up relatively easily, using a surgical instrument. The bird can then excrete the fragments in the normal fashion, without feeling discomfort.

V

VALGUS

A condition in which the bone grows at a different rate on either side, resulting in a curvature as the bone grows.

Signs: The bones will show signs of curvature (i.e. a banana-shaped long bone).

Causes: It normally occurs after damage to the growth area of a bone.

Treatment: Surgical correction is required, the technique used depending on whether the bone has stopped growing or whether more can be expected. If more growth is expected, the bone surface (periosteum) may be surgically removed on the faster-growing side, which has the effect of slowing or stopping growth. If growth has stopped, the shorter side may be stretched until the bone, as a whole, is straight.

VENT

(See Cloaca).

VENTRICULUS

The ventriculus is the muscular, grinding organ of the intestinal tract. It is frequently referred to as the second stomach or gizzard.

VESTIBULAR DISEASE
Any inflammatory condition that affects the balance organ of the inner ear.

Signs: Head tilt, loss of balance, squinting, rolling, or flicking of the head (nystagmus), and many other signs symptomatic of general *Nervous Disease.*
Causes: The signs are caused when the bird's balance organ in the ear is affected, although there may be a number of reasons for this, including an ear infection, trauma or tumours.
Treatment: Vestibular disease must be differentiated from other types of nervous disease, as treatment may be different. Your veterinarian will test for the condition and decide on the appropriate treatment once the results of the test are received.

VIRAEMIA
A term relating to blood-borne viral infections.

VIRAL INFECTIONS
The following are serious viral infections that all owners should guard against: *Pacheco's Disease, Paramyxovirus* **or** *Newcastle Disease, Papillomatosis,* **and** *Psittacine Beak and Feather Disease (PBFD).*

VITAMINS
For the sake of classification, vitamins are normally divided into two groups: fat-soluble vitamins (i.e. A, D, E and K), and water-soluble vitamins (i.e. B and C vitamins). Fat-soluble vitamins are stored in the body, while water-soluble vitamins must be provided on a daily basis.

Generally speaking, a bird's vitamin requirements are broadly similar to those of a mammal. One difference is that birds require activated vitamin D_3 (cholecalciferol) rather than D_2 (ergocholecalciferol). Vitamin C is essential to fruit-eating birds only (e.g. the Bulbul).

Described below are the main functions of some of the essential vitamins.

- **Vitamin A:** An essential vitamin for overall healthy body function, playing an important role in the health of the skin, vision, skeletal development and reproduction. Foods high in vitamin A include greens, dark vegetables, sweetcorn, carrot, fish-liver oil, liver, eggs and dried milk.

- **Vitamin D:** Ingested vitamin D precursors (e.g. ergocalciferol) are converted to active D_3 by ultraviolet light. Vitamin D_3 vital for normal calcium metabolism. Foods rich in vitamin D include fish-liver oil, eggs and dried milk.

- **Vitamin E:** This antioxidant is particularly important for male fertility, and for brain and nerve function. Foods high in vitamin E include vegetable oils, sunflower, saffron, and wheat germ.

- **Vitamin K:** Synthesised by bacteria living in the gut, vitamin K helps the blood to clot.
- **Vitamin B1 (thiamine):** Required for normal nerve transmission. Thiamine is found in all vegetables, but not in meat.
- **Vitamin B2 (riboflavin):** Important for feather coloration, as well as growth, skin health and intestinal health.
- **Vitamin B6 (niacin and pyridoxine):** Important for normal nerve function.
- **Vitamin B$_{12}$ (cyanocobalamin):** Essential for protein, fat and carbohydrate synthesis.
- **Choline:** Responsible for metabolism, cartilage production, and prevention of the fatty build-up in the liver. Choline is widespread in most foods.
- **Folic acid:** Important for carbon metabolism and uric acid synthesis. Foods rich in folic acid include cereals and yeast products.
- **Pantothenic acid and biotin:** Essential for normal metabolism, liver function, and beak and feather growth. Egg yolk and yeast products contain both pantothenic acid and biotin.

VITAMIN DEFICIENCIES AND TOXICOSIS

Vitamin deficiencies and toxicosis are very common among pet birds, and are normally caused by poor diet.

As water-soluble vitamins are not stored in the body, it is often one of these vitamins in which a bird becomes deficient. However, for the same reason, it is extremely difficult to determine which vitamin is deficient. As fat-soluble vitamins are stored in the body, they can quickly rise to toxic levels in the event of oversupplementation.

Signs: Clinical signs vary, depending on which vitamin is deficient or being stored in excessive levels. However, the following are common signs – loss of appetite, poor growth, weakness, *Diarrhoea,* skin problems, *Anaemia,* skin and bone lesions, poor feathering/coloration, failure of eggs to hatch, signs of *Nervous Disease, Kidney Disease* or *Liver Disease,* and, in some cases, the sudden, apparently unexplained death of the bird.

Causes: In the vast majority of cases, a poor diet is responsible. Some rare conditions, or an imbalance in bacteria living in the gut, may also cause problems.

Treatment: Attention must be paid to the bird's diet, and your veterinarian will be happy to advise you about this. In some cases, it may be necessary to add vitamin supplements to the diet.

VITAMIN DEFICIENCIES AND TOXICOSIS: VITAMIN A

A shortage of vitamin A normally results in a condition known as Hypovitaminosis A.

Signs: Common early warning signs of a deficiency include swellings that resemble abscesses under the tongue, frequent minor infections (particularly fungal infections of the mouth, such as thrush), a gradual reduction of vision, sneezing, increased drinking, reduced fertility, and loss of skin foot pattern on the underside of foot. A long-term effect is the development of bumps around the area of the sinuses, which contain cheesy white deposits, and a yellow pigmentation of the skin. Toxicity normally presents as bone abnormalities.

Causes: Most vitamin A deficiencies are the result of poor diet, although there are some rare conditions that prevent absorption of vitamin A from the diet. For example, *Liver Disease* can reduce the availability of vitamin A. Toxicity occurs only if vitamin levels exceed 100 times the required level for extended periods.

Treatment: Initially, the veterinarian will probably give weekly injections of vitamin A for three weeks, while also recommending dietary changes. This can be further supplemented by a good vitamin supplement, which contains both vitamin A and D_3. There are several of these manufactured specifically for birds/parrots, although you should always consult with your veterinarian before giving your bird any dietary supplements. Birds suffering from toxic levels of vitamin A will require a lot of supportive care – *Fluid Therapy,* pain relief and nutritional support.

VITAMIN DEFICIENCIES AND TOXICOSIS: D
Vitamin D deficiencies and toxicosis are common among pet birds.
Signs: Vitamin D deficiency normally presents with lack of mineralisation, soft bones, curvature of bones, often accompanied by fractures, and thin-shelled or soft eggs. Excessive vitamin D normally produces signs of *Kidney Disease.*
Causes: Insufficient vitamin D results in the body's failure to metabolise calcium, which is why bone abnormalities are the usual result. Vitamin D toxicity, on the other hand, leads to mineralisation of soft tissues, which is why *Kidney Disease* is a common consequence.
Treatment: Your veterinarian will treat the signs of toxicity, where possible, and provide advice about increasing the level of vitamin D in the diet in cases of deficiency. Further supplementation may also be advised.

VOICE
A psittacine's voice is produced by the *Syrinx*.

VOMITING AND REGURGITATION
Vomiting and regurgitation are among the most common signs that an owner will first notice when their bird becomes unwell.
Signs: Initially, vomiting and regurgitation will be noticed because of food staining around the beak and head feathers. The owner may actually witness the bird vomiting. Other signs include tail bobbing and weight loss.
Causes: There are many potential causes, including infection, parasites,

irritants, metabolic organ failure, foreign bodies, toxic agents, nerve malfunction, food allergies, and some behavioural problems.

Treatment: Any bird vomiting should be presented to an experienced avian veterinarian as soon as possible. Diagnosis is based on recent history, the collection and testing of samples from the gut, *Radiology, Endoscopy,* and faecal examination. It is important that, wherever possible, a specific diagnosis is made. In the interim, symptomatic treatment (such as *Fluid Therapy),* antivomiting drugs, and antibiotics should be administered.

W

WARFARIN
(See Toxicity: Anticoagulants).

WHITE BLOOD CELLS
(See Blood: White Blood Cells).

X

XANTHOMAS
(See Neoplasia: Xanthomas).

Y

YEAST
(See Candidiasis).

YEW
(See Toxicity: Plants).

YOLK SAC: UNRETRACTED
At hatch, the yolk sac should have been retracted into the chick's body. When this does not happen, it is referred to as an unretracted yolk sac.

Signs: A yellow, mushroom-shaped swelling at the umbilicus.

Causes: It is caused most commonly by a slightly high incubation temperature.

Treatment: This is an emergency situation and requires immediate veterinary attention. If a small amount of yolk remains, a suture should be placed around the exposed yolk sac. The outer part will quickly dry up and drop off. If a large amount of yolk sac remains, this should be cleaned, disinfected, and gently pushed back into the abdomen if possible. If the exposed yolk sac is damaged or contaminated, a ligature is placed around the umbilicus, the yolk sac contents sucked out, and the excess tissue trimmed off. Unfortunately, the survival rate for such chicks is low.

Z

ZINC POISONING
(See Toxicity: Heavy Metals).

APPENDIX

USEFUL CONTACTS

1. Websites
2. Useful addresses

1. WEBSITES

There is now a wealth of parrot websites on the Internet. Listed below are just a few of the good, non-commercial sites, from which you will find links to many others worldwide.

World Parrot Trust
www.worldparrottrust.org

Bird Clubs of America Alliance
www.oldstone.com

The Gabriel Foundation (Rescue Sanctuary)
www.thegabrielfoundation.org

Loro Parque Fundacion (Tenerife)
www.loroparque-fundacion.org

Australian Parrot Society
www.parrotsociety.org.au

Belgian Parrot Society
www.parkieten-revue.com

New Zealand Parrot Society
www.parrot.co.nz

The Parrot Society (UK)
www.theparrotsocietyuk.org

Parrot-link UK
www.parrot-link.co.uk

Parrot Pages
www.parrotsfirst.com

Liz Wilson, Parrot Psychologist
www.upatsix.com/liz

Parrot Talk
www.parrottalk.com

Pet Station: Bird Barn
www.petstation.com

Dave Poole: Safe/unsafe Foods for Birds
www.petcraft.com/docs/safebird.html

The Aviary: Your Avian Info Center
www.theaviary.com/map.shtml

Birds 'n' Ways
www.birdsnways.com

The Blue Macaws
www.bluemacaws.org

Cyprus Parrot Rescue Centre
www.nuts-about-birds.com

Kathy Johnson's Home Page
www.ddc.com/~kjohnson

Macaw Landing Foundation
www.macawlanding.org

Parrot Parrot
www.parrotparrot.com/

Parrots Canada
www.parrotscanada.com/

Poicephalus Parrots
www.poicephalus.org/

Quaker Parrots
www.quakerparrots.com/

European College of Avian Medicine and Surgery
www.ecams-online.org

An Amateur's Guide to Keeping Parrots
www.geocities.com/Heartland/4545/

Society of Parrot Breeders and Exhibitors
www.spbe.org/

Parrots of the World – A Checklist
www.interaktv.com/BIRDS/Part.html

Canadian World Parrot Trust
www.canadianparrottrust.org

Nancy's Parrot Sanctuary
www.parrot-sanctuary.org/

The Pet Bird Page
www.petbirdpage.com/

Testing for Zinc in Parrot Toys
www.synnovation.com/zinctesting.html

Lexicon of Parrotswww.arndt-verlag.com/index.html

The African Grey Parrot
www.minorkey.com/grey.html

African Grey Parrot
www.wingscc.com/aps/grey.htm

African Grey Parrots
www.oz.net/~fur/greyparrot/

African Parrot Society
www.wingscc.com/aps/

All About Wild Parrots
www.birding.about.com

AvianWeb
www.avianweb.com

2. USEFUL ADDRESSES

GENERAL
CITES Secretariat,
15, Chemin des Anemones,
1219 Chatelaine,
Geneva,
Switzerland.
Tel: + 4122 917 8139/40

International Parrot Convention,
Loro Parque,
Puerto de la Cruz,
Tenerife,
Spain.

WORLD PARROT TRUST
OFFICES

AFRICA
V Dennison,
PO Box 1758,
Link Hills, Natal 3652,
South Africa.
Tel: +27 31763 4054
Fax: +27 31763 3811

ASIA
Catherine Carlton,
Hong Kong.
Tel: + 85 29235 6300
E-mail: asia@worldparrottrust.org

AUSTRALIA
Mike Owen,
7 Monteray Street,
Mooloolaba,
Queensland 4557,
Australia.
Tel: + 61 75478 0454
E-mail:
australia@worldparrottrust.org

BELGIUM
Enquiries to Romain Bejstrup
(Tel: + 32 3252 6773)

CANADA
Sandra Metzger,
PO Box 29,
Mount Hope,
Ontario L0R 1WO0,
Canada.
Tel/Fax: + 15 19823 8941
E-mail: canada@worldparrottrust.org
Website:
http://www.canadianparrottrust.org

DENMARK (SCANDINAVIA)
Michael Iversen,
Hyldevang 4,
Buresoe,
3550 Slangerup,
Denmark.
Tel: + 45 4818 1710
E-mail:
denmark@worldparrottrust.org
Website:
http://www.image.dk/fpewpt

FRANCE
J. & G. Prin,
55 Rue de la Fassiere,
45140 Ingre,
France.
Tel: + 33 23843 6287
Fax: + 33 23843 9718

ITALY
Cristiana Senni,
WPT Italia,
CP 15021,
00143 Roma,
Italy.
E-mail: italy@worldparrottrust.org
Website:
http://www.worldparrottrust.org/italia

NETHERLANDS
Peter de Vries (Membership
Secretary),
Jagershof 91,
7064 DG Silvolde,

Netherlands.
Tel: + 31 315327418
E-mail:
benelux@worldparrottrust.org
Enquiries to: Ruud Vonk (Tel: + 31 16847 2715)

SPAIN
Marin and Ana Matesanz,
C/Cambados No 1,
2Dcha,
28925 Alcorcon,
Madrid,
Spain.
Tel: +34 91642 5130
E-mail: spain@worldparrottrust.org

SWITZERLAND
Lars Lepperhoff,
Lutschenstrasse 15,
3063 Ittigen,
Switzerland.
Tel: + 41 31922 3902

UK
Karen Whitley, Administrator,
Glanmor House,
Hayle,
Cornwall,
TR27 4HB,
United Kingdom.
Tel: 01736 751026
Fax: 01736 751028
E-mail: uk@worldparrottrust.org
Mike Reynolds e-mail:
reynolds@worldparrottrust.org

US
Joanna Eckles,
Administrator,
WPT-USA,
PO Box 353,
Stillwater,
MN 55082,
United States of America.
Tel: + 1 651-275-1877

Fax: + 1 651-275-1891
E-mail: usa@worldparrottrust.org
Jamie Gilardi e-mail:
gilardi@worldparrottrust.org

AUSTRALIAN ADDRESSES
Parrot Society of Australia,
PO Box 75,
Salisbury,
Qld 4107.

Birds Australia: Parrot Association,
415 Riversdale Road,
Hawthorn East,
Victoria 3123.

CANADIAN ADDRESSES
The Parrot Association of Canada,
60 Bristol Road East, Suite 316,
Mississagua,
Ontario L42 3K8.
Fax: 51 9699 544

NEW ZEALAND ADDRESSES
Parrot Society of New Zealand,
PO Box 79-202 Royal Heights,
Auckland.
Tel: +64 9424 3224
E-mail: parrots@parrotsociety.org.nz

UK ADDRESSES
The Parrot Society,
108B Fenlake Road,
Bedford,
MK42 0EU.
Tel: 01234 358922

The National Council for Aviculture,
4 Haven Crescent,
Werrington,
Stoke-on-Trent,
Staffordshire,
ST9 0EY.
Tel/Fax: 01782 305042

**The Amazona Society UK
(TASUK),**
PO Box 36,
Carmarthen,
SA33 6YG.

The Foreign Bird League,
48 Twickenham Road,
Newton Abbot,
Devon,
TQ12 4JF.
Tel: 01626 352699

**The Society for Conservation in
Aviculture**
Tel: 01733 241494

RSPCA,
Causeway,
Horsham,
West Sussex,
RH12 1HG.
Tel: 01403 264181

Colour Breeding,
Jim Hayward.
Tel: 01993 841736

Parrot Behaviourist Greg Glendell.
Tel: 01630 685518
E-mail:
greg@petparrot.freeserve.co.uk

US ADDRESSES
**American Federation of
Aviculturists,**
PO Box 56218,
Phoenix,
AZ 85079-6218.
Tel: 60 2484 0931
E-mail: afa.birds.org

The Amazona Society,
235 North Walnut Street,
Bryan,
Ohio 43506.

**Association of Avian Veterinarians
(AAV)**
Central Office,
PO Box 811720,
Boca Raton,
FL 33481.
Tel: 56 1393 8901

**North American Parrot Society
Inc.,**
PO Box 404,
Salem,
OH 44460.
Tel: 33 7367 3188

North American Cockatiel Society,
PO Box 1363,
Avon,
CT 06001-1363.

Bird Clubs of America,
PO Box 2005,
Yorktown,
VA 23692.
Tel: 75 7898 5090

International Aviculturists Society,
PO Box 2232,
LaBelle,
FL 33975.